Information Systems

While the subject of information systems (IS) has the potential to widen our view of the world, it often has the opposite effect by limiting our ability to interact, facilitating managerial and state surveillance or instituting strict hierarchies and personal control. In this book, Bernd Stahl offers an alternative and critical perspective on the subject, arguing that the ongoing problems in this area could be caused by the misconceptualisation of the nature and role of IS.

Stahl discusses the question of how IS can be used to actually overcome oppression and promote emancipation, breaking the book into four parts. The first part covers the theory of critical research in IS, giving a central place for the subject of ethics. The second part discusses the philosophical underpinnings of this critical research. The third and largest part gives examples of the application of critical work in IS. The final part then reflects on the approach and suggests ways for further development.

This book will be of interest to students and researchers engaged with critical aspects of IS and the ethics of information, as well as scholars and practitioners looking for alternative ways to approach and understand the use of ICT in society and organisations.

Bernd Carsten Stahl is a Reader in Critical Research in Technology in the Centre for Computing and Social Responsibility at De Montfort University in Leicester.

Routledge studies in organization and systems

Edited by Nandish V. Patel

Director, Brunel Organization and Systems Design Centre [BOSdc], Brunel University

1 Information Systems
Critical perspectives
Bernd Stahl

Information Systems
Critical perspectives

Bernd Carsten Stahl

Routledge
Taylor & Francis Group

LONDON AND NEW YORK

First published 2008
by Routledge
2 Park Square, Milton Park, Abingdon, Oxon OX14 4RN

Simultaneously published in the USA and Canada
by Routledge
270 Madison Ave, New York, NY 10016

Routledge is an imprint of the Taylor & Francis Group, an informa business

© 2008 Bernd Carsten Stahl

Typeset in Times by Wearset Ltd, Boldon, Tyne and Wear
Printed and bound in Great Britain by TJI Digital, Padstow, Cornwall

British Library Cataloguing in Publication Data
A catalogue record for this book is available from the British Library

Library of Congress Cataloging in Publication Data
A catalog record for this book has been requested

ISBN10: 0-415-43378-9 (hbk)
ISBN10: 0-203-92793-1 (ebk)

ISBN13: 978-0-415-43378-5 (hbk)
ISBN13: 978-0-203-92793-9 (ebk)

Contents

Tables

Foreword

The Routledge Studies in Organization and Systems series is a series of research outputs and research monographs covering e-business systems and information systems development for businesses. It encourages researchers to contribute to the designing of organisation and its information technology (IT) systems, which have come to define the data, information, and, recently, knowledge leveraged by businesses.

The present need is for a logical connection between organisational design and IT systems design, including the design of information systems. There is a need for a science of the designing of organisation and its systems. New concepts, design formalisms and technologies are required in order for organisation and its IT systems to be designed coherently.

The series welcomes research monographs on the social, technical, political and ethical aspects of such design and implementation. The present focus on technical design neglects the centrally important social, political and ethical considerations that make business organisations acceptable in our society.

Information Systems: Critical perspectives is thus to be welcomed, as it can contribute to a better understanding of the power and ethical relations linked to information systems. As information technology, the internet and information systems become increasingly the fabric on which businesses design work and commerce systems, the means by which governments deliver services, and the platforms we choose for entertainment, we require greater clarity on the implications for humans.

Is it possible to have information systems without information technology? Bernd Carsten Stahl ponders technology as rationality applied to human problems. The highest point at which technology can fail us is its lack of social, political and ethical value to us. Alternatively, if such technology is not available to us, it is possible to have impressive, highly effective and efficient, information systems nevertheless. The humble and impoverished Mumbai *tiffin-wallas* have designed an organisation and information system that makes use of just a six-category code to deliver 175,000 lunches or *tiffins*. They make only one error in two months, or in 16 million transactions, which exceeds a Six Sigma performance. Most importantly, it has empowered them and made them into a case study for prestigious management schools.

Yet no solution to human problems can be totally devoid of material techno-logy, even the *tiffinwallas* write the symbols on tiffin lids. For us, information technology and information systems make our solutions sophisticated, but also, most importantly, they enhance us as humans. We thus need both solutions that are effective and empowering.

Nandish V. Patel
Director, Brunel Organization and Systems Design Centre [BOSdc]
Brunel University

Preface

This book has developed from a collection of ideas and thoughts, some of which have been published in a variety of books and journals. Many of the papers and presentations that form the basis of some chapters of the book were attempts to shine light on some aspect of the theory or practice of information systems. Like many others, I have come to the field of information systems (IS) by chance rather than by design. And to this day I am not sure whether IS is a field, a discipline or just a muddled-up adhocracy. And I am not sure, either, whether I am part of it, an observer, or possibly a parasite. Or whether any of this matters.

What does matter to me is that technology is all around us, possibly a part of what it means to be human. However, we are often not very good at understanding and using it in ways that are of most benefit to ourselves. This is true in particular for information and communication technologies (ICTs). ICTs have some characteristics that seem to allow human beings to live better private and public lives but, at the same time, they often constrain us and contribute to social arrangements that are problematic. In order to address this problem, this book attempts to combine three different strands of literature that have the potential to improve our understanding and use of ICT and IS: traditional IS literature, critical research in IS, and computer and information ethics. From early on in my IS career I felt that mainstream IS literature is usually too narrow in scope and interest and that it needs to be supplemented with a more socially aware theoretical approach. This is where the second stream of literature comes in, namely critical theory. I am, of course, not the first to link IS and critical theory and I therefore draw heavily on sources that have done the same. These are now often referred to as critical research in information systems (CRIS). Publications that can be classed under the heading of CRIS go back at least to the 1984 IFIP WG 8.2 conference in Manchester, but interest in this approach has started to intensify much more recently. It appears that this is the first single-authored book on CRIS.

One of the problems of writing a book that emphasises critical perspectives on information systems is that the number of possible topics, theories and issues to discuss exceeds the confines of most books. I believe that critical research is ethically motivated, an argument I will develop in more depth as the book progresses. Critical research tends to concentrate on issues of high ethical relevance, such as power, gender, surveillance, etc. At the same time, there is a body of literature that explicitly addresses ethical issues with regard to information and ICT, namely the field of computer and information ethics. This literature is the third stream of work that the current book will focus on.

The academic rationale for this approach is easy to state. Critical research in general and CRIS in particular are interventionist enterprises that aim to promote emancipation. This raises many problems, some of which I will discuss below. It also means, however, that critical research is built on ethical assumptions that need to be made explicit. The unique contribution of this book will thus be to go beyond a general discussion of critical perspectives of information systems and to concentrate on the role that ethics plays in these perspectives as well as offering an ethical evaluation of CRIS. I am happy to argue that ethical considerations are increasingly being perceived as relevant in a number of fields, including IS. This book will therefore contribute not only to the debate on critical theory and information systems, but also to the role of IS in society and the larger question of how liberal democracies can and should view and use the technologies at their disposal, in order to promote the ethical aim of furthering our individual and collective abilities to lead a good life.

Acknowledgements

The book draws on a number of contributions without which it would not have been possible to produce the present narrative. A number of colleagues have given me their permission to use texts that were originally prepared or published as jointly authored papers. I would like to thank Ibrahim Elbeltagi and Neil McBride for their permission to draw upon the empirical research and the theoretical development concerning the ICT strategy in Egypt. At this point I want to underline that the critical conclusions concerning Egyptian policy are mine. It was Bruno Zelic who originally suggested the idea of investigating the role of ontology in the failure of e-voting in Ireland. I need to thank Alison Adam for her contribution to the idea of heroic management and its application to privacy and surveillance in organisations. My discussions and collaboration with Björn Niehaves have greatly clarified my view of the concept of paradigms in information systems.

In addition, I should thank all those who have made it possible for me to write this book. This includes my line managers, who, should they ever read this book, will find out that my general appreciation of management is limited, but should not interpret this as a personal insult. Thanks are also due to the members of the Centre for Computing and Social Responsibility and the Information Society Doctoral Programme, which have provided fora for discussing many of the issues treated here. Special thanks go to Simon Rogerson and Ben Fairweather for the many stimulating debates we have had. And I would also like to include our research students, whose work and contributions to discussions have often forced me to become more precise in my reasoning and clearer in its expression.

Thanks are finally due to the following for their kind permission to reproduce copyright material or material that has previously been published in other outlets:

Springer Science and Business Media:
Stahl, Bernd Carsten (2006): 'Emancipation in Cross-Cultural IS Research: The Fine Line between Relativism and Dictatorship of the Intellectual' *Ethics and Information Technology* (8:3), special issue on 'Bridging Cultures: Computer

Ethics, Culture, and Information and Communication Technologies', edited by Charles Ess: 97–108

Zelic, Bruno and Stahl, Bernd Carsten (2005): 'Does Ontology Influence Technological Projects? The Case of Irish Electronic Voting.' In: *Lecture Notes in Computer Science*, vol. 3782/2005, Professional Knowledge Management: Third Biennial Conference, WM 2005, Kaiserslautern, Germany, 10–13 April 2005, Revised Selected Papers Editors: Klaus-Dieter Althoff, Andreas Dengel, Ralph Bergmann, Markus Nick and Thomas Roth-Berghofer: 657–667

Stahl, Bernd Carsten (2006): 'Positivism or Non-positivism – Tertium Non Datur: A Critique of Philosophical Syncretism in IS Research.' In: Kishore, Rajiv; Ramesh, Ram and Sharman, Raj (eds), *Ontologies: A Handbook of Principles, Concepts and Applications in Information Systems*. Springer, New York

The *Journal of Information Systems in Education*:
Stahl, Bernd Carsten (2004): 'E-Teaching: The Economic Threat to the Ethical Legitimacy of Education?' In: *Journal of Information Systems in Education* (15:2), 155–162

IEEE:
Stahl, Bernd Carsten (2007): 'Privacy and Security as Ideology'. *IEEE Technology and Society*, special issue on 'Usable Security and Privacy', edited by L. Jean Camp: 35–45

The Informing Science Institute:
Stahl, Bernd Carsten (2006): 'On the Difference or Equality of Information, Misinformation, and Disinformation: A Critical Perspective'. In: *Informing Science Journal* (9), 83–96, available at: http://inform.nu/Articles/Vol9/ v9p083–096Stahl65.pdf

Academic conferences:
Stahl, Bernd Carsten (2005): 'The Ethical Problem of Framing E-Government in Terms of E-Commerce'. In: *Electronic Journal of E-Government* (3:2), 77–86

Blackwell:
Stahl, Bernd Carsten (2008): 'The Ethical Nature of Critical Research in Information Systems'. *Information Systems Journal*, special issue on 'Exploring the Critical Agenda in IS Research', edited by Carole Brooke, Dubravka Cecez-Kecmanovic and Heinz K. Klein (forthcoming)

Introduction

A book that purports to offer critical perspectives on information systems should probably start out with a definition of these terms and an explanation of why such critical perspectives are necessary, required or warranted. This, in turn, will require a brief discussion of the concepts involved and their recent history. As much of the book will deal with questions concerning critical theory and critical research, I will use this introduction to outline the field of information systems and the recent history of critical research in information systems.

Information systems (IS), sometimes called management information systems, is an academic field that was first established in the 1960s. It originally drew on computer science, management and organisation theory, operations research, and accounting, but went beyond these in its explicit focus on the use of computers in society and organisations (Hirschheim and Klein, 2003). In a narrow view, information systems as a field of inquiry is interested in the optimal use and allocation of computing and related resources for the purpose of promoting organisational aims, such as efficiency and the optimal control of business processes. From the outset of the establishment of IS there has been much critique of such a narrow definition of the discipline. There are several reasons for this. The scope and limitation of IS to profit-generating organisations is difficult to sustain, given the prevalence of computing technology in all sorts of organisations, including not-for-profit, non-governmental but also public organisations. Since the different types of organisations follow vastly different goals, it is difficult to limit IS considerations to narrow business issues that eventually promote the maximisation of profits. Furthermore, there is the issue of the aims and larger context of organisations in society. Going back to the bases of market-oriented ways of organising economies and societies as set out by Adam Smith in *The Wealth of Nations* (Smith, 1986), one should keep in mind that businesses are not ends in themselves but function in a social framework that is tailored to promote society's goals. To put it differently, society allows companies to pursue the aim of profit maximisation because it expects some greater good from this. If computing technology is used for such purposes, then its implications for the greater good to flow should be considered in order to avoid inconsistencies.

Another problem in the definition of IS as a field of study is the reference to computing technology. In the early days of the field, computers were clearly recognisable and posed challenges that were comparatively easy to define. While computer sciences and related fields concentrated on the technical side of such problems, IS focused on organisational issues. In the early twenty-first century it is more difficult to define the relevant technology. Computing technology is becoming pervasive and it is increasingly embedded in other technologies – and it has a wide-ranging influence on social interaction. Not only are there clearly business-linked phenomena such as e-business and e-commerce that IS scholars have to consider, but there are issues such as emerging technologies (often summarised under the heading of web 2.0), social software, ambient intelligence, affective computing and many others that have an influence on the field. It is very difficult to clearly delimit the subject field, even if one follows Orlikowski and Iacono's (2001) call to concentrate more explicitly on the IT artefact. A related problem is that of an appropriate theory of technology that would allow a clear demarcation of technology and thus of information technology. If one prefers a wider understanding of technology as the application of a particular type of rationality to specific types of problems, then information technology may not require an artefact at all, thus rendering attempts to define IS via technology deeply problematic.

One aspect that most IS researchers seem to agree on is that, other than computer science, software engineering, etc., IS has a strong focus on the human element in technology (Argyris, 1971; Lyytinen and Hirschheim, 1988). Definitions such as Laudon and Laudon's (1999, p. 13) are common. These authors describe IS as 'composed of machines, devices, and "hard" physical technology', and requiring 'substantial social, organizational, and intellectual investments to make them work properly'. However, not all IS research is necessarily engaged in all of these aspects, and, again, there is a rather functional view implied when IS are seen as something that can and should be made to work properly.

Another possible avenue to gain a workable definition of IS is the concept of 'system'. The idea of a system is strongly linked to the technological development of computers, which from the outset were linked to the idea of cybernetics as put forward and developed by Norbert Wiener and others. At the same time, there has been much interest in the idea of social systems and resulting concepts such as autopoiesis and the description of living organisms and even societies as systems. There have been calls for an increased emphasis on the idea of systems in IS research, similar to the earlier-cited call for a concentration on technology (Lee, 2004). However, a problem with this is that systems are not inherently given but arguably constituted by observation (Nygaard, 2002). Moreover, many IS researchers have neither a formal background in systems theory nor much interest in it.

A further problem of IS as an academic discipline is that it has developed from a variety of existing disciplines and that there is much overlap with these, and also with other disciplines that are interested in similar issues. Questions to do with the use of ICT in organisations and society can equally well be raised in sociology, psychology or philosophy, leaving little that is unique about IS. This has led to an 'identity crisis in the IS discipline' (Benbasat and Zmud, 2003). This problem is partly a theoretical one, but it has massive practical implications in terms of career prospects and abilities to publish findings, and it has thus been controversially discussed by members of the discipline (Ives *et al.*, 2004). While it is not the main intention of this book to contribute to this discussion, it will be a necessary by-product to engage with these questions. Much critical work in IS is motivated by the perceived self-imposed limitations of the field and aims to overcome them. Given the problems of finding a generally agreed and accept-able definition of IS, I follow Willcocks (2004) and use a loose view that is devoid of any material content and relies exclusively on the self-referential property of members of the discipline as individuals who describe themselves as members by attending IS conferences and publishing in IS outlets.

I have already indicated that there are quite a few members of this loosely defined group of IS scholars who are not happy with the way the discipline has viewed itself and is viewed from the outside. Issues raised have to do with the philosophical underpinnings, the choice of appropriate theories, the scope of admissible research questions and the general purpose of the field. One stream of research that is sceptical about current IS research draws on figures of thought that were established by scholars engaged in what is often called critical theory or critical research. I will spend a considerable amount of space on the question of what exactly that might be, so at this stage I will confine myself to a brief history of critical research in IS. Depending on one's definition of critical research, one can find traces of it going back to the very beginning of the field. It began to emerge as a coherent body of work in the early and mid-1980s and is most famously linked to the 1984 IFIP WG 8.2 conference in Manchester (Mumford *et al.*, 1985), where many of the most important figures of thought were first formulated. Despite these well-established roots, relatively little IS research was undertaken that was explicitly critical. Notwithstanding some high-profile publications (Lee, 1994; Hirschheim and Klein, 1994), critical research in IS remained a minor activity and did not develop into a coherent body of work.

However, that position has started to change in recent years. There have now been several special issues on CRIS, starting with a special issue of the *Journal of Information Technology* in 2002 and followed by two special issues in 2006, one in the journal *Information Technology and People* and the other in the *International Journal of Technology and Human Interaction*. A further special issue in the *Information Systems Journal* is expected for 2008. In 2005, Howcroft and Trauth edited the first book-length account of CRIS, which will be followed by at least one further edited volume to be edited by Brooke in 2008. The present book, to the best of my knowledge, is the first single-authored volume that explicitly deals with the topic area of critical research in information systems.

As will become clear quickly, CRIS in many ways still is very much in an early state of development. There is little agreement on what should count as critical as opposed to non-critical research in IS. CRIS scholars have diverging views on the purpose of the activity and where it should be heading. Theoretical roots and reference disciplines are many, and the community spends much time discussing these. On the other hand, there seems to be an increasingly visible wish by members of the CRIS community to establish it as an accepted and legitimate part of the IS field, which may be strong enough to override internal differences. The CRIS community is sufficiently small to allow for much personal interaction but it is also sufficiently wide to find world-wide representation and thus allow for potential growth.

In order to provide a good overview of CRIS and, at the same time, develop a useful contribution to the debate, I will concentrate on the aspects that seem most relevant to CRIS. The structure of the book reflects these main areas. The book is divided into four main parts, each of which will discuss one aspect in some depth. Part I will deal with the theory of CRIS. It will start out with a definition of CRIS and a rooting of CRIS work in the literature on critical research. It will then elaborate on some of the dominant theoretical streams in CRIS, focusing on a comparison of the two theorists who, arguably, have influenced CRIS the most, namely Michel Foucault and Jürgen Habermas. The attempt to cover the theoretical basis of CRIS will also start to touch on one of the main contributions of the book, namely the link between CRIS and ethics. Some of the open theoretical questions will be addressed, notably the question of how critical research that claims to be emancipatory can avoid the problem of forcing emancipation on subjects who do not wish to be emancipated, which could render the liberating idea of emancipation an act of intellectual oppression. This theoretical part of the book will also touch on questions of culture and critical research, and attempt to reinterpret some established critical theories from the critical point of view.

Part II will address philosophical issues arising from the theoretical foundations of CRIS. The three main questions of this section will refer to the ontology, epistemology and methodology of CRIS. Critical researchers tend to have particular views on all these issues, and those views give rise to conclusions that can support the entire critical approach but that should be reflected critically.

IS is typically seen as an applied field. This is reflected in CRIS, where a lack of empirical studies is often lamented. Part III of the book is therefore dedicated to applications of CRIS. It gives examples of critical work in a variety of areas related to information systems. Not all the 'applications' are empirical. Some are examples of the application of critical thought to existing discourses in IS. Others draw either on pieces of research that I have undertaken myself or on research done by colleagues who have kindly allowed me to use their material. Overall, this part of the book should give an indication of the many different avenues that CRIS can take.

Part IV, the final part, is then dedicated to a reflection on CRIS. It is often claimed that reflexivity is a defining feature of critical work, including CRIS. Reflection can refer to honesty and transparency concerning the researcher's own bias, but also to considerations of the consistency and coherence of the work undertaken. Critical research arguably raises more questions than it answers. CRIS scholars will need to face some important issues. How will the field continue to develop? Can we agree on what should or should not count as critical? Does CRIS claim to be radical? If so, how can it be radical and still remain an academic discipline? How can we measure the successes or outcomes of critical work, or do we not need to do so? Are there solutions or recommendations that can follow from CRIS? These and other questions will need to be addressed by the community and the current book will, hopefully, contribute to the debate.

Part I

Theory

Critical research tends to be theory driven. At the same time, the question of appropriate theory is a continuous source of debate in critical research. To a large degree, the choice of theory defines research as critical. In addition, there is an ongoing debate about theory, its meaning, its role and its choice in the area of information systems (Gregor, 2006; Truex *et al.*, 2006). It is therefore fitting that the first main part of a book on critical research in information systems will be dedicated to the topic of theory.

An appropriate starting point will be the topic of a theory of critical research in IS. As indicated earlier, it is problematic to define CRIS in a sentence or two. In order to explore what we mean by CRIS, it will be useful to choose a theoretical approach that allows for the description of several facets and nuances. The first chapter in Part I will therefore aim to give a comprehensive view of CRIS, one that is consistent with the current literature but goes beyond it in several ways. This theory of CRIS will also be important later on in the book when a connection between CRIS and other theories and the concept of ethics will be established.

The subsequent chapters of Part I will be used to explore the link between CRIS and other theories or to explore problems that arise from the theory of CRIS. First I offer a detailed discussion of two of the main theories used in CRIS, namely the work of Habermas and Foucault respectively. It has been argued that Habermas has a dominant role in CRIS (Brooke, 2002a) and that other approaches should find more of an audience. I am not sure that this is still true and that Habermas does indeed dominate the discourse, but he certainly plays a central role. Foucault is similarly well established, and one can see the two as representatives of two main streams of critical theory, with Habermas representing the modernist Frankfurt School perspective and Foucault the postmodern view of critical research. Discussing their relationship will be useful for understanding open issues in the critical tradition.

Subsequent to this, I will establish a link between CRIS and ethics. This is one aspect where I believe the book makes a substantial contribution to knowledge because the relationship between CRIS and ethics, albeit arguably obvious, is rarely made explicit. While CRIS is motivated and supported by ethical ideas, this does not mean that it endorses an uncritical morality. Indeed, morality has been observed to be one of the strongest carriers of ideologies that serve to cement the status quo and thus one of the most important impediments to critical reflection. The subsequent chapter will take this thought and apply it to one of the central concepts in CRIS, namely emancipation. Emancipating people requires an ethical intention, but at the same time the attempt to emancipate others carries the risk of alienating them or, worse, of turning into a different kind of domination. Emancipation thus requires an awareness of the limitations of critical work. At the same time, the problems of emancipation should not lead us to the conclusion that criticalists should refrain from striving for it.

1 Critical research in information systems

The attempt to give a clear and unambiguous definition of any concept is always problematic, as it presupposes the possibility of giving a fixed meaning to a term, even though language is always in motion. This is particularly true for contested terms, including many that we know from the social sciences. And it is even worse for the term 'critical research' or 'critical theory', where it can be argued that the very attempt to determine fixed characteristics of the term goes against the basics and beliefs that scholars engaged in it hold (Kincheloe and McLaren, 2005). It will nevertheless be necessary to describe what we mean by 'critical' in the specific area of information systems. Critical research in the field of information systems is often described as an alternative research approach, one that complements the more established positivist and interpretivist positions (Trauth, 2001). This is based on Orlikowski and Baroudi's (1991) seminal paper, which was built on Chua's (1986) work. This, in turn, can best be understood as a reaction to the dichotomous categorisation of social science research by Burrell and Morgan (1979). Critical research in this context is a paradigm[1] or a world-view that consists of beliefs about physical and social reality (ontology, social relations, human rationality), knowledge (epistemology, methodology), and the relationship between theory and practice. The value of this view is that it allows alternatives to the prevailing paradigm of positivist research to be discussed. At the same time it is misleading because it implies that the three paradigms are mutually exclusive and comprehensive. Neither implication is correct.

In order to avoid the problems raised by the view of critical research as a paradigm, I propose the definition of critical research as research characterised by an intention to change the status quo, overcome injustice and alienation, and promote emancipation. This is the heart of critical research and it allows the identification of further characteristics such as typical topics, theories and methodologies. I wish to emphasise that this definition is not the only one possible. Harvey (1990, p. 19), for example, has suggested the characteristics of 'abstraction, totality, essence, praxis, ideology, history and structure'. My suggested and competing definitions should be seen as complementary. Harvey's view, for example, reflects my emphasis on the critical intention when he says that '[c]ritical social research includes an overt political struggle against oppressive social structures' (1990, p. 20). The added value of the definition proposed in this chapter is that it offers a different account of critical research and allows for a view with differing emphasis, which will be useful for the discussion of theoretical and philosophical implications of CRIS, including the link between CRIS and ethics.

Critical intention

The most important characteristic of critical research in information systems is its critical intention, which means the fact that critical researchers aim at initiating and promoting change (Cecez-Kecmanovic, 2005). This is the heart of Chua's and Orlikowski and Baroudi's claim that critical research is an alternative to positivist and interpretivist research. Both of the latter research approaches can be purely descriptive, whereas critical research aspires to change social realities. As we will see later, this normative characteristic is closely linked with critical topics and theories. It is based on the Marxist view of history as a history of class struggles and a negative perception of capitalism (Marx, 1969; Hirschheim and Klein, 1989; Orlikowski and Baroudi, 1991). The injustices and inequities inherent in given social structures require the researcher to search for better, freer, less alienating and more emancipated ones. Few critical IS researchers would call themselves Marxist, but most share a suspicion that current social arrangements are not in everyone's interest and need to be improved. Global injustices and unequal distribution are an important factor in motivating IS scholars to adopt a critical stance (Walsham, 2005b).

The critical intention thus mirrors Marx's (1964 I, p. 141) view that philosophy (or, in our case, IS research) has always merely interpreted the world differently, while it is important to change it. Critical research thus seeks knowledge, but not for its own sake. Critical research aims to be practical but in a specific way (Walsham, 2005a), namely to change social practices in such a way that the negative effects of the way society and organisations are run will be minimised. 'The critical social theory approach was never intended to be an abstract philosophy. It was to bring about real change in the human condition' (Ngwenyama, 1991, p. 276). Critical research will therefore rarely aim at improving managerial tools or practices for the sake of efficiency. Or, to use Fournier and Grey's (2000) terms, CRIS is 'non-performative'. Instead, it tries to keep the bigger picture of the role of the economic system and individuals in society in mind.

The critical intention is central to critical research because it influences all other aspects. Most of the defining features of critical research found in the literature are consequences of the intention. An important example of this is reflexivity, which is often seen as a central aspect (Alvesson and Willmott, 1992; Alvesson and Deetz, 2000; Cecez-Kecmanovic, 2001a; Waring, 2004). Reflexivity means that critical researchers are willing to be critical about their own assumptions, beliefs and ideologies and render these open to debate. If the intention is to promote emancipation, the researchers need to allow a critique of their own viewpoint. This may help identify obstacles that preclude successful emancipation. Similarly, reflexivity requires researchers to consider whether the aim of their research is realistic. Research with well-meaning emancipatory aims that stands no chance of making a practical difference thus cannot claim to be critical. This raises a range of epistemological and political problems that should considered by critical researchers. One result of reflexivity is that critical scholars need to reflect on and be open about their own background and aims. Doing so requires them to admit that they cannot be neutral, that a value-neutral position is impossible and that the critical intention requires them to own up to their political agendas, which are often linked to critical work (Richardson, 2005). This book will emphasise the feature of reflexivity in its final part, Part IV, which will undertake a reflection of the arguments presented here and of the conclusions that can be drawn from them.

Critical topics

On the basis of the critical intention to change society or parts thereof, critical research is interested in those areas where our social structures are in need of attention. These areas are what I call 'critical topics'. Critical topics can thus be defined as objects of research which facilitate furthering of the critical intention. This definition includes and goes beyond Harvey's (1990) suggested topics of class, gender (Adam, 2005) and race. Because of the importance of power structures for the individual and that individual's ability to live a life according to his or her own criteria, power is probably the most important critical topic (Brooke, 2002b). Much critical IS research concentrates on the situation of the individual. A central critical topic is therefore individual empowerment. Critical IS researchers discuss how information systems can disempower people and how, conversely, they can be used to empower individuals (Lyytinen and Hirschheim, 1988; Brooke, 2002a). Empowerment can play a role wherever IS are used, including traditional profit-oriented capitalist companies, virtual organisations (Levary and Niederman, 2003) or educational institutions (Dawson and Newman, 2002). For the critical researcher, those uses of IS that exploit, dominate, oppress, or disempower people are misuses, and the aim is to 'promote liberating and empowering IS design and use' (Cecez-Kecmanovic, 2001a). Following the Marxist tradition, critical research is worried about the alienating effects of current labour relations (Orlikowski and Baroudi, 1991; Varey *et al.*, 2002).

Another critical topic, closely related to and sometimes used synonymously with empowerment, is emancipation. Emancipation is one of the most frequently cited topics of critical IS research (McAulay *et al.*, 2002; Ulrich, 2001a; Cecez-Kecmanovic, 2001b; Klein and Myers, 1999; Cecez-Kecmanovic *et al.*, 2002). Capitalist work structures not only enslave and alienate labourers but also systematically take away their ability to develop and prosper. Emancipation is a slightly wider concept than empowerment because it needs to address the question of how the individual's abilities can be developed and its potential achieved. Emancipation looks into psychological as well as organisational issues

(Hirschheim and Klein, 1994). Related concepts are authenticity (Probert, 2002a) and autonomy, which also concern individuals' ability to interact with their environment. While the primary interest of emancipation is to aid the individual to achieve his or her potential, it has also been framed in terms of common interest. A workforce consisting of empowered and emancipated individuals can achieve better results and is thus in the interest of the employer (Mumford, 2003). This interpretation relies on the belief that the goals of capital and labour, or employers and employees, are compatible, however, and is therefore contentious in critical research.

Apart from the fundamental topics of power, empowerment and emancipation, critical research is also interested in areas of information systems where these basic questions lead to practical consequences. Among the topics for CRIS one can find problems ranging from the organisational level, such as failure of information systems (Introna, 1997; Doherty and King, 2001; Mitev, 2005), to the level of society, such as gender and discrimination (Adam, 2001a; Robinson and Watson, 2001), and international problems such as access and the digital divide (Kvasny and Trauth, 2003; Tavani, 2003).

Furthermore, there are topics related to the underlying social structures, which tend to be critical of capitalism and demonstrate the problems resulting from capitalist social and economic structure. Some authors are interested in the fundamental contradictions and conflicts within capitalist society (Saravanamuthu, 2002a), but the majority of scholars interested in this area of critical topics look at consequences of capitalism, such as the commodification of information (Ladd, 2000; Floridi, 1999), privacy (Davison *et al.*, 2003), labour (Giddens, 1984; Knights and Willmott, 1999), or humans and their activity in general (Klein and Lyytinen, 1985; Brooke, 2002b). Not all critical scholars reject capitalism outright, and there has been some recognition that, at least for some, capitalism can be rewarding and emancipating. Capitalism has furthermore managed to appropriate many critical arguments, thus acquiring the ability to pre-empt critical attacks (Thrift, 2005). As this has been at least partly a result of critical management education, there is a growing awareness of the importance of education in critical work (Grey, 2005).

Finally, there is the critical topic of how capitalism and its alienating conditions came to power and retain a high level of legitimacy. This question is closely linked to the relationship of economic practice and its scientific justification. The underlying problem here seems to be a certain kind of purposive rationality, which is widespread in information systems and thus constitutes another topic of interest for critical research (White, 1985; Hirschheim and Newman, 1991; Wastell, 1996; Wynn, 2001; Cecez-Kecmanovic *et al.*, 2002; Saravanamuthu, 2002a, b; Varey *et al.*, 2002; McAulay *et al.*, 2002; Hirschheim and Klein, 2003; Westrup, 2005; Klecun, 2005).

The area covered by critical topics is clearly quite wide and it will not be possible to discuss the whole field in detail. A sound understanding of CRIS will require an awareness of possible critical approaches and arguments that refer to the critical topics. Part III of the book will therefore be dedicated to applications of CRIS, where a range of topics will be discussed in more depth. These are consciously chosen to represent a wide array of possible technologies and their uses to show that CRIS has relevance beyond a narrow understanding of the term 'information systems'. This part of the book will look at managerial issues but it will go beyond them by including questions of e-teaching and e-learning, electronic government and the use of ICT for development. It will develop conceptual and empirically supported arguments concerning organisational practice as well as issues arising from research in IS, issues that touch on concepts such as trust, privacy, security, ideology and reification.

Critical theories

Interest in the critical topics is usually linked to preferences for certain theories. Theory can be understood as 'a way of seeing and thinking about the world rather than an abstract representation of it' (Alvesson and Deetz, 2000, p. 37). Critical research uses the term 'theory' in this wide sense, rather than the narrow empiricist understanding which is prevalent in positivist IS or business research. The reason for the importance of theory for CRIS is that the choice of theory influences the type of research topic and methodology. The chosen theory also has considerable influence on possible conclusions and practical outcomes. As will be indicated in the discussion of the critical intention, the historical roots of critical research are to be found in the Marxist critique of capitalism. Consequentially, many critical theories go back to Marxist theories, to historical or dialectical materialism (Brooke, 2002a). Critical thoughts aimed at opposing oppression can of course be found in pre-Marx philosophy, including 'Plato, Aristotle, Socrates, Machiavelli, Hobbes, Locke, Saint-Simon...' (Harvey, 1990, p. 14). And the development of critical theory took place in discourse with other philosophical streams, including Nietzschean nihilism (an important influence on Foucault; see Mahon, 1992) and phenomenology (which is relevant for the later Habermas). Other philosophical roots can be found in Kant's call for enlightenment (Kant, 1985), which can be seen as a precursor to and starting point of the critical interest in emancipation. One should see, however, that – at least in continental European philosophy – critical theory means theory whose development takes its historical starting point from Marx. According to Harvey (1990), this close link to Marxism is absent from the Anglo-American understanding of the term, which is more closely linked to pragmatism.

The most prominent representatives of critical theory in the twentieth century were located in the Frankfurt School, among whose main protagonists were Horkheimer, Adorno, Marcuse and Bloch (see Wiggershaus, 2001). While the original scholars of the Frankfurt School are sometimes cited in IS research, most critical research in IS referring to it emphasises the works of Karl-Otto Apel and, more importantly, of Jürgen Habermas. In critical IS research, Habermas's theory of communicative action (TCA) plays a central role (Habermas, 1981). The basis of this use of TCA in IS was laid down by Lyytinen and Klein (1985) and Lyytinen and Hirschheim (1988).

Habermas may be read as a representative of a 'modernist' reading of critique, which arguably appeals to critical IS researchers because it offers the hope of emancipation despite the theoretical and practical problems that arose during the twentieth century. However, there is also strong criticism of this approach, and particularly of Habermas, in critical research (Wilson, 1997). One theoretical stream that is sceptical of modernist enlightenment promises arose from French philosophy in the second half of the twentieth century, from existentialism to postmodernism (Burrell, 1994; Calás and Smircich, 1999). There are further theories that seem to be conducive to the critical intention and that do not always fit well with the modernist perspective, such as postcolonialism, which has also been used in IS research (Mayasandra *et al.*, 2006). Further theoretical approaches open to critical researchers include critical realism (Mingers, 2001a), which tries to overcome the dichotomy of positivism and interpretivism, and opens avenues of understanding of critical issues and critical approaches deriving from different traditions, such as Rorty's neo-pragmatism (1989).

It will not be possible to discuss all these possible theoretical bases of CRIS comprehensively. However, in order to point out some of the relevant arguments, I will discuss the relationship between Habermas's and Foucault's theoretical contributions to CRIS in Chapter 2, which will, hopefully, give an impression of the type of theoretical issues that critical research addresses.

Very briefly, my characterisation of CRIS emphasises the critical faculties of seeking change and improving the status quo by promoting the emancipation of individuals and groups who are in some way affected by ICT. The critical intention has consequences for the types of topics that CRIS scholars tend to be interested in, as well as the choice of theory that they are likely to use. A comprehensive and all-encompassing definition is thus not likely to be forthcoming. However, the description of CRIS I have provided in this chapter should be enough to give an indication of which research can be considered critical and what consequences it may have. The following chapter will now be dedicated to a central question of CRIS, namely the question of the appropriate theory.

2 Theoretical discourses

A comparison of the Foucauldian and Habermasian concepts of discourse in CRIS

Theories that carry the attribute 'critical' abound. Whether a theory is critical or not is often hotly debated. Howcroft and Trauth (2005, p. 2) list the Frankfurt school of critical theory, actor–network theory, Marxism, feminist theory and the work of Bourdieu, Dooyeweerd, Foucault and Heidegger as possible candidates. Fournier and Grey (2000, p. 16) complement this list by naming 'neo-Marxism (labour process theory, Frankfurt School of Critical Theory, Gramscian "hegemony theory"), post-structuralism, deconstructionism, literary criticism, feminism, psychoanalysis, cultural studies, environmentalism'. More recent theoretical developments such as postcolonialism and queer theory also find a place under the umbrella of critical theory. This list cannot claim to be exhaustive but it can be quite exhausting. There are few, if any, individuals who can claim to be familiar with all of these streams of critical theory.

More important than a mere listing of such critical fields and the names of critical researchers who have produced theories in them is probably the meaning and use of theory that render it critical. Critical and non-critical theories can be distinguished according to their ability to promote the critical intention, to overcome injustice and promote emancipation. For Cecez-Kecmanovic (2005, p. 35), a critical theory is a way of being in the world that allows relevant phenomena to be dealt with. The main functions of critical theory, according to Alvesson and Deetz (2000), are directing attention, organising experience and enabling useful responses.

Two theoretical bodies of literature that are generally recognised as critical theories are derived from the work of Jürgen Habermas and Michel Foucault respectively. They share the critical attributes of questioning accepted reality and providing alternative views. They are also arguably the most frequently used theories in CRIS and thus a useful starting point for a more detailed discussion of theoretical issues. For both Habermas and Foucault, the concept of 'discourse' is of central importance. I have thus chosen this term as the focus around which I have organised the discussion and comparison of these two critical theories.

Information systems, as the academic discipline that is interested in the mutual influence of technology, individuals and social entities, has long since discovered the importance of discourses. Discourses play a role in understanding what information and communication technology is, how it can be used, how different interpretations affect use, etc. On a more fundamental level it has been argued that ICT is even constituted by discourses (Gergen, 1999).

At the same time, however, it is not always clear what a discourse is. It has something to do with communication, with the exchange of ideas and views. But does that mean that every act of communication is a discourse? If not, what are the criteria that define discourses and distinguish them from chat, idle talk or other forms of communication? Are there conditions of discourses? What is the purpose of discourses?

The concept of discourse

This section will attempt to clarify what the term 'discourse' means in the theories of Foucault and Habermas. A useful starting point is the etymology of the term 'discourse'. The Latin root of the term is the verb *discurrere*, which means literally 'to run apart', from *currere*, 'to run'. '*Diskursus*' thus means 'to run to and fro' (*Encarta*, 1999, p. 538), which has developed into the idea of an exchange of ideas. The English, French and German uses of the term differ slightly. The French '*le discours*' is slightly less formal than the English 'discourse'. While it still refers to serious statements, it is more part of the ordinary use of language. *Donner un discours*, for example, means to give a speech or presentation. *Discours* therefore does not necessarily refer to an immediate exchange of ideas. On the other hand, the German term '*Diskurs*', as used by Habermas, is probably even more formal in its use than the English term. The use of *Diskurs* in German stands for a clearly defined debate about a specific topic. What we should keep in mind is that Foucault's *le discours* and Habermas's *der Diskurs* are not identical in their everyday uses of the terms.

Foucault's discourse

Foucault is interested in discourse as the societal process of understanding and self-definition. His research concentrates on the way discourses are organised and, more specifically, on who gets to participate and contribute and who is excluded. This question of inclusion or exclusion from discourse is the central theme of his work and it can be identified in most of his diverse writings. The procedures that control and organise discourses are manifold, but include, among others, truth, conversational taboos, madness, doctrine and (scientific) discipline (Foucault, 1971).

Foucault wants to show that the European idea of universal communication is a myth and that access to communication is regulated by rituals that are not subject of discourses and that are not rationally defined or defended. Despite the fact that our societies appear to honour discourses, they are in fact afraid of the word. Foucault tries to show the lack of rationality of discourses and to demonstrate their character as events rather than continuous developments. Discourses are discontinuous, risky and overlapping. We are actually using discourses as a form of violence (Foucault, 1971, p. 55).

Using this background, Foucault's concept of discourse has been widely received in social sciences, including business studies and information systems. Researchers who refer to Foucault's view of discourse tend to recognise that it is not a precise definition of the term that is of interest to him but rather the procedures and social interactions that shape communication. Drawing on Foucault, Knights and Morgan (1991, p. 253), for example, see discourse as a 'set of ideas and practices which condition our ways of relating to, and acting upon, particular phenomena'.

A central aspect of Foucauldian discourses is power. Power is recognised to be a core constituent of all discourses, and one of the reasons why one participates in discourses (Foucault, 1971, p. 12). Power also has to do with madness and wisdom. Power produces and defines knowledge. Power and knowledge imply one another (Foucault, 1975, p. 32). Discourses produce power but they can also expose it and render it fragile (Foucault, 1976, p. 133). An important issue concerning power relationships in discourses is the question of inclusion or exclusion. Foucault is interested in the criteria according to which specific views are considered legitimate contributions and individuals are allowed to participate in particular discourses. Power shapes and directs discourses, and it influences the meaning of concepts. Foucault's writings are relevant here because they suggest that terminology is central to the functioning of discourses but that it is not neutral. The power to define terms determines the outcome of discourses.

Related to Foucault's concept of power is another concept that seems to exert great power over the imagination of IS scholars, namely the Panopticon. The term 'Panopticon' describes a prison where all the prisoners are constantly under covert observation. Bentham, who coined the term, saw it as an improvement over traditional methods of punishment. It was meant to modify convicts' behaviour and to allow them to be reintegrated into society. Foucault's recasting of Bentham's idea of the Panopticon is of interest because it links the ideas of power, discipline, education, and access to discourses. At the same time, it seems to strike a chord with IS scholars because organisational use of information and communication technology (ICT) seems almost predestined to re-enact new versions of the Panopticon (see Goold, 2003).

Despite, or maybe because of, the importance of the concept of power for Foucault's idea of discourse, it is important to note that he does not talk about power as we know it from political theory: the ability to force others to do one's bidding. It is more than mere repression (Foucault, 1994a). Power is not a thing that can be possessed, nor is it necessarily negative (Knights and Willmott, 1999). Power has something to do with discipline – discipline over the human body as well as academic disciplines (see Introna, 1997). It tends to be spread throughout discourses and can affect those at the top of the apparent hierarchy as well as those at the bottom (see Wong, 2002). Discursive power is linked, via the idea of the Panopticon, to technology and its organisational or societal use (see Edenius, 2003). Discourses in this view are not universal exchanges of ideas but can better be compared with markets and negotiations, where different stakeholders have different market power and the production of discourse depends on the social, technical and other capital.

Foucault's concept of discourse is critical because it analyses and deconstructs our Enlightenment ideas of rational communication. It questions our self-image and shows some of the underlying realities of modern societies. Foucault develops powerful analytical tools, and he arguably does so in order to improve social reality. Of importance for academic writing but also for social interaction is the idea of regimes of truth. Regimes of truth are the circumscribed discourses that define particular issues as relevant, particular actors as worth listening to and particular propositions as capable of being true. Regimes of truth define what is to be considered true and what is not. The very idea of regimes of truth goes against the common-sense concept of truth as objective and constant. It gives critical scholars an opening to question shared consensus and thus to explore ideologies, reifications, etc., as I shall argue. Most interestingly, it shows that power and truth cannot simply be divided (Avgerou and McGrath, 2005). It has also been used to expose the power constellations within the IS discipline, where certain attempts to define the nature of the field can easily be understood as attempts to define discourses and thus exert power over competing interpretations of the field (Introna, 2003a).

Habermas's discourse

The concept of discourse is as central in Habermas's work as it is in Foucault's, but it takes on a different meaning. Habermas's central work, 'The Theory of Communicative Action' (1981), explains the concept and function of discourses. Communicative action is distinguished from other types of action such as pragmatic action or strategic action and it is characterised by the fact that it takes the other seriously and accepts him or her as an equal, and deserving of respect. Communicative action thus always has an ethical side to it. The background to this is the conception of humans as social beings who need to interact in order to survive and prosper. We need to collaborate, and by employing communicative action we do so in a moral fashion.

Whenever we communicate, in every speech act, the speaker implies at least three validity claims (*Geltunsansprüche*). These are truth, (normative) rightness and authenticity. This means that no matter what a speaker says, it is implied that the content of the statement is true, that it conforms to normative rules and that the speaker is veracious (that is, the speaker means what he or she says). There will, of course, frequently be cases where it can be doubted whether a statement is true, whether it is allowed or whether the speaker is authentic in saying it. In such situations, discourses play a central role. Discourses are the means or the medium (Habermas, 1981) that interlocutors use to clarify contentious validity claims (Ulrich, 2001a). In a discourse, all the parties affected by the claim have the chance to discuss it, with the aim of resolving their differences and arriving at a consensus regarding the claim. The result of the discourse is a claim whose validity is accepted by all the participants in the discourse (Ess, 1996). It is important to note that Habermas does not produce material rules for the evaluation of speech acts. His theory only provides procedures that, if adhered to, will guarantee the validity of claims. This formal character of Habermasian discourses allows the inclusion of all aspects of a disputed claim that seem relevant to participants, including historical or local particularities that are important for a given problem.

As I have already indicated, an important aspect of discourses is that they are inherently ethical. Normative validity claims are part of all speech acts and there is no value-neutrality in communication. This is caused by our social nature and the resulting vulnerability of human beings, which ethics is meant to alleviate. Discourses do not create norms but they are used to check existing norms for validity (Habermas, 1983, p. 132).

Habermas sees communicative action as an expression of rationality (Cecez-Kecmanovic *et al.*, 2002). He defines rationality as a disposition of subjects who are capable of speech and action. Rationality is expressed in behaviour for which good reasons exist (Habermas, 1981). The normative term 'rational' is to be used for those discourses in which contentious validity claims are discussed under certain conditions. These conditions are supposed to ensure that the better argument wins (Habermas, 1998a, pp. 138–139). This idea of the better argument that convinces the participants in the discourse is central to Habermas's theory and it is also in clear contradiction to Foucault's discourse, where power and discipline dominate.

The idea that there are better arguments and that these are recognisable and of universal validity is a strong restatement of the hopes of the Enlightenment that reason can enable us to understand the world. However, Habermas reformulates it in such a way that it reflects the 'linguistic turn' of philosophy and overcomes the solipsist dangers of, for example, Kantian thinking. At the same time, Habermas realises that real discourses are often skewed and that the factors which are the focus of Foucault's investigation may have a stronger influence on the outcome of discourses than rationality and good arguments. He therefore defines the conditions under which rational agents would be able to find a consensus by using the exchange of arguments (Habermas, 1998a, p. 278). These conditions are usually called the 'ideal speech situation'. This is defined by a number of factors. The most important ones, according to Habermas, are that (a) nobody can be excluded from the discourse, (b) everybody has the same chance to contribute, (c) participants must mean what they say, and (d) the communication must be free of external as well as internal constraints (Habermas, 1996, p. 62; 1998a, p. 282; 1984, p. 160; Hirschheim and Klein, 1994).

Habermas has often been criticised for this construct of the ideal speech situation, which will rarely, if ever, be realised (Silva, 2005). Such criticism is based on a misunderstanding of the meaning of the construct, whose main contribution is counterfactual and transcendental. That means that it is a condition of the possibility of discourse. Participants in everyday communication need to have the ideal speech situation in mind in order for communication to make sense

(Introna, 1997). Otherwise, if interlocutors assumed that the other does not speak the truth, does not have the legitimacy to say what he or she says and does not mean what he or she says, then there would be little point in engaging in communication.

Discourses in information systems

The previous section gave an overview of the concepts of discourse as we find them in the writings of Foucault and Habermas. Briefly, Foucault stands for the investigation of the influence of power and bodily discipline on historical discourses whereas Habermas stands for the normative explication of the validity and acceptability of discourses. Foucault can be read as an attack on the universalistic idea of scientific rationality whereas Habermas tries to uphold the power of reason and the validity of norms despite the problems with grand narratives.

Foucauldian discourses in IS

There are a wealth of references to Foucault's understanding of discourses in the literature on information systems. The reason for this may be that the organisational use of ICT provides decision makers with numerous possibilities to exert power, to change discourses, to discipline and normalise users. All these are central themes for Foucault, and consequently there seems to be a good fit between Foucault and (critical) IS research (Avgerou and McGrath, 2007).

As Foucault's framework aims to expose the hidden influences on discourses, the power relations and the normalising effect, it can be used to analyse the influence of the use of ICT on communication. Edenius (2003), for example, discusses the way email shapes our discourses. A somewhat more general overview of the effects of computer-mediated communication is offered by Yoon (1996). Since Foucault's approach is highly critical of established institutions, his view of discourses is often utilised in research that aims to critique the status quo. One such area is that of exclusion. While the rhetoric of ICT is often highly inclusive and paints utopias of universal access, the reality is frequently that ICT excludes certain groups or individuals from discourse. This is the problem area of the 'digital divide', or of access (Kvasny and Trauth, 2003; Thompson, 2003; Wastell, 2003; Trauth *et al.*, 2006).

Another discourse that lends itself to a Foucauldian interpretation is that of management fashions. Management fashions are of great importance concerning the adoption and use of technology (Westrup, 2005). They shape our perception and define what is seen as rational. At the same time, they are results of discourses (Doorewaard and van Bijsterveld, 2001). Foucauldian discourse analysis can thus help us understand the development and trajectory of management fashions such as enterprise resource planning (ERP) (Westrup, 2003), supply chain management (SCM) and total quality management (TQM).

Finally, we find applications of Foucault's view of discourse in research regarding singular organisational occurrences such as the introduction of a new system in the London ambulance service (McGrath, 2003) or a specific use of a particular word with defining power for discourses, such as the 'surgical strike' in modern technology-supported warfare (Bissett, 2002).

Using a Foucauldian approach can also be problematic. Foucault's concept of power is so wide that it is hard to distinguish from mere influence (Habermas, 1994a). Another serious problem is the theoretical basis of his critique. Foucault criticises all discourses, including his own. He does not give us a way of determining which discourses are more desirable than others or which use of power is more legitimate than another. This is why Habermas can call him a 'fortunate positivist' for whom validity is expressed in terms of power alone (Habermas, 1994b, p. 88). This also explains why Habermas accuses Foucault of relativism. Furthermore, Foucault's writings, albeit self-critical, are arguably not applicable to themselves. They do not analyse their own genealogical roots in the same way they apply genealogy to other discourses.

Summarising the problems, one could say that Foucault offers great perspectives for the analysis and critique of extant social structures and that he sharpens the perceptions of pathologies of discourses but he offers no means to redress them.

Habermasian discourses in IS

Discursive communicative action is meant to promote co-operation and arrive at generally acceptable principles (Lyytinen and Hirschheim, 1988). Consequently, one can frequently find references to Habermasian discourses in research that addresses issues of ethical importance. Given the formal character of Habermas's theory of discourse, the application of this theory concentrates on the processes of achieving validity of claims rather than on the content of particular claims. A typical question would be how discourses can be instituted that achieve consensus regarding contested validity claims.

A prominent example of this would be the application of ICT in government and democracy. Democratic processes determine rights and obligations. They affect norms and the type of interaction between individuals. Democracy itself can be viewed as an attempt to institute a large-scale discourse. It is therefore not surprising that researchers who are interested in the impact of ICT on democratic processes use the Habermasian lens. It has been found that ICT has an ambivalent impact on e-government or e-democracy. On the one hand, it can improve discourses and help approximate the ideal speech situation (Heng and de Moor, 2003). On the other hand, ICT can also skew discourses, and hide inequalities and unacceptable outcomes (see Ess, 1996; Kolb, 1996). Another example of the Habermasian concept of discourse as a theoretical framework for studying the use of technology in organisational settings is that of e-learning or e-teaching, where the Habermasian view allows for an understanding of the predominant discussions of technology and pedagogy (Settle and Berthiaume, 2002).

Even though Habermasian discourse seems tailor-made for addressing issues that have an obvious ethical angle, one can also find Habermasian or similar approaches in more traditional IS research. One example is that of a rather conventionally motivated information systems development where Habermas's theory of discourse is used to determine user requirements. The argument for Habermas in this type of situation is that it is useful because it maximises the amount of information and minimises the risk of failure (see Elkjaer *et al.*, 1991; Metcalfe and Lynch, 2003). One can observe attempts to take these normative and factual considerations and turn them into applicable IS methodologies such as ETHICS, which is implicitly based on Habermas's ideal speech situation (Hirschheim and Klein, 1994; Stahl, 2007).

There are several problems with the application of Habermas's theories in IS. One of them is the difference between ideal and real discourse. Real discourses are binding only when they approximate ideal discourses, which is always only possible to a certain degree. The question is when real discourses are sufficiently close to ideal discourses to exert normative power and produce acceptable results. A related problem is that of the realisation of discourses. In many cases it will simply not be possible to include all the parties who would have an interest in the discourse. In the case of IS research this problem can arise because commercial entities tend to be based on rigid hierarchies, which by definition exclude the possibility of a free exchange of ideas where the better argument wins. Similarly, using IS as a means of discourse can also be problematic because of the change in communication structures it may entail (see Lyytinen and Hirschheim, 1988).

Another problem of Habermasian discourses is their reliance on consensus. While Habermas recognises that the consensus is to be found in the realm of the ideal speech situation rather than in real discourse, he believes that consensuses can be achieved. It may be that the only available consensus is that no consensus is achievable. There is nevertheless some criticism of the very idea that communication is meant to lead to consensus, because an observation of real communication might just as well give rise to the idea that communication is about disagreement.

A last problem that results from the use of discourses for technical purposes such as IS development is that of the instrumentalisation of discourses. Discourses as expressions of communicative action must be open to the better argument in a power-free zone. Apart from the practicalities of determining the better argument, there is the problem that instrumental use of discourses for specific purposes, such as IS development, runs counter to the very idea of discourses. This is a theoretical problem but it also has practical implications (Howcroft and Wilson, 2003).

The relationship between Habermasian and Foucauldian discourse in IS research

The relationship between the two views of discourse is complex. Habermas and Foucault briefly engaged in a debate about their different views (see Kelly, 1994). This debate was somewhat one-sided because Foucault died soon after starting to consider the Habermasian viewpoint whereas Habermas had time to develop his arguments in more depth. An important difference between the two is that Habermas's theory is more reflective, that it considers its own ontological and epistemological roots, whereas Foucault is less clear about these. It is not possible to reiterate this entire debate here (see Kelly, 1994, and Ashendon and Owen, 1999). I will concentrate on spelling out its meaning for IS researchers.

Using Foucault's discourse theory implies that the researcher is interested in the way discourses are structured, in the processes that allow or disallow access, and in the genealogy of the discourse. The central point of interest tends to be that of power and of the bodily means of exerting power. Scholars who want to utilise Foucault's ideas as a basis of research will need to be critical of their research object in the sense that the creation and constitution of the object need to be considered. Questions of power, discipline and rationality are of central interest, particularly those that are not obvious and can be discovered only by looking at hidden backgrounds and tacit assumptions.

In contrast to a Foucauldian researcher, who is interested in the structure and genealogy of discourses, a Habermasian researcher would concentrate on their content and validity. The comparison of real discourses with the normative construct of the ideal speech situation allows the identification of shortcomings of real speech situations. This 'critical turn' can be applied to information systems (see Ulrich, 2001a, b) where it looks at the content of discourses and at the different validity claims rather than the origin and social environments of statements. Choosing a Habermasian approach goes beyond an objective analysis of discourses and requires the researcher to understand him- or herself as part of an ongoing discourse.

Choosing a Habermasian approach is highly demanding for IS researchers. They are required to be critical and emancipatory, to participate in discourses and to be open to discussion. They should realise the ethical implications of their research and act on them. This means that validity claims should become transparent, that the affected parties should be able to participate in discourses, and that differences in the ability to be heard should be minimised (see Apel, 1988).

The relationship between the two concepts of discourse is not easily captured. On the one hand, one could argue that they are contradictory. Foucault's concentration on power and bodily discipline in real discourses seems to be incommensurable with Habermas's emphasis on acceptability. The underlying concepts of rationality seem to contradict each other. A Foucauldian discourse analysis cannot capture the difference between legitimate and illegitimate uses of power. It treats the individual as a product of its environment and generally does not emphasise the participants' views of power in discourses. One could thus argue that on the basis of a Foucauldian discourse, it is impossible to use a Habermasian perspective and vice versa.

On the other hand, there are similarities between the two. They both see discourses as constitutive of reality, including our individual life-worlds and our collective environments. Individual as well as collective identities are shaped and created by discourses. Probably the most important point where they coincide is the idea of critique. While one can argue that Foucault's critique is theoretically deficient because it offers no alternative, no way of distinguishing acceptable from unacceptable uses of power, it can also be argued that his main motivation was the critique of modern society and the hope to change it (Foucault, 1994b). The most important agreement between Habermas and Foucault can thus be said to be their hope to use their work to improve the social world (Brooke, 2002b).

In this book I will follow the idea that Foucault and Habermas offer theoretical views that are commensurable and complementary. The main line of this answer is that both aim to be critical in order to improve human circumstances. A Foucauldian perspective can be helpful for a Habermasian researcher because it sharpens awareness of non-discursive elements of discourses. Looking at the genealogy of discourses and power constellations that shape them may help one to understand and contextualise validity claims. A Habermasian researcher could use Foucauldian arguments within discourses in order to expose hidden validity claims that have been taken for granted. Participating in and understanding real discourses will often be easier when one takes the Foucauldian perspective into account.

On the other hand, a Foucauldian may need the help of Habermasian ideas in order to fulfil his or her critical intention. Given that Foucault is good at exposing problematic practices but less good at offering alternatives, a Habermasian view may help develop alternatives. Furthermore, Habermas offers an insight into the individual that Foucault neglects. The shape of real discourses is clearly dependent on external power, and it is to Foucault's credit that this has become more explicit. At the same time, it is questionable whether discourses can really be understood without a reflection on the individual's understanding and thus on validity claims. This leads back to critical research, because an understanding of the views of the affected is necessary to develop an idea of improving social realities.

3   Ethics, morality and critical research in IS

Now that I have introduced and discussed in some depth the concept of CRIS and some possible theoretical underpinnings, the next theoretical consideration concerns the link between CRIS and normative theory – that is, ethics and morality. Establishing this link is one of the original contributions of this book, and it is necessary to do so in some depth. I will therefore start this chapter by offering a review of the concepts of ethics and morality. This review will develop two alternative distinctions between the two terms which will allow for an inclusive understanding of ethics and morality, which covers much current ethical thinking and is compatible with a range of philosophical theories on ethics. I will then explain why and how ethics and morality are linked to critical research specifically in IS. They will then follow a discussion of several current CRIS publications, their implicit views on ethics and morality, and the question of how my distinction between the terms can contribute to CRIS research.

Ethics and morality: two possible distinctions

The concept of ethics is an integral part of philosophy. It has been discussed in the Western philosophical tradition at least since the ancient Greeks. Introductory books demonstrate the complexity of the issue. They concentrate either on an exploration of the history of ethical ideas (Hinman, 1998; Brandt, 1959) or on an exposition of the most relevant authors (Dewey and Hurlbutt, 1977).

In order to come to a workable understanding of what ethical issues are, I will discuss two ways of distinguishing between the two terms. On the basis of my earlier work (Stahl, 2004), I call them the French and the German traditions. This way of introducing ethics allows the reader who is not well acquainted with literature on the subject to comprehend the main questions it raises for critical research in IS. At the same time, it should prove to be of interest for readers who have a good knowledge of ethics, because it offers a different approach from the usual discussion of deontology versus teleology or a necessarily eclectic discussion of some relevant ethicists.

Three brief cautionary remarks are in order to preclude unnecessary criticism of the approach. First, the etymology of the two terms 'ethics' and 'morality' does not necessitate a distinction. 'Ethics' has a Greek root whereas 'morality' is derived from Latin. Both can be used to describe customs, good practices or expected behaviour. Indeed, a large part of contemporary Anglo-American literature does not make a clear distinction between them (see Hausman and McPherson, 1996; Johnson, 2001; Ricoeur, 2001). In contrast, I will argue that it will be useful to distinguish between the two and that there are different ways of doing this, but my argument should not be misunderstood as an attempt to prove any other uses 'wrong'. Second, I am using national attributes by labelling my two approaches a 'German' and a 'French' approach respectively. I do so because it provides the reader with an intuitive link to the traditions, which would not materialise if I had used the names of particular scholars. Also, a large number of scholars from France and from Germany do follow the particular approach I have linked to the name of their country, which can be explained by their intellectual heritage. I do not imply that all scholars from those traditions (which would be impossible to delineate clearly in the first place) follow the distinction as explained here. Neither do I mean that the distinction is not used by scholars from different national and intellectual traditions. And finally, the reader should be aware that there are many other ethical traditions which are not covered by this approach.

Ethics and morality in the German tradition

The German tradition can be characterised by three features:

1   Ethics is based on the idea of duty (deontology).
2   Ethics and morality can be understood as the theory and practice of good action respectively.
3   Ethics is based on rationality.

One can only understand the German tradition by taking into account the strong formative role of Immanuel Kant. For Kant, the only good thing is the good will (1995, p. BA 1). The will is good if it is motivated by duty, which means that the maxim of the agent must be universalisable. These thoughts are famously summarised as the Categorical Imperative. The Categorical Imperative states that one should '[a]ct only according to that maxim whereby you can at the same time will that it should become a universal law' (translation: Kemerling, 2000).

Kant's moral philosophy obviously fulfils criteria 1 and 3. It is duty based, and duty can be recognised through the use of reason. In the Anglo-American view, Kant is often described as a rigorous moralist who wants to prescribe every action. This is a misinterpretation based on a lack of attention to point 2, the difference between ethics and morality as theory and practice. Kant's ethics is purely formal. It provides a framework for the evaluation of maxims, which might best be translated as 'frames of mind', and it allows agents to identify maxims that are immoral because they cannot be universalised. It does not create any material duties. This reasoning can be understood only on the basis of the distinction between ethics and morality as theory and practice, which, following Kant, is widespread in German applied ethics and is of pivotal importance for critical research.

Morality, in this tradition, is the set of factually recognised norms which govern individual and collective behaviour. It is a positive fact which can be observed and studied by social sciences. Norms such as 'thou shall not commit adultery' or 'it is bad to copy proprietary software' are part of the canon of morality. This definition of morality is widespread among German ethicists (see Homann and Blome-Drees, 1992; Bayertz, 1993; Steinmann and Löhr, 1994; Ulrich, 1997). According to this definition, morality can include norms that we would consider problematic. Norms such as the Mafia's norm not to collaborate with the police or Al-Qaida's norm to kill as many infidels as possible would be part of a given morality. The question thus is: how can we distinguish between desirable and problematic moralities?

This is where ethics enters the debate. Where morality refers to given and accepted norms, ethics provides the theoretical framework of these norms. Ethics offers criteria that allow us to distinguish between good and bad forms of morality. This can be done by addressing issues of consistency of moralities and, most importantly, by establishing the foundations of moral reasoning, such as Kant's Categorical Imperative. This definition of ethics is again widespread in contemporary applied German ethics (see Lenk, 1991; Hastedt, 1994; Stegmaier, 1995; Ropohl, 1996). However, it is not confined to German scholars and has been reflected in a number of Anglo-American publications as well (see Severson, 1997; Velasquez, 1998; De George, 1999; Marturano, 2002).

This distinction between ethics and morality has several advantages. It allows an explanation of why we can have diverging moral rules and still strive for universal ethical theories, thus addressing the problem of relativity in ethics. It helps distinguish the acceptance of norms from their acceptability. This gives ethicists a place in the debate without making them authoritative or dictatorial figures. The strong reliance on duty captures a moral intuition shared by many of us that good actions must be characterised by more than just good (and possibly accidental) outcomes. Finally, it attributes an important place to rationality, which means that ethical issues can be subject to debate and are not just idiosyncratic whims. The model nevertheless leaves open some questions and ignores some traditions of moral philosophy which are better captured by a different conceptualisation of the terms.

Ethics and morality in the French tradition

Where the German tradition has developed from Kant's thinking, the French tradition is rooted in French moralism, as represented by Michel de Montaigne (1533–1592). The French tradition can be characterised as follows:

1   There is no final foundation of moral norms.
2   Ethics refers to teleology, and morality to deontology.

The historical background of Montaigne's view of ethics (see his Essays, 1910) is the devastation of France in the sixteenth century by internal and external wars and unrest. Montaigne's main philosophical endeavour was a battle against totalising philosophical systems as represented by the predominant Christian theology of his times. He believed that life is infinite and cannot be described in full. Hence, there is no chance of arriving at a systematic foundation for philosophy and ethics. Montaigne's position is hedonistic, which means that he thinks that joy and pleasure are our final ends. There is, however, one permanent danger to our pleasure, namely death, which threatens us constantly. Fear of death limits our ability to lead a fulfilled life. The purpose of philosophy is to allow us to recognise the inevitability of death, to embrace its certainty and thereby overcome our fear. He famously revives Cicero's dictum that engaging in philosophy is learning to die.

These starting assumptions affect the status of philosophy. The traditional distinctions between ontology, epistemology, ethics, etc. are no longer relevant, since all philosophy must contribute to the aim of preparing a good death. Such thinking is subversive for moral systems. When we realise that dying is no evil, we are free from external constraints. This, combined with the impossibility of providing a conclusive foundation of ethics, leads Montaigne to accept current morality as a necessity of social life but without privileging it theoretically. Its main purpose is to establish and protect peace.

Building on these thoughts, the French tradition has developed a different understanding of ethics and morality from the German tradition. There is a general acceptance that abstract reason cannot be the foundation of the distinction between good and bad. Instead, there is a strong assumption that the starting point of ethical considerations must be a recognition of what constitutes a good life. This reflects Aristotelian ethics and also links in with Montaigne's pursuit of happiness. In order for a community or a society to define norms, it must first agree on what it aims to achieve. These considerations are subsumed under the term 'ethics' (*'l'éthique'* in French). This shared perception of the good life is not subject to any higher-level justification. It is the starting point of moral philosophy. It also allows the development of ethical theories based on the interaction with the 'other', as suggested by a range of French philosophers in the twentieth century from Sartre to Levinas (Ricoeur, 1994).

If ethics is concerned with the teleological aim, the vision of the good life (Ricoeur, 1991), then why do we need morality? Morality (*'la morale'*) is understood as a set of rules, as in the German tradition (Russ, 1995). The difference is that the French tradition emphasises the obligatory and constraining nature of morality. The need for morality exists because unconstrained individuals threaten each other with violence and thereby jeopardise the ethical vision of the good life. Morality is thus subordinate to ethics and it is a means of facilitating the ethical aims of a community. There is no further justification of moral rules other than that they allow the avoidance of violence and unhappiness (Weil, 1998) and facilitate the search for the good life. What the good life is or should be is beyond this conception of ethics and morality. This distinction between ethics and morality can be found in a number of French writings on moral philosophy (Wunenburger, 1993; Lenoir, 1991; Ricoeur, 1990, 1991, 1994, 2001).

Contributions and limitations of the French and German traditions to critical research in information systems

The brief introduction to the concepts of ethics and morality in the French and German tradition gives me the conceptual support for the argument that critical research is intrinsically ethical. It should not be misunderstood to imply a comprehensive coverage of the field of ethics. And neither does it imply that the two traditions just outlined are able to address all possible ethical problems. While they cover a range of ethical views, they are united in their focus on the individual human being in a decision situation. Neither can address issues where individual decisions are of low importance, as in the case of environmental ethics, and they are open to a feminist critique of ethics. In many instances they will thus have to be complemented with ethical theories that are less decision centred, such as flourishing ethics (Bynum, 2006) or an ethics of capability (Johnstone, 2007). Table 3.1 summarises the discussion of the two traditions, and will help me establish a link to critical research in IS.

The link between ethics, morality and critical research in information systems

Having provided a framework of ethics and morality allows me to discuss the link they have with critical research in information systems. This discussion is based on the defining features developed so far in this chapter, on the critical intention, topics, and theories.

Table 3.1 The German and French traditions of distinguishing ethics and morality

	German tradition	*French tradition*
Ethics	Theory and justification of morality; based on rationality; emphasises duty	Shared vision of the good life of the community; no final foundation
Morality	Set of accepted rules guiding individual and collective behaviour	Constraints and obligations used to avoid violence and facilitate ethical aims
Problems	• Open question of competing ethical theories • Tradition provides no material 'good'	• Is there a shared vision of the 'good life'? • Obligatory nature of ethics without final foundation
Important aspects	• Relevance of duty in ethics • Formal approach • Distinction between practice and justification	• Material vision of 'good life' is necessary • Obligation and enforcement must be considered

Critical intentions and ethics and morality

The critical intention was introduced as the most important characteristic of critical research. Critical topics, theories and methodologies all follow from the critical intention. The critical intention was defined as the desire to use research to initiate and promote change. Because of it, critical researchers not only want to observe but also want to interact with their research object. This is what sets critical research apart from positivist and interpretive research in the Chua (1986)/Orlikowski and Baroudi (1991) tradition.

This critical intention must have a direct link with ethics. The formal reason for this is that it is prescriptive and, as Hume (1948) has argued, prescription cannot be deduced from description. There is an implicit normative premise in the critical starting point that the world should be changed. That premise would read something like the following: 'When injustice is being done, critical research should change it.' This premise is clearly of an ethical nature. While the suggested formulation may be debatable and could be replaced by an alternative, it will retain its ethical quality. It needs to refer to what should be done in order to justify the critical intention.

A material link between the critical intention and ethics is that the aim of critical research is to 'make things better' in a wide sense of the word. This 'better' is a moral notion, since it implies an improvement of the human condition and is directly based on anthropological assumptions concerning the environments and circumstances which will benefit humans. Gregor (2006, p. 612) agrees that critical theory 'explicitly addresses ethical and moral questions, by seeking to be emancipatory and bring about improvements in the human condition [...].' Without value judgements referring to human nature and the possibility of improving society, critical work is simply not possible (Marcuse, 1964).

Viewed from the German tradition, the critical intention implies a sense of duty to change an undesirable reality. It is a formal approach that relies on the possibility of rationally identifying ethical issues. However, the distinction between moral practice and ethical theory is not clear, as will be discussed in the next section. The French tradition informs the critical intention through its vision of a 'good life'. Or, more to the point, critical researchers would probably find it easier to agree on the 'bad life', the alienating existence in a capitalist system, which should be overcome. Finally, the French tradition stresses the importance of avoiding violence by instituting moral rules. The critical intention *per se* does not indicate how this can or should be done.

Critical topics and ethics and morality

While the argument for the ethical quality of the critical intention is relatively straightforward, discussing the ethical quality of critical topics is much more complex, owing to the variety of critical topics. This chapter can offer only a cursory glance at the possible arguments. For most of the critical topics introduced earlier, however, it is easy to argue that they are of ethical relevance.

The most important critical topic is power. Power is a complex term but in most cases it refers to the ability an agent has to influence another agent's behaviour, to make one do another's bidding. Power thus implies obligations, rules and norms, all of which have an ethical nature. This does not mean that power is intrinsically bad (or good), just that its exertion has ethical consequences (Giddens, 1984). This is true for political power (Rawls, 2001), economic power (Galbraith, 1998) as well as information as power (Mason *et al.*, 1995). The argument extends to attempts to free the individual from power as summarised under the concept of emancipation. While it is arguably impossible to free oneself completely from power relationships (Gergen, 1999), critical research attempts to identify and analyse those effects of capitalist societies that alienate individuals (Myers and Avison, 2002) and limit their options. The emphasis on power is linked to the concept of emancipation, which is central to critical research. Going back to the German tradition, it is not clear whether emancipation is a moral (practical) or an ethical (theoretical, justificatory) concept. It seems to promise clear and identifiable results, which would put it in the realm of morality, but at the same time it seems to be a justification for action, rendering it an ethical notion. In the French tradition, emancipation could be seen as a representation of the good life.

The other critical topics which characterise critical research are also closely linked to ethics and morality. The digital divide, for example, is a topic of interest for critical researchers because it disempowers some, and precludes them from living up to their potential (Rookby, 2006). Britz (1999, p. 25) points out that 'access to Information is the most important ethical question in the information age'. Apart from the immediate ethical importance, access is also ethically relevant because it affects the way society is organised, for example through e-democracy or e-government (Breen, 1999). This argument leads easily to other critical topics such as the problem of gender in IT. The central question is who gets access to which resources and on what grounds. This, in turn, determines chances and obligation, and is therefore a moral question (Wheeler, 2001; Stewart *et al.*, 2001; Adam, 2002). Questions of information systems failure derive part of their interest to critical researchers from the ethical effects they have. IS failures are partly an economic or technical problem but their importance originates from the ethical impact they have. Failures waste money and other resources, thereby limiting the freedom of the agents involved. At the same time, failure is often caused by non-technical problems, most of which are related to ethics. These include organisational politics, recognition of legitimate stakeholders, or a lack of respect for others (see Wilson, 2003; Wilson and Howcroft, 2002; Schiller, 1999; Keil *et al.*, 2002).

The topics of critical research are united in that they have a moral nature. What is much less clear is how the argument supporting the moral nature of critical topics can be supported by ethical theory. It appears that critical research very much relies on moral intuition ('it is bad that people are alienated, disempowered, have no access, ...') but that there is little explicit reflection on why it is bad or why one should concentrate exactly on those issues. From the point of view of the French tradition, these topics are of an ethical nature because they refer to how the good life should be lived, but few indications of resulting moral norms are given.

Critical theory and ethics and morality

The question of the ethical quality of critical theory can be addressed by looking at one widely shared root: at Marx. The orthodox reading of Marx (at least the later Marx) suggests that he rejected ethics, believing that society was a social system in which ethics plays no role. Marx's emphasis on the importance of the material world as a determinant for society but also for consciousness can be read this way (Marx, 1998). However, a different reading of Marx is also possible (Wolff, 2003). The early Marx was clearly interested in ethical questions, but one can also see the later Marx as ethical. Rorty (1998) argues that the *Communist Manifesto* is an expression of hope for a better society, comparable with the New Testament and equally based on an ethical view of human nature. Another stream of thought asks what the relevance of property in means of production is, if it is not of an ethical nature (Kambartel, 1998). Similarly, how can one explain Marx's interest in alienation and emancipation, if not on an ethical basis (Wynn, 2001)? Looking at the overall theoretical and political system based on Marx, one can therefore conclude that 'Marxism–Leninism is not only an economic system but a moral theory; a theory of production and a system of ethics' (Vallance, 1992, p. 40).

Given the variety of critical theorists, it is not possible to present a comprehensive description of the link between critical theories and ethics and morality. In order to support the argument that there is such a link, I argue that critical theorists can be placed within the German and the French tradition of ethics and morality. For this purpose I will concentrate on Jürgen Habermas and Michel Foucault, but I will also touch on other critical researchers.

The German tradition of ethics and morality in critical theory

I have referred to Habermas as a critical theorist and also used his work to support the view that there is a German tradition in distinguishing between ethics and morality (Stahl, 2004). Habermas's 'discourse ethics' (1983, 1991) is inextricably linked to his theory of communicative action (TCA) (1981). It builds on the validity claims introduced above, which accompany each speech act.

The second of these, the claim to legitimacy, has an ethical quality. It is the starting point of discourse ethics. Habermas, like Kant, believes that rationality points the way to ethical understanding. However, he believes that the individual is not capable of satisfying the Categorical Imperative (Habermas, 1996, p. 48). The idea of the discourse thus replaces Kant's internal check of universalisability (Habermas, 1983).

Habermas's ethical theory fulfils the criteria of the German tradition. He uses the terms with slightly different meanings: morality (*Moral*) for him is the impartial general good, whereas ethics (*Ethik*) stands for the individual plan of a good life. What we have called morality, the existing set of accepted norms, he terms *Sittlichkeit*. However, he clearly distinguishes between existing norms and their ethical justification, which is done through discourses. His ethical theory, discourse ethics, is purely formal and implies a duty, namely to be willing to participate in discourses. Using Habermas's theories as the basis for critical research in IS therefore establishes a direct link to ethical questions.

A very similar argument could be made for Karl-Otto Apel, who introduced the concept of 'discourse ethics' and whose ethical stance is comparable to that of Habermas (see Apel, 1980). A more difficult question is whether the first generation of Frankfurt School scholars also conform to the ethical definition laid out here. This is a relevant question in this chapter since there have been some attempts to draw on them for purposes of IS research (Probert, 2002b, 2004a, b). Adorno, on whom Probert draws predominantly, is no doubt deeply influenced by ethical considerations. He was forced to flee Germany under the Nazi regime and wrote a considerable part of his work in American exile. Like most German Jews who survived the Shoah, he suffered immense personal losses. In the light of these events, he was deeply pessimistic about our ability to overcome the destructive traits of humanity. An argument for the relevance of ethical issues for Adorno can be made, similar to the argument for Marx's ethics. It rests on the question of what critical theory is good for if it does not contribute to the improvement of the world. However, Adorno shows a deep scepticism concerning the ability of reason to provide the means for a better world and therefore does not fully conform with the German tradition.

The French tradition of ethics and morality in critical theory

A similar argument concerning the ethical quality of Foucault's writings is a little more difficult to construct. One can read Foucault as being highly sceptical of moral claims. Indeed, much of his analyses of discourses investigates the use of morality as a means to exclude individuals or groups from participation. The main aim of his 'History of Sexuality' (1976), for example, is to capture the development of sexual morality and to find out how Christian morality has developed and differs from classical Greek morality. In 'Discipline and Punish' (1975), he looks at the way members of society are socialised into following the governing order, and moral norms are an important weapon in the arsenal of subjugation. Foucault is thus highly sceptical of overt moral claims. However, that does not mean that his theoretical endeavours cannot be classed as being in the tradition of moral philosophy. Indeed, probably one of the most important tasks of ethics is to criticise morality.

One can construct an argument about Foucault similar to the one made about the ethical qualities of Marx. While Foucault is sceptical about moral claims, there is no reason for him to engage in the genealogy of knowledge, were it not in the hope of creating a better future. One aspect of this is Foucault's notion of power. Power is central to Foucault's work, which means that it is amenable to questions of empowerment. Also, power is not necessarily a morally bad issue, but rather is constitutive of all social relations (Gomart and Hennion, 1999).

Foucault's ethical position can be categorised in terms of the two traditions. He is clearly a member of the French tradition in that he does not believe that rationality can be the final grounding of ethics. What makes it somewhat difficult to determine his position is that he does not give clear indications of what he takes the ethical *telos* of life to be. He gives much attention to the moral rules which society has created. He engages in a genealogy of moral rules, which he criticises, without disclosing how he envisages the good society to be. This, as mentioned above, is one of the main points of critique of Habermas against Foucault, namely that he is incapable of providing a positive alternative to the moral practices he deconstructs (Ashenden and Owen, 1999).

One could counter such an attack by pointing out that Foucault's implicit ethical vision is indeed one of emancipation, understood as the increasing ability of autonomy and self-determination. This is, for example, reflected in Foucault's preferred method of genealogy, which Owen (1999, p. 36) describes as an 'ethical practice' which 'orients our thinking to an immanent ideal which is nothing other than the [endless] process of developing and exercising our capacity for self-government'. For this reason, one can place Foucault alongside Habermas as successors of the project of enlightenment, of whose inherent problems both are aware and to which they react with different means (Conway, 1999). Without the ethical and critical intention to improve people's life, neither Habermas's nor Foucault's work is comprehensible.

Similar arguments can be made for several of his French contemporaries. Foucault was part of a politically active circle of French intellectuals, including Sartre and Bourdieu, who used their strong political influence to stimulate public debate. Despite philosophical differences between them, their attempt to raise issues publicly can be seen as the expression of the ethical nature of the critical intention to change social reality. Their activities as public intellectuals can also be seen as an attempt to help shape and define the ethical vision that is the basis of the French tradition. Finally, they share a deep scepticism regarding the possibility of a final justification of ethics, and particularly of individual reason as its possible basis.

Table 3.2 offers a summary of the relationship between ethics, morality and critical research.

Examples of the ethical nature of critical research

If the argument just presented is correct and critical research in information systems has an irreducible ethical aspect, then examples of critical research should display ethical characteristics. In order to support the argument that there is a strong link between ethics, morality and CRIS, I chose three recent papers which could be clearly identified as belonging to the critical research tradition in IS and which reflect current thinking in the area. I will briefly introduce each of

Table 3.2 Link between defining attributes of critical research in information systems and ethics/morality

Properties of criticality	Link to ethics and morality in the German tradition	Link to ethics and morality in the French tradition
Intention: change reality, promote emancipation	Critical intention is prescriptive, aims at better society. Change is a duty for critical research	Change of reality requires a vision of the good life. Overcoming violence is a condition of emancipation
Topic: share moral nature, intuition of injustice	E.g. power: power is not morally bad but requires rational reflection and justified rules to fulfil ethical	E.g. power: power is required to lead a good life in society. Power provides the constraints to violence but must itself be constrained
Theory	E.g. Habermas: clear link in Habermas. TCA implies discourse ethics. Ethical links are less clear in the older Frankfurt School	E.g. Foucault: Foucault is critical of conventional morality as a means of coercion, but his research implies a desire to create a better society and to emancipate individuals

these papers and point out where they intersect with ethical issues. I will then outline how the German and French tradition of ethics and morality can help identify shortcomings of the papers and lead to possible improvements.

The work of Janson and Cecez-Kecmanovic (2005) represents a typical example of critical research in IS. Their paper uses Habermas's TCA in order to analyse the interaction between buyers and sellers in e-commerce in the vehicle retail industry. The paper conforms to our definition of critical research. It has a critical intention despite the fact that it is primarily descriptive. The authors hope that the development of a Habermasian framework in e-commerce will allow buyers and sellers to use communicative action, which will emancipate both from the current alienating practices of the used car industry. While their topic is e-commerce, they concentrate on issues such as power relationships between buyers and sellers.

The paper involves a variety of ethical assumptions and implications. The intention of investigating e-commerce as social interaction reveals the view that a technical reading of e-commerce is insufficient. Such a view is based on an implicit ethical understanding of how research should proceed. The topic of relationships and interaction between online buyers and sellers is relevant from the point of view of TCA only if the current state of these relationships is morally doubtful. The methodology, finally, is based on the communicative action between researchers and research subjects, which means it requires the acceptance of the ethical value of the subjects.

While Janson and Cecez-Kecmanovic's (2005) paper can thus be integrated in the view of critical research as ethical research, it also displays some of the shortcomings of the German tradition. It assumes that a certain rationality will lead to ethically desirable outcomes and it adopts Habermas's procedural approach to ethics. It lacks the material view of the good life and therefore fails to criticise the context of the research. A different critical researcher could argue that the US used car market is a primary example for alienation and exploitation and for the commercial dominance of current society. Their approach does not allow Janson and Cecez-Kecmanovic to criticise an economic system where people are led to believe that owning a highly dangerous and polluting piece of technology will improve their well-being. They also fail to discuss the issue of how technically mediated communication, which could be read as an example of Habermas's systems theory, can lead to true communicative action. This may be a theoretical shortcoming of the paper or a problem of the TCA itself.

A good example of a completely different critical approach is provided by Edenius (2003), who relies on a Foucauldian angle to understand the use of email in discourses. Edenius focuses on the use of knowledge in email and draws on Foucault's notion of discipline. The intention of his paper is to change our perception of reality by pointing out that email functions as disciplinary power, limiting the ability to participate in discourses. This intention is critical in that it will change social reality by demonstrating discursive closures that we face, which, by being exposed, become open to modification. Following Foucault, Edenius does not openly claim to advance emancipation but implicitly does so by addressing discursive reifications. Among the topics he addresses we can find the typical critical candidates of power and meaning. In order to illustrate the arguments, Edenius uses a multiple case study approach, including interviews.

Edenius's paper exhibits critical intention, topics, and theory. Ethical assumptions can be identified in all of them. The paper aims to raise awareness of the alienating properties of current disciplines and discourses surrounding email. The paper argues that email is used to exert power by strategically using and distributing knowledge, and it continues to argue that this use of email is intrinsically contradictory because it leads to information overload. It can be read as an expression of the French tradition of ethics and morality in that it implies that there is a lack of a shared ethical vision, which it invites us in its closing sentences to start to develop. The second step of the French tradition, namely the development of moral rules to support the ethical vision, is not developed in the paper. However, it is relatively easy to see that such rules would have to result from an agreement on the ethical vision.

Fleshing out the ethics of Edenius's paper following the French tradition shows that there is a lack of distinction between moral practice and ethical theory. Edenius admits that his work, like that of Foucault, could be faulted for not providing a positive view. What is more, the approach does not allow the distinction between a desirable moral plan and an ethical procedure to check the acceptability of such a plan. The lack of a final foundation for ethics, which is characteristic of the French tradition, makes it difficult to develop a constructive analysis.

A final example of critical research is supplied by Klecun and Cornford (2005). They apply a critical view to the evaluation of systems in the healthcare sector in the United Kingdom. Unlike the other two examples, they do not explicitly draw on a specific theorist. Their critical intention is to change the way IS evaluation is perceived. They argue that current approaches to evaluation are too narrow, concentrating on technical criteria or considering only privileged users, whereas the nature of healthcare systems requires a wide range of opinions to be considered in evaluation. Their topic is thus the empowerment of the individuals who have to deal with and suffer from systems, including healthcare professionals and patients. The theoretical basis of their work draws on the Frankfurt School but includes other approaches such as the socio-technical approach, social constructivism and hermeneutics. From these different theoretical positions they extract principles of critical research which they then apply to their area of interest. Their method of investigation is a stakeholder approach based on interviews.

The argument for the ethical quality of intention and topic of this study is similar to that for the other two examples. The wish to review the dominant approach to evaluation can be explained by the moral desire to improve IS practices. The purpose is to empower individuals who are currently silenced by the established evaluation practices. The case for the ethical quality of their theoretical background is more difficult to make because they use a broad approach drawing on several research traditions. What all of these have in common, however, is that they emphasise the human element of technology and the importance of human interaction for the construction of meaning and understanding. This carries the ethical implication that humans' views are equally valuable and need to be considered if the validity of evaluation is to be established. Their case study/stakeholder methodology allows a similar conclusion of the ethical relevance of the individual research subject. This is well established for stakeholder approaches, which are frequently used in business ethics research (Bowie, 1999; Donaldson and Dunfee, 1999; Gibson, 2000).

Klecun and Cornford provide a good example of critical research whose ethical assumptions are quite obvious. They are nevertheless not sufficiently developed to support further action. The approach strongly suggests an ethics of respect for the individual, but it does not operationalise this in any way. From the German tradition they could learn the importance of distinguishing between moral practice and its ethical justification, which would help them justify their critical approach. The French tradition would help them to see the relevance of developing a positive ethical vision, but at the same time support and enforce it with moral rules. Both approaches would be supportive in drawing practical conclusions from the evaluation of IS projects.

These three brief examples are meant to support the argument that critical research does indeed share critical intention, topics and theories, and that all of these are linked with issues of ethics and morality. The discussion of the examples cannot claim to do the authors justice but it does show that ethical implications tend to underlie critical research yet are often not made explicit. Making them explicit reveals problems of consistency and raises new issues that need to be addressed. The French and German traditions can help us understand what these issues are and how they can be addressed.

Ethical lessons for critical research in information systems

In this chapter I have introduced some of the ideas of philosophical ethics by discussing the differences between the concepts of ethics and morality in the French and German traditions respectively. On this basis I argued that critical research is based on ethical assumptions and aims to follow ethical objectives. If we accept this conclusion, then the next question concerns the implications this has for critical research. These can be divided into theoretical and practical ones. The theoretical implications relate to the fact that critical research in IS rarely incorporates ethical theory explicitly. For critical research as ethical research, this is not tenable. Critical researchers must render their ethical assumptions and presuppositions open to scrutiny. This is particularly important in that ethical theory is always complicated and there is no ethical theory without weaknesses or counter-arguments. A critical researcher who follows the critical intention to change reality and wants to promote emancipation will have to reflect on the reasons for this intention. How could social reality be improved, what does it mean to be emancipated and why is it better to be emancipated than not? What can the researcher do if people resist being emancipated and is it possible to promote emancipation across cultural boundaries? These are difficult questions which can only be answered if the normative theoretical background is made explicit.

The German and French traditions can be helpful when considering these questions because they offer hints of what aspects of ethics or morality should be considered. The German tradition reminds critical researchers that there is a difference between factual moral norms and their ethical justification, both of which they must reflect on. It also emphasises the importance of a formal approach to ethical issues at a time when all material moralities seem to be contested. From the French tradition, researchers can learn the importance of the traditional Aristotelian 'good life', which is a necessity in ethics. Indeed, the critical intention can be seen as the expression of a vision of the good life because it implies that there is a better alternative to the reality we live in. At the same time, the French tradition shows that the good life is no guarantee of the achievement of ethical ideals if matters of material moral duties are neglected. Ethical visions need moral enforcement. This is of great relevance for critical research which assumes that it is possible to come to a better state of the world by facilitating emancipation but often neglects to consider what rules will be required to achieve such aims and how they can be enforced. The two ethical traditions will thus offer some answers to important questions, but, as the discussion of the examples has shown, they are not comprehensive, and additional ethical theories may offer further help in some situations. Computer or information ethics as a discipline that explicitly deals with ethical and moral questions with regards to ICT should thus be taken into consideration by critical IS researchers (Adam, 2005).

These theoretical considerations thus have practical consequences. If it is the intention of critical research to improve social reality, then logical and ethical consistency require that the practical consequences of such research must be considered in evaluating its success. Or, more simply, we need to ask whether critical research that has no practical consequences can be considered critical research at all. This raises a range of epistemological and methodological questions, many of which have ethical angles. If critical researchers aim to make the world better, then how can they know they have succeeded? What are they to do if they do not succeed, or if their efforts have an inverse effect? This leads to other difficult questions, such as the question of realisability. How much effort must critical researchers expend on deliberating whether the aims of their research can be realised at all? I will return to this question in the concluding reflections of the book.

All these questions are difficult to answer. That should not distract us from their importance. The success of critical research can be ensured and evaluated only if the criteria of success are clearly defined, and those criteria must include a clear understanding of ethical implications and presumptions. Extending critical research in IS into the ethical domain will further complicate already complicated matters. However, a failure to do so is likely to burden the critical endeavour with conceptual confusion. One problem is that critical researchers are not necessarily conversant with ethical theory and its use in ICT. Fortunately, there are parallel discourses to the ones in information systems, for example those on computer and information ethics, which critical IS researchers can draw upon to incorporate existing ethical discourses in their work (Bell and Adam, 2004). I hope that this book, having argued that critical research is linked to ethics and morality, will broaden the discourse on critical research in information systems and help critical researchers avoid making the mistake of neglecting reflection on their ethical premises and implications. In doing so, the book displays the characteristics of critical research. It aims to change the status quo (neglect of ethical issues in CRIS) and promotes emancipation (of researchers, who will be freer to engage in ethical discourses). Using a conceptual and reflective approach, the book should have ethical consequences because, by promoting discourse on ethics and raising awareness of moral questions, outcomes of critical research will be more morally sensitive and ethically justifiable.

4 Emancipation across cultural boundaries

A fundamental problem of critical research in information systems

Now that I have established the concept of critical research in information systems, some of the dominant theories and also its ethical and moral background, this chapter will be dedicated to the discussion of one of the resulting problems. The narrative so far could be construed as being relatively linear and unproblematic. However, there are fundamental problems arising from the combination of ethical awareness, the critical intention to emancipate, the role of critical scholars in society and many other factors. This chapter will discuss one such issue in depth, namely the issue of emancipation across cultural boundaries.

I have already mentioned that digital divides are one of the topics of CRIS. When doing research in this area, the researcher is often confronted with the vast inequalities that exist between different countries or between different groups within and between countries. The attempt to apply the critical emancipatory intention in such circumstances where there is more than one dominant culture is at the heart of this chapter. My central question is: is there anything culturally invariant about emancipation? The importance of this question is easily understood. Since critical research wants to make a difference, wants to effect a 'transformative praxis' (Kincheloe and McLaren, 2005, p. 323), the critical researcher needs to have a clear idea as to what difference he or she wants to make, and why. If emancipation is universal and culturally invariant, then the researcher might draw up a desirable path to emancipation, and if the research subjects follow the path, emancipation will be realised and the research can be considered successful.

However, most critical researchers will be suspicious of such a simplistic approach. One reason for this is the problem of the cross-cultural validity of perceptions of moral reality. What counts as good and desirable in one cultural setting may be bad and deplorable in the next. How are we to know that our understanding of emancipation is viewed as providing real emancipation by the people we are trying to emancipate? History provides us with a wealth of examples that warn against the dangers of the good will to improve people's lot – that is, as these instances backfire and sometimes only worsen people's lives and circumstances. It is therefore important to investigate whether cross-cultural emancipation is viable at all.

Cross-cultural research in ICT

In this section I will first define the concept of culture and then briefly review some of the areas where culture is of relevance for research on ICT. The heart of the section will be the question as to whether and in what way cultures are similar or whether they are completely disparate.

The concept of culture

Defining culture is a highly ambitious endeavour and, owing to the multitude of possible definitions from different disciplines (see Rey, 2001), it is not likely to be successful. The current definition of culture is thus based on the literature that refers to questions of the relationship of ICT and culture. It does not claim to cover all possible aspects of culture.

The central aspect of culture for our purposes has to do with shared meanings and interpretations. It 'refers to the socially learned behaviours, beliefs, and values that the members of a group or society share' (Maitland and Bauer, 2001, p. 88). Walsham (2002, p. 362) defines culture, at its most basic level, as 'shared symbols, norms, and values in a social collectivity such as a country'. Values and norms can be shared only on the basis of a common understanding of some basic factor such as the nature of human beings, the nature of reality, the nature of knowledge, etc. Culture is thus a set of fundamental shared assumptions that allow the members of the culture to understand each other. Culture is based on communication and is expressed through symbolic interaction (Walsham, 1993; Ward and Peppard, 1996; Castells, 2000a).

Such a shared set of symbols is necessary for the functioning of any group or society. It contains a number of assumptions and explicit as well as implicit rules. This includes some sort of shared morality (Ricoeur, 1983). As Robey and Azevedo (1994, p. 26) put it, 'the distinctive feature of culture is its normative character; culture guides people in the correct ways to think, feel, and act'.

While culture can thus be described as the set of shared meanings and interpretations of a group, one of the central problems is that no group ever agrees on all interpretations and meanings. Furthermore, most individuals are members of different groups that share different cultures. One aspect of this is the difference between national and organisational culture. These different cultures can be similar but they can also be contradictory. They are also locally situated and subject to ongoing negotiations (Weisinger and Trauth, 2002). For researchers, it is thus difficult to materially describe a culture because it can never be captured completely and it evolves during, and sometimes because of, the research activity.

Finally, critical researchers face another problem with culture, namely the fact that culture is also the anchor of ideology. Culture contains those ideological assumptions that critical researchers find problematic and try to expose. It is at least partly on the basis of culture that people are exploited, dominated and alienated (see Schultze and Leidner, 2002).

An important aspect of culture is its relationship to technology. If we follow Gehlen (1997; and see Höffe, 1995) in his description of human beings as tool-using animals, then it is clear that culture must be related to technology. Human beings require technology (in the widest sense of the word) to survive and thrive. Technology is therefore an important part of the symbolic universe that surrounds humans and thus an integral part of culture. The type of technology we use and the purposes we use it for are in large parts determined by our culture. Conversely, cultures can be classified by the types of technologies they use (Postman, 1992).

Universality versus particularity of culture

The central question of this chapter is whether the idea of emancipation is applicable across cultural boundaries. In order to be able to discuss this question in depth, it is important to consider whether there is anything that all cultures have in common. If there is not, then it stands to reason that the concept of emancipation developed in one culture will simply not be applicable to other cultures, and cross-cultural critical research is faced with a serious problem. There are two possible answers to the question of whether cultures have something in common, which I will call universality and particularity.

It is plain to see that cultures differ. Our interpretations and symbolic interactions are endowed with different meanings, which are often hard to translate. A good example familiar to most readers is that of academic cultures. In academia many people find it hard to interact with members of other academic sub-communities simply because concepts are used differently and there are different expectations levelled at validity claims. This book is probably a case in point since the central concepts, critical research and culture will be defined differently in different disciplines. These different cultures may diverge to the point that successful communication becomes impossible. The point of view of particularity is that these differences run so deep that there is nothing that all cultures have in common. There is no common root that we could agree on, given the factual differences between cultures.

If one subscribes to such a strong view of particularity of culture, then one has to admit that in many cases communication will not be possible and the best one can hope for is that the lack of mutual understanding will not lead to outright war. However, such a hope would not be well founded. There are proponents of such a strong view of particularity, for example Huntington and his concept of the clash of civilisations (Huntington, 1993), which at its base is in our terminology a clash of cultures. Another observation that might support a strong view of particularity is that different cultures have different moral and ethical systems which often seem to be irreconcilable. One culture may believe in forgiveness and loving one's enemies, whereas the next may prescribe revenge. Moral codes, for example with regard to sexuality, are so different that they seem to suggest incompatibility.

On the other hand, such a strong view of cultural particularity is difficult to sustain in the light of the fact that – despite all difficulties – we are able to communicate across cultural barriers. This is true on a national level, where there have always been interlopers between cultures who were conversant in different interpretatory schemes as well as on a local or organisational level. With a bit of goodwill it is possible for the physicist to understand the sociologist, at least to the point where one can agree on disagreement. Another empirical phenomenon that supports the idea of universality of at least some aspects of culture is globalisation (Beck, 1998). We seem to live in a world that is becoming more and more homogeneous. This may in some parts be the result of cultural imperialism (McDonaldisation of the world – e.g. Barber, 1995), but such cultural imperialism can work only on the basis that some aspects of culture can be translated.

One reason why there may be universals that underlie cultures despite their material differences is that there are universal aspects of human nature. One universal aspect of humans seems to be that we have a culture, however different various cultures may be. We need a symbolic environment that allows us to grasp and interact with our world. One could call humans the cultured animal (see Lenoir, 1991; Weber, 1994). We also share other aspects that are part of being a human. From an existentialist viewpoint, one can underline the facts that we are bodily beings who live in a world structured by communication. We can recognise the other as someone who is fundamentally similar to us and who deserves respect. We also know of our coming death and can sympathise with others on the basis of these shared aspects of existence. This is the basis of existentialist ethical positions from Sartre to Levinas. Elsewhere (Stahl and Elbeltagi, 2004) we have used a Habermasian framework to argue that there are universals that all cultures share. These include the fact that culture is a human constant, that cultures are communicatively constructed and that they have to consider the human nature as being-in-the-world (to use a Heideggerian term).

Culture, research and ICT

Given everything that I have said so far, it is plain to see that there are interdependencies between culture, ICT and research (Trauth and O'Connor, 1991). ICT is part of the technology that forms an integral part of all cultures. It thus provides us with our background knowledge of shared meanings. At the same time, culture influences the way we perceive and use technology, including ICT. Both aspects have been discussed in the research literature on ICT and IS.

The influence of ICT on organisational culture is a central part of IS research. Computers and other types of ICT have had an important impact on the way we organise work and the way organisations in general are run. These changes run so deep that ICT has been likened to other central inventions such as the steam engine (Floridi, 1999). ICT is often used as a means to produce change intentionally, which is why it is linked to change management approaches such as business process re-engineering.

The influence of ICT on organisational as well as national culture goes beyond such instrumental uses, however. Given that culture is about shared interpretations and symbolic interaction, the use of and familiarity with ICT offer new ways of conceptualising the world. The widespread use of a highly logical and formal technology thus supports a technological and logical view of reality, and thereby the instrumental rationality that underlies capitalism. At the same time, it offers a way of interpreting human behaviour in terms of machines (Weizenbaum, 1976). The ICT that we observe in Western democracies is thus a supporting influence on the organisation of society. An important aspect of this is capitalism, which is partly facilitated and expanded by technology (Castells, 2000a, b). ICT thus provides a metaphor that allows us to reinterpret our environment. This includes the basic constituents of our world, including our view of humans and ontological constructions such as the nature of God and religion (Berne, 2003; Ess, 2001).

This influence of ICT on culture is certainly not one-sided. Since our actions are structured by the culturally transmitted symbolic universe we live in, the use of technology depends on cultural beliefs. The very definition of what we believe technology (and ICT) to be depends on culture. Orlikowski and Iacono (2001, p. 132) believe that researchers have to conceptualise IT artefacts as 'multiple, fragmented, partial, and provisional'. Certain technologies, such as the internet, 'do not provide the same material and cultural properties in each local time or context of use'. As Wyatt *et al.* put it, all 'technologies are imbued with cultural significance' (2002, p. 39).

This is again true for national as well as organisational or other local cultures. It also goes a long way towards explaining why certain types of ICT are used successfully in one context, yet fail in a different one. Examples are easy to find. Riis (1997), for example, offers the example of the Danish strategy of developing the internet infrastructure, which was sensitive to the Danish culture of social development. The internet is probably a good example of a technology with cultural significance since it is available in many places in different cultural circumstances, which leads to widely differing uses and interpretations.

Critical research on ICT in cross-cultural contexts

On the conceptual basis developed so far, we now need to question whether critical research on ICT is possible across cultural barriers. It will depend on one's view of culture – on whether one subscribes to the particularist or the universal view of culture – whether the answer will be negative or positive. I will now present both sides of the argument.

Problems of cross-cultural research

To make this question more accessible, let us imagine an example. A growing area of interest for researchers in ICT is the relationship between ICT and development. Many countries spend large amounts of money on ICT in the hope that it will help them achieve a higher level of development. Similarly, many of the more developed countries make aid available for the procurement of ICT. Such initiatives are often highly problematic. In many cases they do not deliver the desired outcome, possibly because they may be based on biases and uncertain concepts (i.e. 'development') that render them hard to grasp.

This is an area that interests many researchers. There are journals and conferences exclusively dedicated to ICT in global/development contexts, and even journals that look at specific aspects of such technology use, namely in education (e.g. the *International Journal of Education and Development using ICT* (http://ijedict.dec.uwi.edu/)). The question this chapter wants to explore is: is it possible to do critical research, including the express orientation towards emancipation, in such cross-cultural contexts? Or, to put the question more bluntly, can we as Western researchers tell the users and decision makers in ICT in developing countries what to do in order to become emancipated?

The attempt to realise emancipatory critical research across cultural boundaries is fraught with numerous problems. Some of them are related directly to the underlying concepts. As I mentioned earlier, there is no consensus on what critical research should aim for and what the term 'emancipation' actually means (Brooke, 2002b). A similar problem related to the above example is that we are not too clear about the meaning of development. There is an argument to be had that speaking of development is a self-fulfilling prophecy and that the division in more and less developed countries is an act of cultural imperialism. The current understanding of development seems to be one centred on capitalist economic production and liberal social and political philosophy. It is very much controlled by actors from states that perceive themselves as 'developed' and that label others as 'under-developed' or 'developing'. The central assumption is that it is desirable to be in a situation similar to that of the 'developed' states. The debate structures the problem area in a particular way and leaves little room for alternative conceptions of development or the potential for the 'developed' to learn from the 'developing'. Such research may thus produce the very problem it aims to solve. Even if these conceptual problems were solved and if the researcher knew what emancipation means, it stands to reason that it will be a social process that will produce losers as well as winners (Alvesson and Willmott, 1992). Emancipation of some may lead to the disempowerment of others (which is not to suggest that it is necessarily and always a zero-sum game), a fact that is related to the idea that critical research needs to engage in politics if it is to make a difference, which leads to the conclusion that there will most likely be stakeholders who will resist critical research (Mingers, 1992).

A different problem is that of the acceptance of different cultures. Since emancipation is likely to translate into a different perception of reality and different conceptualisations of the environment, it is likely to change culture. Who are we as researchers to say that other cultures should be changed? For example, consider traditional societies which are governed by traditional structures and mores. Behaviour is regulated by the community, and individuals are under strong expectations to follow certain behaviours. Emancipation as an individual approach is likely to weaken the power of such traditions and thereby change the very structure of the culture. This may happen even through descriptive research, where the mere contact with different ways of life can destroy a culture. There are examples of indigenous cultures that were destroyed in this way. Critical research that intends to change behaviour may be even more likely to have this effect.

A related problem is that of understanding different cultures. Certain practices may appear highly dominating and alienating to the western researcher, and he or she may perceive a justification to change these. Examples of this could be the religiously justified suppression of women or minorities in some cultures. While such practices may look dominating from the outside, it is unclear what they like from the inside. A good example of this is the ongoing debate about Muslim women's headscarves in several areas of Europe, most notably in France and Germany. The argument of the opponents to the scarf is that it is a cultural sign of the subjugation of women and that it symbolises their inferior status. In a free and democratic society such signs are not welcome. The proponents argue that the opposite is true, that headscarves are a voluntary display of certain religious beliefs, that they are thus a sign of freedom and that they also allow women to interact more freely with men because it protects them from unwanted advances. The question for us is whether there is a way for critical researchers to judge such debates and come to a coherent position *qua* critical researcher.

A critical researcher will usually not be of the opinion that culture is something that is to be preserved as an end in itself. Moreover, culture as the system of meaning-making and interaction is affected by research as well as technology, and therefore the very act of research will affect culture. Also, culture is often the object of intentional manipulation, at least in western market democracies (Burrell and Dale, 2003). As such, culture can be a legitimate target for change and emancipation. The question still remains, however, whether there are cultures which researchers can or should not change.

Cultures are not simply given social arrangements that are value free. I have already mentioned earlier that cultures are intrinsically linked to moral rules and their ethical justification. One aspect of this is that cultures entail narratives about what it means to live a good life. Cultures are thus inherently utopian in the sense that they assume a vision about a desirable society. Critical research, by its nature of intending to change social reality, offers another utopian version of how we should live together. These utopias are often contradictory. The critical researcher thus needs to ask him- or herself whether the critical utopia is more desirable than the given utopia of the culture in question. This refers us back to the question of universalisability. How can the critical researcher defend the claim that his or her vision of the good life is universally applicable and should supersede the internal vision of members of the culture in question?

By choosing the term 'utopia', I have already pointed to another problem of critical research, namely the question of how the desire to change society can be justified. 'Utopia', etymologically meaning 'nowhere', was Thomas More's vision of a desirable world. However, the term has taken on a more negative connotation. It is now associated with the idea of enforcing one's vision of a good life by all possible means. It is therefore linked to terror and destruction (Castells, 2000b).

Another fundamental problem of critical research refers to the possibility of emancipation in and through ICT. In a considerable part of the critical literature on IS, emancipation is translated as the participative design and use of systems. In a very lucid critique of this approach, Wilson (1997) points out that such emancipatory strategies have problems justifying their own agenda as better than alternative conceptions. He describes the alternative for critical research as either remaining idealistic but unclear or admitting to having a specific agenda, which can then no longer claim to be universally acceptable.

A different charge regarding the impossibility of empowerment comes from postmodernism. Postmodernist objection to grand narratives can be translated into a strong cultural particularism, which renders the hope to be able to find common ground for emancipation futile (Walsham, 1993). And then there is the empirical observation of contradictory moralities, which, given the moral nature of emancipation and the strong link of culture with morality, can also be seen as a reason for the incompatibility of the researcher's view of emancipation and the research subject's understanding of the world.

All these arguments can be taken as a fatal critique of the critical intention to emancipate. If they are true, then it seems unlikely that emancipatory concerns can be realised across cultural boundaries. Worse, the very attempt to emancipate people from different cultures can then be seen as cultural imperialism. Given the inability to do justice to other cultures, emancipation can quickly become a utopia in the worst sense – that is, one supporting terror and repression, not liberation. Thought through to the end, it can mean that foreign intellectuals design a path that is not compatible with a culture and destroys traditional ways of living and turns into outright terror. The conclusion could thus be that we need to move away from the idea of emancipation and thus from critical research.

Justification of cross-cultural research

I do not support such a negative conclusion, however. While all the considerations are valid to some degree, they overlook one central factor, namely that we interact with other cultures anyway and that all research – both that which is explicitly critical and that which is not – has the potential to change cultures and societies. By explicitly considering the idea of emancipation, critical researchers are forced to think about the results of their research and are therefore more sensitive to these issues than other researchers. The only alternative to affecting cultures through research is no longer to do any intercultural research. But even this would be a conscious decision with consequences for other cultures. It would be a conservative choice based on the assumption that all cultures are equally valid and that there is nothing we can learn from or teach to other cultures. Such a stance is logically consistent but it is also deeply relativist. It assumes that a democratic culture that values human rights is fundamentally equal to a headhunter and cannibal society. Moreover, such a stance would seem to imply that research must be restricted to within the boundaries of one's own culture – a conclusion most researchers, especially in an era of globalisation fostered by ICTs that make the crossing of boundaries so easy, are not likely to accept. For those of us who do not accept it, critical research can offer a way out that is preferable to purely descriptive research.

Critical researchers nevertheless need to be aware of the fact that emancipation is not easily defined. An even more serious issue is that there is no simple and straightforward way to apply critical thoughts, and neither do we have an agreed methodology to go about promoting emancipation (McGrath, 2005). To some degree this is not problematic for critical research because it is an approach that claims to be reflective and thus critical of its own assumptions anyway. The question is how the objections to emancipatory research across cultures can be accommodated and, more specifically, how this can be done with regard to ICT and IS.

The solution to me seems to be a formal approach. All material descriptions or emancipatory practices run the risk of overlooking local particularities and thus becoming unworkable or self-contradictory. In order for the researcher to find out what emancipation with or through ICT can mean in a different culture, it is necessary to create procedures that allow the individuals or groups in question to develop their own vision of emancipation or empowerment. Researchers do not necessarily have to accept these at face value, and they can interact with such visions. But a researcher does not have the authority to prescribe them. A possible example of this is the use of anonymity in group decision support systems (GDSS). This feature is often described as liberating, and thus emancipatory in western contexts. However, in other cultural settings it may be seen as counter to the culture of 'saving face' and therefore against the interests of the participants and thus not emancipatory (see Abdat and Pervan, 2000). The conclusion should thus be that critical researchers will not prescribe certain features that they believe to be emancipatory, but instead give the research subjects the chance to define their version of emancipation.

A resulting question is whether such formal approaches imply material conclusions. Is there anything that a critical researcher can prescribe to the research subjects in the name of emancipation? I believe that the Habermasian discourse approach can give us some answers. A Habermasian discourse is formal in the sense described in that it does not tell people what emancipation will look like for them. At the same time, it explicates the conditions of successful discourses that are summarised under the headings of the 'ideal speech situation'. These conditions, in turn, can be used to create material conditions that allow the formal approach to emancipation. In more practical terms this means that there are situations and circumstances that critical researchers should promote in the name of emancipation, such as democratic participation, freedom of speech, or stakeholder inclusion. These do not constitute emancipation but they are the necessary condition of determining what emancipation means. A current example of this can be seen in the area of the use of ICT for government and democratic purposes. Such uses can be promoted as beneficial when and where they lead to the ability of individuals to interact, and widen the spaces for possible discourses (see Heng and de Moor, 2003). What form the resulting emancipation that can develop from such interactions will take cannot be predicted. It may go against the wishes of those who provide the technology by giving power to political parties that promote policies contrary to those imagined by critical researchers. Similar examples can easily be imagined on an organisational level. In terms of critical research in IS this means that the participative approaches that are often associated with Habermasian ideas do indeed seem to be a promising way to address emancipatory issues – not because they represent successful emancipation, but rather because they allow for an acceptable definition of emancipation.

This brings us back to the critique of critical research and emancipatory practices as voiced by Wilson and others. Can critical research claim to be anything other than a particular special interest? First, the question may be misleading, because critical research reflects on its biases but does not claim to be free of biases. It is based on the assumption that emancipation is possible and desirable. But second, and more important, critical research recognises that there is no objective description of the world anyway. The researcher thus is not faced with the supposed dilemma of choosing between conducting either value-free or emancipatory research. Rather, given the choice between different values, including emancipation or conservativism, critical researchers make the conscious choice to make a critical intervention. It therefore seems to me that the only alternative to critical emancipatory research is that of relativism, which I do not believe to be theoretically tenable or practically desirable.

Part II

Philosophy

In Part I I have outlined some of the relevant theoretical aspects of CRIS. Apart from the definition and functions of the field, I discussed the two most important theoretical approaches that currently dominate critical IS research. I put forward the argument that there is a strong and intrinsic link between critical research and ethics that criticalists need to consider. And finally, I explored some of the complications that can result from the theoretical make-up of the field by exploring how emancipation across different cultures needs to be conceptualised. All these topics have philosophical implications, but there are several further philosophical issues of central importance that we have not yet explored in any depth.

This second part of the book will therefore be dedicated to an analysis of some of the philosophical issues of critical research. It will review some of the literature but it will also use philosophical thoughts to further the critical arguments. I will use three classical philosophical terms as headings of the chapters in this sections: ontology, epistemology and methodology. These refer respectively to the nature of being or reality, to our ability to gain knowledge about it and to the way in which such knowledge can be gathered. The three arc interrelated, and a critical approach requires an appreciation of the most important positions. More importantly, there are implications following from the characteristics of critical research, such as its aim to change the status quo and promote emancipation, that link in with some of the philosophical underpinnings of the approach. An understanding of these will be important for the subsequent discussion of examples and applications of critical research in IS.

5 Ontology

On positivism, realism, and their relevance for critical IS research

I have already touched on the debate between positivism and interpretivism in the social sciences in general and in IS in particular. This debate is central to the definition of the field of information systems and also to the standing of different positions within this field. It is crucial for the acceptance of research agendas and it determines what counts as legitimate knowledge and what does not. This importance has led to a ubiquity of related debates that have elicited negative reactions to the very question of paradigm. Ron Weber (2004, p. xi), for example, wishes to 'assign the rhetoric of positivism versus interpretivism to the scrap heap' because it serves no purpose and leads to schisms. There are nevertheless good reasons to return to this debate and look at it from a different angle. First, CRIS is often described as an alternative to positivism and interpretivism. For a book such as this, it is thus of central importance to understand whether this classification is tenable. I believe that this is not the case for reasons having to do with issues of ontology. Furthermore, there are increasingly calls for a combination of different approaches and paradigms whose philosophical underpinnings are rarely questioned. One can frequently hear calls for multi-paradigm or multi-method research in IS, which typically imply that the positivism–interpretivism dichotomy is being ignored and that the research should incorporate aspects from both. Again, this is important for critical research, which is part of neither positivism nor interpretivism and could thus play the role of combining them. In this chapter I will touch on these issues and argue that there are two basic ontological positions that one can follow and that these are closely linked to the research paradigms that are available. I will furthermore argue that these two ontological positions are contradictory, which will have implications for a variety of questions that influence the choice of research strategy and methodology, but also the choice of topics and possible outcomes.

The chapter thus aims to clarify some questions of general philosophical ontology and their use in the area of information systems. One should note that such a general ontology is of central importance if one wants to discuss regional ontologies, as suggested by Kishore *et al.* (2004a, b). Regional ontologies and the universes of discourse they are based upon rely on a general understanding of ontology. This is important to realise if one wants to come to an understanding of computational ontologies. Such computational ontologies are often the subject of discussion when IS scholars talk about ontology (see Kishore *et al.*, 2007). Computational ontologies, which could better be described as taxonomies of information entities, are still closely linked to philosophical ontology.

Ontology and paradigms

Ontology, which etymologically means 'speaking of being', is the philosophical discipline that asks 'what is?' and 'what does it mean to be' (see Heidegger, 1993). It deals with the fundamental questions of being, and thus, in everyday parlance, one could say that it studies the nature of reality. Ontological assumptions form one of the most important building blocks of our world-view and they are so fundamental that we rarely question them. They are therefore of central importance to any research in any discipline (see Klein *et al.*, 1991). One needs to know what is or what exists in order to research it.

There are profoundly different ontological theories. They are integral parts of research paradigms. The concept of positivism, for example, is inextricably linked to its realist ontological assumptions. Ontological questions are at the basis of many of our epistemological and methodological differences. There are numerous questions of importance to be found in the history of ontology. For the purposes of this chapter I will concentrate only on the question of whether reality is independent of the observer or not. The ontological position that supports such observer-independence of reality is that of realism; opposing views will be called anti-realism. The issue of observer-dependence of reality is an old philosophical question that is also discussed under the headings of idealism versus materialism, or rationalism versus empiricism. The history of these debates is much richer than I can do justice to here, and I will thus emphasise the seemingly simple question of whether there is a world beyond us, the observers.

Realism and positivism

The definition of realism used in this chapter is that it is the ontological doctrine that reality is independent of the observer. Realism is the prevailing ontological position of the positivist paradigm. Most scholars interested in the philosophy of IS research agree with this definition. The independent and objective existence of reality can be found as a definition of positivism in a number of texts (Orlikowski and Baroudi, 1991; Visala, 1991; Jönsson, 1991; Landry and Banville, 1992; Darke *et al.*, 1998; Iivari *et al.*, 1998; Myers and Avison, 2002; Varey *et al.*, 2002). Some authors use different terms to denote this ontological position, such as 'objectivism' (Burrell and Morgan, 1979; Hirschheim, 1985; Chua, 1986; Hirschheim and Klein, 1989). Where positivism is described as a paradigm, it is typically also linked to epistemological (Olaison, 1991; Lee, 1991; Walsham, 1995a), methodological (Benbasat and Weber, 1996) and sometimes other philosophical aspects, such as ethical ones (Wynn, 2001). In this chapter I am exclusively interested in the ontological underpinnings of positivism.

The ontological question that divides positivism from alternative research approaches should not be underestimated. The question of whether reality exists may appear to be a rather dry and possibly useless one, and many scholars prefer to simply ignore it because the answer seems obvious (Hjørland, 2004). However, such fundamental philosophical questions are highly relevant to a large number of debates that have the potential to affect some of our most important self-descriptions. As a historical tendency, one can say that the division between positivism and interpretivism, whose root I argue to be the question of ontology, has gone beyond differing ontological views. In fact, many non-positivists – and this usually includes critical scholars – have a tendency disqualify much of the dominant positivist research as unreflected and conservative (Cecez-Kecmanovic, 2005). The underlying division between positivism and non-positivism is so deep that the very term 'positivism' has taken on a pejorative meaning for non-positivist (Burrell and Morgan, 1979; Lee, 2001). It seems to be used predominantly by opponents of the idea, whereas proponents prefer the adjective 'positive' instead of 'positivist' (see Friedman, 1994a; Westland, 2004).

It is not the purpose of this chapter to discuss the shortcomings of positivism and realism. Intellectual honesty requires nevertheless that some of the main arguments against them be reviewed to render the thrust of the argument comprehensible to the reader. Positivism, especially the elaborate set of theories developed by the Vienna Circle called 'logical positivism', has largely been discredited in the philosophy of sciences. It nevertheless continues to be a strong 'logic in use' (Landry and Banville, 1992), and its underlying realism is an important 'ontology in use' (Lee, 2004) in the social sciences, and information systems. Probably the most important critique of positivism in information systems is that its ontology, which posits an independent reality and the consequent impartial observation of this reality, do not lead to an adequate understanding of the phenomena in question (Adam, 2001b). This often implies a distinction between natural and social reality. Positivism seems to be a deficient basis for research, at least in the latter realm (Nissen, 1985; Orlikowski and Baroudi, 1991). Other points of critique address the epistemological problems resulting from a positivist ontology. There are problems of induction and generalisation (Pettigrew, 1985; Lee and Baskerville, 2003). Even scholars who are fundamentally in favour of a realist ontology have to admit that philosophy has not found a convincing explanation of how the mind can adequately represent a mind-independent reality (Khlentzos, 2004). Then there is the charge that positivism is self-contradictory because it is not itself a natural occurrence independent of the observer. This raises the question of the final foundation of positivism (Quine, 1980). Resulting from this, it can be argued that positivism is structurally circular and that despite its alleged objectivity, it can only investigate phenomena that are determined by the investigator.

Anti-realism and non-positivism

If realism is not the only ontological position, as was suggested in the preceding subsection, then the question arises as to what alternatives there are. In the light of our definition of realism, the alternatives are those ontological positions that do not believe that reality is independent of the observer. The history of philosophy offers a number of different non-realist ontological viewpoints. Michael Dummett (1963) has suggested the term 'anti-realism' to capture these views. There are other positions that disagree with realist ontology, such as that of rationalism (Hollis, 1994), which is based on the idea that the observer's mind must be involved in the constitution of reality. The field of anti-realism is wide and contains many different theories. One is the doctrine that the observer constructs reality and that, at the extreme, all of reality is just a figment of the individual's imagination. This is mirrored in radical constructivism (Glasersfeld, 2000; Watzlawik, 2001). Another anti-realist stream of thought that was hugely influential in the philosophy of the nineteenth and twentieth centuries is idealism, or more specifically German idealism. It is linked with the names of Hegel, Schelling, Fichte and others who argued for the supremacy of the mind or spirit over any external reality. A shared basis for these different anti-realist positions is Kant's ontology, which posits a difference between the (realist) things as such, or *noumena*, and our perceptions of these things, or *phenomena*. Kant believed that the things as such exist but that the world we live in is the world of phenomena, which is constituted and shaped by our mental faculties.

These ontological positions do not play a major role in contemporary IS research. They can be seen, however, as the basis of some of the ontological alternatives to the realism that is implied in prevalent positivism. One of the most important such concepts is constructionism. Constructionism (or social constructivism) holds that reality is constructed by the observer, but, in opposition to (radical) constructivism, it states that reality is a collective construction. It emphasises the role of interaction and communication in the process of constructing reality (Gergen, 1999). Its intellectual history can be traced back to idealism (Burrell and Morgan, 1979). IS researchers who subscribe to the constructionist ontology typically call themselves interpretivists rather than constructionists. The categorical difference between these is that interpretivism is usually seen as a paradigm, and thus as a broader term that includes an ontological position, usually a socially constructivist one. Furthermore, constructionists are more radical and extend their ontological views to all aspects of reality, whereas interpretivists limit it to social reality. Since IS researchers are usually interested in aspects of technology having to do with social phenomena, they can mostly refrain from defending the more contentious claims of constructionism and concentrate on those aspects of reality that are easily recognisable as socially constituted. One should note, however, that there are a number of research approaches to technology that emphasise its constructed character and promote the constructivist ontology to varying degrees (Mitev, 2005).

In current IS research, interpretivism is the most important alternative to positivism. I argue that this is the case because at the heart of interpretivism is an ontological position which views reality as a social construct. The constructionist ontology of interpretivism is referred to in many texts on interpretivism (Orlikoswki and Baroudi, 1991; Walsham, 1995a; Darke *et al.*, 1998; Varey *et al.*, 2002). The concept of interpretivism used in the sense of a paradigm has to contend with some of the same problems as positivism in that it often refers to epistemological (Myers and Avison, 2002; Klein and Myers, 2001; Trauth and Jessup, 2000; Walsham, 1995b) and methodological (Lee, 1991; Yin, 2003) aspects of research simultaneously. The term 'interpretivism' is often not sharply defined. Also, 'interpretivism' is a term that is relatively new but at the same time ubiquitous among non-positivist IS researchers.

Tertium non datur

The chapter has so far been set up to sharpen the contradiction between positivism and non-positivism, based on the difference between the underlying ontologies of realism and anti-realism. It has defined positivism as based on the realist ontological claim that reality is independent of the observer and non-positivism as the logically contradictory view based on the anti-realist ontological claim that reality depends on the observer. This definition is somewhat problematic because it equates paradigms with ontological positions, which is not always correct. The concept of paradigm is constructed in such a way as to admit some variability in the different components it refers to, and the link between paradigm and ontology is thus not conclusive. The approach can nevertheless be defended by the rather clear link between positivism and realism and the fact that the main non-positivist view in IS, namely interpretivism, is generally accepted as being based on the non-realist ontology of social constructivism. I will return to the issue of paradigms at the end of this main section.

The advantage of the above definition is that it allows the application of a fundamental logical axiom, namely the proposition of the excluded third. This proposition was developed by Aristotle in his *Metaphysics*. It states that a logical proposition (a statement) must be true or false. In the notation of propositional logic it can be represented as follows:

$$\neg(p \wedge \neg p)$$

(that is, it is false that p and non-p are true simultaneously). The history of logic has give rise to several attempts to show that this axiom is not sufficient and that logical states do not have to be bivalent. Examples of such non-bivalent logics are modal logic, deontic logic (Garson, 2003) and fuzzy logic (Hajek, 2002). The proposition is nevertheless widely accepted and forms one of the basic tenets of our scientific system. An example can easily show the strength of the axiom. If A is the proposition 'X is a dog', then $\neg$A is the proposition that 'X is not a dog', and so *tertium non datur* informs us that it is impossible that A and

¬A are true, thus that X cannot be a dog and not a dog (or a non-dog: ¬dog) at the same time.

If the proposition A means 'reality is independent of the observer', then ¬A can be translated as 'reality is not independent of (thus dependent on) the observer'. According to *tertium non datur*, both cannot simultaneously be true. This statement is the heart of the argument. The irreconcilable opposition between realism and anti-realism is simply based on a logical axiom and the ontological root of the terms. If, as was suggested above, positivism is directly linked to realism, and interpretivism is directly linked to social constructivism, then this at least constitutes a problem for people who wish to do away with the debate about them. It is no longer possible to simply say that the two are fundamentally the same, namely attempts to improve our understanding of reality, if they differ in terms of their understanding of reality.

The argument just developed does not solve all ontological problems in IS research, but it allows for a much more precise discussion of several issues. We can now say, for example, that a researcher cannot follow a positivist and an interpretivist research approach at the same time – at least, not if the paradigms include strong ontological views. That does not mean that all researchers must be either positivists or interpretivists. Similarly, if a cat is a non-dog, then X cannot be a dog and a cat. X does not have to be either a cat or a dog, however, since X might be, say, a fish. An analogous conclusion is that an IS researcher can choose a non-positivist paradigm that is not interpretivist.

This position should not be equated with some of the theories concerning the relationship between positivism and its alternatives viewed as paradigms, such as purism (Petter and Gallivan, 2004), supremacism (Klein *et al.*, 1991) or paradigm incommensurability (Brooke, 2002a; Mingers, 2001b). It only states that the ontological assumptions of positivism and interpretivism are not commensurable. What this means for research epistemology and methodology will be explored in subsequent chapters.

Ontology and critical research

The discussion in the previous section of ontological questions concerning research paradigms leaves open the question of where critical research fits in this regard. I have started this book by offering a definition of CRIS that is not based on paradigms, and the ontological argument of *tertium non datur* has now given a further reason for this. If one can be either realist or anti-realist, then there is no space for a third option and one has to decide which side one wants to be on. This view is of course somewhat simplistic, as there are many possible positions on both sides of the divide. This does not change the fact, however, that the ontological divide is fundamentally a dichotomy. If that is the case, then critical researchers have to decide whether they want to side with positivists or with interpretivists in terms of ontology.

Following the definition of CRIS developed in the first section, one can state that of the defining features – critical intention, wish to emancipate, critical topics or theory – none provides a very strong pointer as to where criticalists should position themselves. In practice it seems that the vast majority of critical researchers are strongly opposed to positivism. A critique of positivism has long been a constant feature of critical work, including the work of many of the Frankfurt School classics such as Horkheimer, Adorno or Marcuse. As a result, one could conclude that, ontologically, critical researchers should use anti-realist viewpoints. This contention is supported by the emphasis that current critical research puts on language and the importance of linguistic structures for social relationships, including relationships of oppression and domination. Most of the examples of critical research that I will give in the next main section will draw on this and argue that linguistic reifications are a central problem of the use of technology.

The equation of critical equals anti-realist equals non-positivist is nevertheless too simple. First, one should be aware that the idea of positivism is linked to the Enlightenment aim of overcoming obscurantism and replacing it by a rational access to the world. The history of positivism can thus be read to follow the aim of emancipation, and its origins can even be viewed as critical in the sense of the word used here. However, over time positivism has developed its own dynamics, and little work done in positivist social science or information systems still carries the critical intention of emancipation. This may be a contingency of the development of thought, or, as Horkheimer and Adorno have argued in their 'Dialectics of enlightenment' (2004), it may be a structural product of traditional rationality.

Independent of the answer to this question, there is a second and stronger reason why the equation of critical research and anti-realism is problematic. Strong anti-realist ontologies promote the idea that reality is constituted by humans. This raises the problem of how aspects of reality can be explained that do not conform with the social reality of the people involved. Critical research is very much concerned with this exact type of aspects of reality. When critical researchers investigate instances of alienation, domination or oppression, the implicit assumption is that such instances are counter to the wishes of the people involved. If this is so, then one can ask why they admit the construction of impediments to their emancipation. A possible answer would be that the impediments are the product of antagonistic social groups, such as the capitalists in classical Marxist theory. But this requires a high degree of social coordination that is hard to sustain empirically. It is more plausible to argue that the cause of alienation is not intended, but then it seems to become an externally existing aspect of reality, one that is not under the control of any of the parties. Such a view would be much closer to realism than to anti-realism. Indeed, traditional orthodox Marxism with its emphasis on the objective and possibly even necessary consequences of capitalism would seem to be much more at ease with a realist than with an anti-realist ontology.

All this suggests that there is no clear relationship between ontology and critical research. While claims to nature and reality are often thinly veiled attempts to exert power and subjugate others, and thus counter to the critical intention, it is also difficult to deny the existence of relevant factors that are beyond anybody's control and can thus be considered objective or real, no matter whether they were intentionally constructed, created or found. Probably the most important lesson critical researchers can draw from this discussion of ontology is that it is an aspect of their work they need to reflect on. This refers to the reflexivity that criticalists lay claim to and that needs to include their view of ontology, if for no other reason than to rule out the ideological misuse of ontological statements.

Relevance of ontology in critical information systems: the case of Irish electronic voting

If CRIS is about making a difference, then on might ask why we need to spend time on the discussion of ontology. The following case of the Irish experience with e-voting will indicate the importance of ontology for critical researchers in IS. In 2004 the Irish government tried to introduce electronic voting for the local and European elections. This was the first attempt within the European Union to implement electronic voting comprehensively in a general election. Despite strong objections, the Irish government held on to the idea. Eventually, just five weeks before the start of the election, public opposition became so strong that the government was forced to abandon the idea of electronic voting, at a cost to Irish taxpayers of more than €50 million. There are many possible explanations of this case, and the IS failure literature would offer a number of ways of analysing and understanding it. For the purposes of this chapter, I will emphasise the question of ontology and argue that at the basis of a range of problems and failures is a problematic ontological perception of the e-voting technology in question. In order to render this argument convincing, I will use the following subsection to explain the case and subsequently argue for the relevance of ontology in the case.

The case of Irish e-voting

The traditional way of electing democratic representatives is the collection of ballot papers. On the ballot paper a voter indicates his or her preferences. There are three important factors which have to be assured with ballots issued by the government. First, only eligible voters vote. Second, they vote only once. Third, all votes counted are valid votes (McGaley and Gibson, 2003). These three premises have to be achieved while maintaining the voters' privacy – that is, assurance of anonymity of the vote (Mercuri, 2002a). However, the most important aspect during the election process is the protection from manipulation and misuse. One could argue that the loss of voters' privacy or potential to manipulate ballots could jeopardise democratic principles. For all these reasons, electronic voting is of great interest to critical researchers. By influencing democratic processes, it has the potential to emancipate but also to dominate. It is clearly involved with power, one of the most important topics of critical research.

In 2002 the Irish government started to consider the introduction of electronic voting. During the general election of that year, the government piloted electronic voting in three constituencies. Instead of placing a vote in the ballot box in the traditional way, citizens voted electronically. There is considerable literature on electronic voting that discusses the topic from a range of disciplinary perspectives (Pieters, 2006). Suffice it to say that the approach to electronic voting chosen by the Irish government, namely to have voting booths at polling stations in many respects similar to traditional voting, is probably the least contentious one. And, despite minor problems, the government was pleased with the results. The decision was made to introduce electronic voting nation-wide for the local and European elections on 11 June 2004, which would have given Ireland a pioneering role in Europe. For this purpose a Dutch company was employed to provide Ireland with an electronic voting system (McGaley and Gibson, 2003), and the government started to implement the electronic voting system in early 2003.

There were various arguments as to why e-voting should be implemented. Some of the advantages are its relatively easy usage, the accuracy of the results, elimination of spoiled votes, acceleration of the counting process and the modernisation of the electoral system (McGaley and Gibson, 2003). The Irish Minister for the Environment and Local Government, Martin Cullen, was convinced that e-voting would make it easier for the public to vote, would improve efficiency and the administration, would provide earlier results, and also would provide a positive image of Ireland as a pioneer in the usage of information systems in democratic elections. In fact, Mr Cullen was of the opinion that e-voting would modernise the democratic process in all its facets (Environ, 2002).

Despite the euphoria at the pilot stage, a sizeable number of Irish citizens, computer experts and also opposition parties doubted from the start that electronic voting would be feasible at the national level. One opposition party, for instance, pointed out that the system did not have a paper trail and therefore was open to manipulation (Environ, 2003). The lack of a paper trail was also the main reason for the establishment of a lobby group organised by computer experts, called Irish Citizens for Trustworthy E-voting (ICTE). A paper trail that allowed voters to review a printout of their expressed preferences would have added confidence to the system. Without such a paper trail, no independent random check of the system would be possible.

The main complaints regarding e-voting were the competing aims of having a verified audit trail and at the same time safeguarding the privacy of the voter. An electronic voting system should ensure privacy of the vote – that is, not reveal voters' identity. At the same time, the system had to ensure a verified audit trail. An example of a verified trail comes from banking, where in the case of a mistake a money transfer can be traced back and corrected. American computer scientists Mercuri (2002a, b) had previously identified this stumbling block but seemingly with little response from politicians.

A simple solution to avoid the potential jeopardising of voters' privacy would have been to issue a paper-based audit trail. This solution, proposed by Mercuri

(2002a), was supported by the Irish Computer Society (O'Duffy, 2004) and the lobby group ICTE. This concept suggests that during the process of casting the vote the system would print the ballot containing voters' preferences. This ballot could be examined by the voter and then deposited in a ballot box. Doing so would eliminate the chance of possible manipulation. The election would still profit from the accuracy and the counting speed of a computer but the official certification of the election would come later from the paper records.

However, the government's intention, supported by the Dutch contractor, was to eliminate any paper trail. Arguably, adopting the Mercuri method would have removed most of the economic benefit. Indeed, the cost would have actually increased. According to Minister Cullen, who was responsible for the introduction of e-voting in Ireland, six independent studies had verified the security of the system (Environ, 2003). Disregarding the warnings from the opposition, many independent citizens, ICTE and the Irish Computer Society, the Irish government stood by its decision not to have a paper trail. As Mr Cullen (Environ, 2003) emphasised, 'Receipts were not issued under the old system and will not be issued under the new system for the same reason: to protect voters' privacy'.

The source code of the electronic voting system was another issue in the e-voting debate. The source code was not available for the public. Even the Irish government was not in the possession of the source code, which was owned by the Dutch vendor. This meant that a foreign private company had exclusive insight into the source code. In the case of an attempt at manipulation of the source code, the Irish government would not have had any power to monitor and protect the source code.

Despite the growing opposition to the introduction of electronic voting in June 2004, even in February of that year the Irish government was unwilling to concede the validity of opposing arguments. The Irish Minister for Finance, Charly McCreevy, for instance, strongly advocated electronic voting in the Irish parliament. Electronic voting was also strongly supported by the Taoiseach or Irish prime minister, Bertie Ahern. But in February 2004 some senior members of the ruling party started to doubt the feasibility of electronic voting, which had already cost Irish taxpayers more than €40 million.

Finally, as a result of the public resistance to electronic voting, the Irish government decided to establish an independent Commission on Electronic Voting (www.cev.ie/) consisting of five independent members. The task of the commission was to produce an interim report on the secrecy, accuracy and testing of the chosen electronic system. The report (Commission on Electronic Voting, 2004: 7), published on 1 May, stated that 'the Commission finds that it is not in a position to recommend with the requisite degree of confidence the use of the chosen system at elections in Ireland in June 2004'. The majority of the submissions also stated that the electronic voting system was flawed and should be changed radically before being introduced.

The commission's statements on testing, accuracy and secrecy suggested that electronic voting should not be used. Regarding the testing of the system, the commission stated that the tests which had been carried out to date were insufficient to establish the technology's reliability for use at elections. The final software version was not available to the commission, despite the forthcoming deadline of three months. Nor had the commission received the source code of the system. Hence, the commission was not able to make any statement regarding the accuracy issue. In fact, the secrecy of electronic voting was also in danger. During the voting process the machine would have produced certain sounds which meant that an insider would have been able to identify the voter's preferences. The commission underlined also that a verified paper trail, as many had argued (McGaley and Gibson, 2003; Mercuri, 2002a; O'Duffy, 2004), is crucial to assure the integrity of the election.

After the commission's clear recommendation against the introduction of electronic voting the Irish government was forced to rethink its strategy. Minister Cullen, the politician responsible for the Irish electronic voting disaster, was faced with sustained accusations of arrogance, incompetence and neglecting the public voice against electronic voting. Five weeks before the election date, the government abandoned the proposal to carry out the elections electronically and went back to manual voting (Hennessy and Brennock, 2004). The policy had cost the Irish government more than €50 million.

The government's hope of being able to improve the democratic process by implementing e-voting proved to be impossible to realise. Not only was the episode costly in financial terms but also it massively influenced the local and European elections. The ruling party experienced the worst election results since the 1920s. The question which arises is, how was it possible for the Irish government not to be aware of the various weaknesses of the system before 1 May 2004?

The influence of ontology on the e-voting case

This story of the failure of a large-scale system will sound familiar to many readers who are interested in the development and implementation of information systems. One can see examples of poor management, unclear aims and requirements, lack of communication, non-existing user involvement and, of course, many political issues which are intrinsic to any e-government or e-voting system. There are thus many possible explanations for the failure of the system. I do not want to discuss these but rather to look for underlying causes. There is good reason to argue that the ontological view of an information system is the root cause of many of the problems it encounters and that the Irish e-voting experience provides a good example.

Researchers and practitioners who subscribe to the position of ontological realism see technology as a tool that serves humanity by achieving its inbuilt objectives. While they would concede that technology is created by humans, it eventually matures, freeing itself from human tutelage and leading an existence of its own. The resulting view is that a technological tool is tailored towards a certain task and can be used successfully to address the task and thereby solve the problem. Management of the system thus has to make sure that the right tool for the task at hand is available. Once this has been achieved, the rest is a matter of detail and skilled application. The important observation here is that ontological realism can lead to the attribution of fixed characteristics to technology, characteristics that are intrinsic to the technology and independent of the user.

A further consequence, which does not follow necessarily from realism but which is easy to support, is that of technological determinism. If technology exists independently of its use and if it has objective characteristics, then one can conclude that the use of a certain technology will lead to predetermined consequences. Technological determinism is a problematic figure of thought, and few would defend strong technological determinist positions. It is nevertheless often implied in a realist and positivist approach to technology, which uses functional forms of rationality to effect desired outcomes by using or introducing specific technologies. Technological determinism is also a description of technology that hides social influences and can thus be used to exert power and oppress people without allowing discursive access to the social aspect of technology. For this reason, technological determinism is among the ideas that are opposed by critical research in IS (Cecez-Kecmanovic, 2005).

The case of the Irish e-voting failure fits several aspects of this description of the consequences of realism and determinism. How else can one explain the fact that the Irish government believed that it could go ahead with the new technology? The government ignored societal resistance and the fact that the technology had never been used successfully on a nation-wide scale. The opposition that the Irish government faced could only be overcome (or ignored) on the basis of a strong conviction that e-voting, once installed, would eventually be successful and the opposing voices would slowly disappear. Empirical tests prior to the independent commission's investigations were used to support this conviction. None of these considerations would be tenable without the implicit belief in technological determinism, in this case of the e-voting approach in general and of the chosen technology in particular. And this determinism is not coherent if it is not built on the ontological assumption that technology has fixed, observer-independent features.

One needs to concede that the case is problematic even from a realist position, for several reasons. First, the voting system did not truly exist even five weeks before the election. It thus did not have an objective existence by the best of standards. Second, neither the government nor the commission had access to the source code. The fact that the supplier retained the code meant that it was impossible to verify whether the system actually did what it was supposed to do and how it did so. One can thus argue that the main problem of the project was bad management and oversight as well as political insensitivity. Yet an inadequate ontology is one of the underlying reasons for the problem – and if that is true, then one should ask what the alternative would have been.

Had the Irish government (or, more specifically, Minister Martin Cullen) been of a constructivist persuasion, then the entire project would have presented itself in a different light. Constructivists do not believe in the independent existence of technology but see it in the social context, where technology is being constantly constructed and reconstructed through its use and interaction. The constructivist ontology assumes that technology is not determined by engineers or designers but negotiated by all stakeholders. Consequently, apart from responsible politicians and technical consultants, the input of public opinion and independent computer experts would have been crucial in decision-making.

With the constructivist position in mind, the objections raised by the opposition and by interest groups would have been interpreted not as politically motivated attempts to stop the use of a good system but as a legitimate intervention concerning the character of the technology. Different stakeholders would furthermore have had a legitimate voice in a critical discourse regarding the system. Through the social construction of electronic voting, the participants in the discourse would have shaped the actual manifestation of the e-voting system as well as the interpretation and understanding thereof.

One example of the constructivist alternative could be the status of the source code. The vendor had a legitimate interest in protecting the source code in order to be able to sell the system to other governments. However, the users, and technical specialists among them, had an equally legitimate interest in gaining access to the source code in order to understand it and rule out malfunction and manipulation. The character of the system would then have been constructed through the discourse of these viewpoints. Comparable processes in other countries have led to the installation of systems based on open source code.

Similar processes of negotiation could be used to solve the main stumbling block between Minister Cullen and the public opposition, namely the paper trail. The realist ontology supports the position of using e-voting for rational and economic purposes such as acceleration of the counting process, accurate results and elimination of the paper trail. Irish experts also welcomed the technical advantages such as the accuracy and speed of e-voting. At the same time, they argued that elimination of the paper trail could endanger Irish democratic principles. One can argue that the constructivist ontology would put democratic principles first, accepting the higher costs if necessary. A constructivist would advocate that e-voting should be adjusted to the public requirements, and not vice versa.

The interesting aspect of this analysis of the Irish e-voting case is that it is not confined to ontological matters. In fact, one could counter-argue that the solutions suggested here under the heading of a constructivist ontology have little to do with ontology but are social, organisational, political and possibly even ethical in nature and have to do with the use of technology but not with its ontological nature. Such an argument would miss the point, however, that the use of technology is based on a perception of its nature, and that this perception is derived from implicit ontological positions. While there is no reason why an ontological realist cannot use technology for democratic purposes, the scope of democratic deliberation will be different. Realists and technological determinists can wish to improve the working of society, including voting processes, but they will do so by resorting to specific technological tools with fixed features, whose use has predictable consequences. They are thus more likely to miss issues of unintended use and to disqualify dissenting voices. Discourses will consequently be more limited and are likely to miss important points. At the same time, it appears that anti-realist ontological positions require greater attention to be paid to a variety of stakcholders, which renders them fundamentally more democratic, and arguably more legitimate. Ontology, to summarise, is thus important because it affects our shared understanding of the world, but also because it can have numerous consequences in other areas where they may not be immediately suspected. For both these reasons, critical researchers should pay attention to ontology in their research.

This leads us to the next philosophical aspect, one which is closely linked to ontology, namely to epistemology.

6 Epistemology

On information, knowledge and truth

Epistemology is, according to the *Oxford English Dictionary* of 2004, the 'theory or science of the method or grounds of knowledge'. If research aims to produce knowledge, then it has to rely on an implicit or explicit epistemology. I follow Chua (1986) in distinguishing between epistemology and methodology, where the former refers to the principles of knowledge, the latter to ways of acquiring it. Epistemology is closely linked to ontology. One can only gain knowledge about entities that exist. In return, one needs to have a way of gaining knowledge in order to make statements about whether something exists. While the exact relationship between given ontologies and epistemologies is not always clear-cut, it is important to note that every epistemology requires a corresponding ontology (Iivari *et al.*, 1998). There is no ontology-free epistemology (see Feyerabend, 1980).

If epistemology is the philosophical discipline concerned with knowledge, then it needs to define what knowledge is. One definition sometimes used by philosophers is that knowledge is 'true, justified beliefs' (Steup, 2001). This is helpful because it allows us to distinguish the question of when a statement is true from the question of when we are justified in believing a statement to be true. While the latter question is much discussed in IS research, the former, arguably more important, one, is usually ignored.

Matters of knowledge and truth are clearly important for all research which arguably aims to produce knowledge, and critical researchers thus need to be aware of possible positions. Critical research builds on implicit truth claims of statements. Examples of contested critical claims are that people are oppressed and can be emancipated, that functional and purposive rationality are problematic or that truth statements themselves can be problematic. One reason why critical scholars need to be even more aware of epistemological matters than mainstream positivists is that one important stream of critical arguments attacks exactly those positivist truth claims that are the basis of much mainstream research. It has been an ongoing task of critical research to show the limits of positivist truth claims, with possibly the most stringent argument having been developed by Habermas (1969) in his exposure of technology and science as means of ideology. Habermas shows that knowledge interests are never neutral; they are always built on particular social constellations and connected to consequences that go beyond the apparently neutral pursuit of knowledge.

In this chapter I will give a brief overview of some of the most important epistemological positions to be found in information systems. On this basis, I will then discuss the question of information and truth from the critical perspective.

Epistemological positions in information systems

The history of philosophy has produced a large number of epistemological positions that allow us to understand and compare how knowledge and truth are defined and how they can be achieved. As in the case of ontology, I cannot claim to do these complex debates justice. The purpose of the chapter is to introduce the dominant epistemological positions that can be found in the field of IS, in order for us to understand what a critical position in the question of epistemology and truth may be.

Empiricism

Among the different ways of acquiring knowledge and defending the claim for truth, the most prominent one is probably empiricism. Empiricism can be defined as the 'doctrine that experience rather than reason is the source of our knowledge of the world' (Morick, 1980, p. 1; see Gergen, 1999). Empiricism is the traditional epistemology of the natural sciences (Ciborra, 2002), where it usually searches for causal relationships. It tries to discover the laws governing reality and uses a hypothetico-deductive approach (Vitalari, 1985). Empiricists set up hypotheses which they then try to prove or falsify (Popper, 1980). The ultimate aim of empiricist research is to be able to make well-founded predictions (Orlikowski and Baroudi, 1991; Westland, 2004).

Empiricism is closely associated with several assumptions about the nature of scientific inquiry. First, it holds that observation is objective (Klein and Myers, 1999) and value free (Walsham, 1995a). It is also seen as a universally valid approach to knowledge, which means that it is often associated with calls for a unity of science which would include the natural sciences as well as the arts, humanities and social sciences. Objectivity can be assured through an observer who is detached from the object of observation and who does not interfere (Introna, 1997; Yin, 2003). An important ingredient of this kind of approach to academic inquiry is a certain kind of detached and aloof rationality which is interested in relationships without being intimately involved in them (Wilson, 2003).

As a reaction to the perceived weaknesses of empiricism, which includes the problem of the possibility of objectivity in social science, the question of appropriateness of empirical observation of humans, the alleged circularity of empiricism, the complexities of the notion of causality, a resistance to the underlying rationality, and other problems, other epistemological approaches have been developed.

Phenomenology

Phenomenology is an ambiguous term because it can refer to a general first-person description of human experience or, more specifically, to a philosophical method for analysing consciousness developed by Edmund Husserl (Beavers, 2002). The term was used by Kant and Hegel, but Husserl redefined it in reaction to the detached academic discussion in the nineteenth century. Heidegger, possibly the most prominent phenomenologist, defines the term 'phenomenon' using its Greek etymology as 'that which shows itself in itself, the manifest' (Heidegger, 1993, p. 28; and see Moran, 2000).

Heidegger sees phenomenology as an ontology, but it can also be understood as an epistemology. The central idea of phenomenology is that the world is opened up by consciousness. Every perception is a conscious act. Phenomena are given to consciousness, and phenomenology tries to go back to the things themselves. These things are not objectively given things, but rather the content of consciousness (Lyotard, 1993). The phenomenologist tries to bracket out the non-essential aspects of perception to end up with the essence of the phenomenon.

In phenomenology the essences of the objects of research cannot be divided from the subject who researches them. The classical subject–object dichotomy of empiricism is not valid here (Moran, 2000). An important aspect emphasised by Heidegger is that the subject of perception is never an independent entity but, rather, a human with all the lived experiences and background, what he calls being-in-the-world, and for which he uses the term '*Dasein*'. *Dasein* has to contend with the realities of human existence. It is embodied, it faces death, it is lonely and at the same time subjected to fashions, to the One (*das Man*), as Heidegger calls it (Dreyfus, 1993; Introna, 1997; Capurro and Pingel, 2002; Stuart, 2002; Introna and Whittaker, 2003). Since humans cannot live a detached and objective existence, they live in their own, partly idiosyncratic world, which Husserl calls the life-world. The life-world is the strange thing that disintegrates before our eyes. It is the horizon within which we always move (Habermas, 1985).

Phenomenology is a way of achieving knowledge and can be seen as an epistemology. It differs essentially from empiricism and is based on completely different assumptions regarding what knowledge is and how it can be acquired. But it is not the only possible alternative to empiricism.

Hermeneutics

Hermeneutics is another alternative to empiricism as a way of acquiring knowledge. Etymologically it is derived from the Greek word for 'to interpret' (Hirschheim and Klein, 1989). The original purpose of hermeneutics was the understanding of religious texts, more specifically of the Bible. It has developed into a general approach to the understanding of texts. The underlying problem is that every reader of a text has a different understanding of that text depending on his or her own experiences and life-world. This understanding differs from the understanding of the author. Originally, hermeneutics tried to find ways of determining the true sense of the text as intended by the author (or God). Hermeneutics has moved away from the idea of such a 'correct' understanding and has expanded into the art of understanding all communication, not just written text.

One important aspect of contemporary hermeneutics is the hermeneutic circle. The idea behind this is that there is a circular relationship between the prior knowledge of a recipient of a text and his or her understanding of the same text. A text can be read only if the reader has a general understanding of its content, but this understanding will be modified through the reading of the text (see Gadamer, 1990).

The current version of hermeneutics was explicitly developed to counter the natural science approach to humanities and social sciences. The opposition to natural sciences can best be demonstrated by looking at a pair of concepts associated with the German words *erklären* and *verstehen* (Hausman, 1994). *Erklären*, literally 'to explain', refers to the natural sciences, where causal relations can be established which can be used to explain phenomena. Such causal explanations are not useful in the humanities and social sciences because they neglect agents' ability to act. An explanation of human actions is thus not an application of natural laws but rather a description of humans that allows the reader to understand what the agent did and why she did it. This is what *verstehen*, literally 'to understand', will achieve. Hermeneutics aims at facilitating this understanding. According to this view of hermeneutics, there can be no unity of sciences. Social and natural sciences have different research objects and thus need different epistemologies (see Ricoeur, 1983).

According to this description of hermeneutics, the role of the researcher must be different from that in empiricism. The researcher cannot be detached, and needs to admit that his or her understanding of the situation affects the outcome of the research (Myers and Avison, 2002).

A final remark on the relationship between hermeneutics and phenomenology: in its current form, hermeneutics has been shaped by phenomenology. The most important hermeneutic philosophers, among them Gadamer and Ricoeur, were strongly influenced by phenomenology. If the phenomenon in question is a social one, as is typically the case in IS research, then a phenomenological researcher needs to acquire an understanding of the social exchange that constitutes it. For this, the researcher must apply hermeneutic means. He or she must follow the hermeneutic circle by starting with a given understanding, engaging with the phenomenon and thereby changing the initial understanding (see Boland, 1985).

Critical epistemology: the question of truth and information

As a rule of thumb, one can state that a realist ontology goes well with an empiricist epistemology, whereas phenomenology and hermeneutics are closer to an anti-realist position. It is thus not surprising that the paradigm of positivism typically includes realism and empiricism, whereas interpretivism tends to cover a constructivist ontology and epistemological views based on hermeneutics and phenomenology. These connections are again not logically necessary (there is, for example, no fundamental reason why hermeneutics should not be based on a realist ontology, as its history as the attempt to find the 'real' meaning of a text shows), but in current social sciences, including information systems, this distinction seems to be widely accepted. This leaves open the question of the position of critical research in terms of epistemology. Instead of attempting a general categorisation of critical research in this respect, I will demonstrate the critical position by looking at the question of what distinguishes truth from untruth, or information from misinformation when looked at from a critical viewpoint. Doing so will require a brief discussion of theories of truth, knowledge and information, which will lead to a reinterpretation of traditional positions from the critical points of view of Foucault's and Habermas's theories.

Information

We allegedly live in an information society and possibly even in the information age. Information surrounds us, powers our economy and makes us information workers. The concept of information is clearly of central relevance for information systems research and practice. There seems to be an assumption that information is central to managerial decision making and that more and higher-quality information will lead to better outcomes. This assumption persists even though Ackoff (1967) argued 40 years ago that it is misleading. One of the reasons for the longevity of this arguably naïve reliance on IS to produce more and better information is a lack of conceptual clarity regarding the very term 'information'.

Brock and Dhillon (2001), having done an in-depth review of the term, come to the conclusion that it is almost everything and anything, and they liken it to the 'ether' of the Middle Ages, which pervades everything but cannot be captured. In a classic definition, Wiener (1954, p. 17) states that 'information is a name for the content of what is exchanged with the outer world as we adjust to it, and make our adjustment felt upon it', thus emphasising the processes involved in information sharing rather than the entity itself.

A typical approach to information in the field of IS is to compare it with the concept of data. Where data are the raw facts of the world, information is then data 'with meaning'. 'When "data" acquires context-dependent meaning and relevance, it becomes information. Furthermore, we obviously expect information to represent valid knowledge on which users can rely for rational action' (Ulrich, 2001a, p. 56). This relationship between data, information and meaning is adopted frequently (see Davenport and Prusak, 1998; Walsham, 2001). It is also problematic. First, there is the problem that data is not simply brute facts of the world but that all data is already processed and gathered. Information thus cannot simply be the injection of meaning into data, because data already has meaning; otherwise it would not be possible to perceive it (see Introna, 1997). The difference between data and information is thus a difference in the level and appreciation of meaning (see Floridi, 1999). Another problem of this definition is that it renders information completely idiosyncratic. Data that may hold meaning for you may be utterly meaningless to me. This would contradict the implicit assumption that information is more generally accessible, which is required for it to be processed it by machines

This raises another problem, namely the relationship between information and technology. The reason why we are currently interested in information is that technology allows us to collect information (or data?) in previously unimaginable amounts. It can be processed automatically and checked for higher-level patterns that would not be discernible without technology. This requires a new information infrastructure, which in turn requires huge investments and therefore novel processes and procedures (Kahin, 1997). The transformation of information in a machine-readable format at the same time produces new problems, for example mobility and reproducibility (Straub and Collins, 1990). The technical use of information also suggests that information must be machine-readable and thus quantifiable (Bloomfield and Coombs, 1992). This returns us to the problem of meaning, because information, seen from a technical point of view, does not seem to offer a link to the concept of meaning as introduced earlier, as central to information (Grim *et al.*, 2004).

Another approach to understanding information would be to look at its function. Information as meaningful data needs to have meaning to (human) agents. Such meaning is relevant only if information can affect actions or perceptions (see Mingers, 2001a). Information without any consequences is arguably not information. If information has a direct influence on humans, then it will also have an ethical impact. Indeed, the ethical importance of information has been recognised for a long time (see Wiener, 1954; Mason, 1986; Stichler, 1998).

This discussion of information could be continued in a variety of directions. One could look at the disadvantages of information (e.g. information overload (see Postman, 1992)) or other, related concepts such as facts, jargon, numbers, opinions (Brooke, 2002a), or resulting developments, such as the informating nature of modern work (Zuboff, 1988). Extending the distinction of data and information, one could discuss further concepts such as knowledge, wisdom, or judgement (see French, 1990). The one aspect I will briefly elaborate on in the next subsection is that of truth.

Information, misinformation and truth

One strong assumption about information is that it is true. If it were not true, then the meaning associated with it would be wrong or misleading. Untrue information can also not inform perception or action. De George (2003a) distinguishes between data and information precisely because data contains no claim to truth, whereas information does. This raises the difficult question of what it means for a statement to be true. It is important to briefly think about the criteria we accept for something to be held true or false, because critical positions differ greatly in this respect from the common-sense understanding we typically use.

Truth is a property of a statement. A sentence or proposition can be true or false. When do we say a statement is true? A typical answer would be: 'A statement is true if it describes a state of the world as it is.' Or we could rephrase by saying that a statement is true if it corresponds with the way the world is. We therefore call this the correspondence theory of truth (Feyerabend, 1980). The correspondence theory would appear to be what has been called the 'natural attitude'. Humans are socialised into believing that one can objectively perceive and make true statements about an external reality. The theory is problematic, however. The most serious problem it has to contend with, and one that even strong supporters cannot overcome, is directly linked to the underlying ontology. It is our inability to explain how an external reality can be equal to a mental representation (Khlentzos, 2004).

Alternative accounts of truth include the pragmatic, consensus and coherence approaches. For adherents of the pragmatic view, a statement is true if it contributes to a desired outcome (Rorty, 1982). A consensus view of truth is based on the conviction that the criterion for the truth of a statement is the consensus of all (or all relevant or all informed) individuals or parties (Rorty, 1996a). Finally, a statement can be seen as true if it conforms to a variety of other statements and does not contradict other known true statements. Such a coherence view of truth is typical for formal languages or mathematics.

The question of truth is important in this chapter because it has to do with the difference between information and mis- or disinformation. Discussing these concepts will make clearer the epistemological position and open epistemological questions of critical research.

The most important distinction between information and misinformation and disinformation is the question of truth. Whereas information is true, misinformation or disinformation is untrue. Following the definition of the *Oxford English Dictionary* (www.oed.com/; accessed 27 October 2005), one can define 'misinformation' as 'wrong or misleading information'. Disinformation is also wrong information, but, unlike misinformation, it is a known falsehood. The OED defines disinformation as 'the dissemination of deliberately false information' and refers specifically to wrong information supplied by governments. For the purposes of this argument I will distinguish between misinformation as accidental falsehood and disinformation as deliberate falsehood.

Truth in critical research

For a critical researcher, truth will usually not be an objective description of an external reality. All perception is always value laden and based on individual and collective prejudices. Following the hermeneutic tradition, critical researchers in IS tend to agree that prejudices cannot be overcome (Gadamer, 1990). Instead, the purpose of research is to expose them and render them open to discursive analysis. This raises serious problem for a critical epistemology. How can we know what is true, if all truth claims can always be contested? And how can critical theory claim to be true, if it fundamentally doubts the existence of eternal truths? The short answer to this is that critical research has to emphasise reflexivity. That means that critical research must question its own assumptions and foundations. Only by remaining open to constant questioning can it be possible to overcome the dilemma of scepticism. (The dilemma of scepticism is that it doubts the existence of truth and thus cannot be true.) And, indeed, an emphasis on reflexivity is central to critical research (Cecez-Kecmanovic, 2001a; Waring, 2004) and will form the basis of the final main section of this book.

Another important aspect of the understanding of truth in CRIS is that truth cannot be value neutral. It is impossible to divide truth claims from normative claims. Following Habermas, one can say that every speech act simultaneously promotes different validity claims, which can be separated for the purpose of analysis but in practical discourses always exist side by side. A presumably value-neutral statement such as 'the Technology Acceptance Model (TAM) offers a good description of ICT user behaviour' is not really value neutral. It implies that the speaker has a right to say this, and that saying it does not limit anyone's rights. It assumes that objective descriptions are possible and good, which is a value statement. Alternative descriptions of reality are curtailed, because the assumed truth of the statement puts the onus on the listener to believe it and use TAM as a description of reality. All of this is meant to show not that this is an immoral statement but rather that it is not value free.

Truth can also be used as an ideology. The worst form of ideology is that which has been recognised as truth and is therefore no longer open to debate. Truths which are generally accepted are therefore the strongest form of ideology. And they are also closely linked to power. If it is true that managers are rational humans who can recognise the needs of the organisation and maximise the overall utility, then there is no need to question the status of managers in the organisation or the role of commercial entities in society. Truth thus cements power and, at the same time, power helps establish truth. This is the meaning of Foucault's regimes of truth. A look at popular discourse about companies and their role in society or the role of ICT in organisations shows that there are numerous 'truths' which stabilise the status quo without there being strong evidence to support them. Among them there is the assumption that economic growth is the panacea to most of society's problems, that economic rationality is the best way to approach questions of distribution, or that the use of ICT will improve organisational processes from commerce and government to education.

Misinformation and disinformation in CRIS

If we go back to the definition of information, then a relevant aspect is that it makes a difference, that it 'in-forms' people and helps them orientate themselves. Given that critical research is interested in emancipation, one can say that from the perspective of CRIS, information is what helps emancipate humans, whereas misinformation and disinformation alienate and disempower. To address this, CRIS can try to point out where information as well as technology hide and propagate ideology. A fitting example of this is provided by Introna (1997), who points out that the information provided by MIS can be described as a status symbol. It allows the user (manager) to lay a claim to rationality, which in our society legitimises the exertion of power. This would not be so bad if it did not mean that it legitimises the manager to make decisions which can alienate others. And it would also be acceptable if the relative nature of such truth claims were clearer. However, the current truth discourse that tries to find universal truths easily turns into (cultural) imperialism.

To return to the difference between misinformation and disinformation, one can say that for a critical researcher misinformation is such claims as inadvertently lead to alienation whereas disinformation is claims which the originator knows to be alienating but nevertheless proposes.

From a Habermasian perspective, misinformation is not problematic. It is simply information that is contentious and that therefore will be analysed in a discourse. The person claiming truth will have to explain the reasons for the claim and will have to answer critique. All of this can be done within the framework of communicative action where people recognise each other as dignified beings and are willing to take each other seriously. Disinformation is more problematic. Since it is information that deliberately alienates or disempowers people, the speaker shows a disregard for the other, who is disempowered. This means that he or she is interacting not in communicative mode but in what Habermas calls 'strategic' mode, where others are used as means to the speaker's ends. From a Habermasian perspective, this would still be subject to discourse, because one could point out to the speaker that he or she is self-contradictory. The problem is, however, that the speaker may simply not care. This is where the Habermasian view of critical research becomes problematic. The hope of such critical research is that by exposing ideology and false claims, these will be rectified. It does not offer any guarantee, however, that this will happen. When disinformation is exposed as such and still not changed, then critical research will have reached its limits and needs to interact with other social institutions such as politics or the law to stimulate change.

The distinction between misinformation and disinformation would look different from a Foucauldian viewpoint. Foucault is much more sceptical about any truth claims than Habermas. A Foucauldian could argue that the distinction between misinformation and disinformation is artificial because it seems to presuppose the existence of a universal truth and the ability, through self-reflectiveness, of speakers to know their her own intentions when speaking. Both may be doubtful. A further problem would be that the idea of emancipation is much less clear and that it is not obvious whether emancipation is not a particular ideology itself.

The Foucauldian approach would therefore be to undertake a genealogy of the information in question and try to understand why some statements are believed to be true or false and why individuals would form propositions that can be construed as false. The emphasis in such a genealogy would be on questions of power and bodily discipline. How are we socialised in order for us to accept certain truths and falsehoods? This Foucauldian approach does not offer any hope of arriving at a clear distinction between truth and untruth, between information and misinformation. However, it seems to be carried by an implicit hope that there are better (i.e. more empowering) accounts of the world and worse ones. Otherwise, there would be little point in undertaking a genealogy.

From the point of view of critical research, the distinction between information, misinformation and disinformation is problematic. It is closely linked to the question of truth, and we should admit that there is no universally accepted theory of truth. The critical approach will help scholars widen their understanding of issues and question their own work. Choosing to do critical research is not a value-neutral stance but requires researchers to reflect actively on their assumptions. It is based on a desire to promote emancipation rather than work in systemic imperatives.

Critical research does not offer any easy answers. By discussing the two competing theoretical approaches of Habermas and Foucault, I have argued that even within critical research there is no unanimous answer to the question of what information is and whether we can detect and address misinformation or disinformation. However, critical research does provide us with ways of thinking about truth and what we hold to be true or false. It stresses the fact that truth is not a natural occurrence and that it is worthwhile to think about where it comes from and who promotes it or benefits from it.

One argument that the chapter certainly does not promote is that critical researchers become the gatekeepers of truth and information. This would only substitute one type of ideology for another. It is not a necessary critical position that there is no truth, which would leave CRIS open to the charges of being relativistic and self-contradictory. Instead, the practical lesson to be learned from the above discussions is that we need to be very careful with regard to truth claims and realise that truth is always open to debate. This means that there is no clear and unambiguous dividing line between information and misinformation. A statement that can serve as useful and clear information when uttered by A in context B can become an outright lie with political intentions when uttered by person C in context D. The only thing that can be done in the light of this uncertainty regarding truth and information is to keep an open mind and remain open to discourses and new arguments.

7 Methodology

Is there a specific critical way to knowledge?

Whereas epistemology deals with the question of what knowledge is, methodology asks how valid knowledge can be acquired. Methodology is thus the study of methods (Mingers, 2001b), and it analyses the different methods used in research. There are numerous attempts to collect and classify research methods. I am referring here to ways of acquiring valid knowledge, which needs to be distinguished from structured approaches to IS development or data modelling. (For a review of the philosophical basics of such methodologies, see Hirschheim *et al.*, 1995.) Jenkins (1985), for example, identifies 13 ways. The most important divide between methods is that between quantitative and qualitative methods. There has been an intensive discussion between proponents of the two sides in IS research for at least the past 20 years. I will not recount this discussion here. Suffice it to say that numbers are signs, which carry meaning in a particular context, just like letters, words, and sentences. All signs require interpretation in order to be understood, which renders the perceived opposition between quantitative and qualitative fairly uninteresting.

The only question with regard to methodologies and methods that I will discuss in this chapter is whether there is such a thing as a critical methodology, a way of acquiring valid knowledge that is unique to critical research.

Critical methodology

The question of a critical methodology keeps being asked in CRIS debates (McGrath, 2005). The reasons why criticalists might wish for a unique methodology are clear. Getting published in respected journals is an important part of an academic career, and in the field of IS there is a strong expectation that any research will follow a specified methodology which will guarantee the acceptability of the findings. Research papers without a methodology section are likely to be rejected. Justifying the chosen methodology in each case is highly laborious, and being able to draw upon established methodologies would leave scholars more space to publish interesting inferences and conclusions.

This description of the reasons for desiring a critical methodology, read in conjunction with the earlier discussion of ontology and epistemology, indicates why there are problems with the very idea of a critical methodology. One of these is the implications of the very term 'methodology'. Looked at more closely, the idea that there can be a clearly defined approach to research that will, if followed correctly, lead to desired outcomes which will produce true statements is fundamentally positivist. It only works on the further assumptions of a realist ontology and a correspondence theory of truth, both of which are highly contentious in critical research. Furthermore, methodologies can hide ideologies by privileging certain aspects (e.g. quantifiable ones) over others, as I will argue in Chapter 11 on trust research in IS. Methodologies are also generally built upon the functionalist rationality that critical research seeks to discredit (Kincheloe and McLaren, 2005).

Where critical researchers reject ontological realism, an added question is that of the status of any research findings. Phenomenology informs us that the phenomena we perceive are creations of the intentional activity of perception of the individual. This means, however, that there is little hope that researchers, even if they research the same phenomenon, will have identical perceptions and, much less, identical conclusions. This then raises the question of why we engage in empirical research in the first place. Indeed, a problem here may be that the English nouns 'science' and 'research' are usually taken to imply empirical work. One should note that this is not necessary and that, for example, the German translations *Wissenschaft* (science) and *Forschung* (research) do not carry this same implication, or at least do so to a lesser degree. From hermeneutics we can learn that the process of producing knowledge has to do with the creation of texts and that the reception and development of texts are what constitutes knowledge.

It may thus not be surprising that much critical research is not empirical. This fact is much bemoaned in CRIS, but it can be observed in the history of critical work, for example in the work of the Frankfurt School, whose initial claim was to support Marxist ideas with empirical research but which found it increasingly hard to live up to this claim. If the aim of critical work is to emancipate and if this is done by intervening in public discourses, then the strength of the work and its success depend on the plausibility of narratives, not on any empirical data, which, as I argued earlier, is always open to interpretation anyway.

However, this argument also leads us back to the wish to work empirically in information systems. The reason for undertaking empirical critical research may not be that there is a truth out there that needs to be unearthed but that empirical work is required to retain the ability to communicate with peers and the wider public whose expectations must be met if critical claims are to find an audience. This has to do with practical political realities that criticalists face in daily life, such as criteria for being published, promoted, etc. Also, there is the plausibility in the eyes of the general public, which, at least in the Anglo-American world, has a strong expectation that social scientists will undertake empirical work. Critical researchers thus face the external constraint that they have to produce empirical data, despite the fact that critical research can never be reduced to empirical data, not least because of its non-empirical ethical underpinnings.

For these reasons, it is probably politically opportune to engage in the debate on critical methodology, rather than just to reject it as irrelevant. Fundamentally, any methodology that allows the collection of relevant data concerning one of the critical topics, using a critical theory aimed at fulfilling the critical intention, can be used in critical research. This includes positivist, empiricist and quantitative approaches. Orthodox Marxist critical research would typically use such approaches to prove the subjugation of labour. Methodology is thus not central to critical research (see Walsham, 2005a; Avgerou, 2005).

In the practice of critical IS research, however, it seems to be the case that there are some methods that are typically used by critical researchers, and these are generally on the qualitative and hermeneutic side. One important aspect of critical research methodologies is that they are reflexive: they reflect on the role of the researcher within the research process (Cecez-Kecmanovic, 2001a). There seem to be two groups of critical methodologies. One aims at determining the social realities of people who are affected by information systems whereas the other concentrates on the use of language.

The first group of research methodologies comprises those research approaches that allow an in-depth understanding of people's view of their situation to be developed. This will usually require intensive interaction. One can therefore find participative approaches (Trauth and O'Connor, 1991; Walsham, 1995a) used in critical research. One example of this is ethnography, which can be used in a critical way, making it 'critical ethnography' (Schultze, 2001). A research method that is based on participant observation and that openly shares the critical intention to change given situations is action research (Gergen, 1999; Mumford, 2001). The other group of research methodologies is more interested in how the use of language hides power influences, how information systems produce ideologies, how discourses lead to disempowerment and how these developments can be counteracted. Here we find methodologies based on the concept of discourses (Ulrich, 2001b). These can be based on assumption analysis (Hirschheim and Klein, 1994), discourse analysis (Schultze and Leidner, 2002; Thompson, 2003) or ideology critique (McAulay *et al.*, 2002). More generally, most hermeneutic and narrative approaches to IS research seem to be well suited to serve as methodologies for critical IS research (Heaton, 2001; van der Blonk, 2003). There remains the difficult question of compatibility of these different research methodologies (Brooke, 2002b), which has to be looked at in each individual case.

8 Philosophical syncretism in IS research

Final remarks on ontology, epistemology and paradigms

I have argued from the beginning of this book that the frequently used distinction of positivist, interpretivist and critical research as the main paradigms for IS research is misleading. Now that we have discussed issues of ontology, epistemology and methodology in some more depth, it should have become clear why this distinction is not helpful.

There are typical combinations of methods, epistemologies and ontologies that we call paradigms, but these are not logically obligatory. Positivists using a correspondence theory of truth and an empiricist epistemology will often use quantitative methods. However, there is no fundamental reason why they could not use qualitative methods (Urquhart, 2001). In order to find out the reality of a social phenomenon and to describe it as it objectively is, it may be helpful to observe agents or interview them, to write 'realist tales' (van der Blonk, 2003). On the other hand, there is the typical interpretive combination of constructionist ontology, consensus theory of truth, hermeneutic/phenomenological epistemology and qualitative methods. Again, there is no a-priori reason why quantitative methods should not be used here. Numbers and statistics can be seen as ways of clarifying meanings and shared realities (Miranda and Saunders, 2003).

Where does all this leave CRIS? Critical research is not independent of positivism or interpretivism, and in many cases it will be based on shared assumptions. Current criticalists tend to share more common ground with interpretivism than with positivism. Some scholars have taken to speaking of 'critical interpretivism' rather than distinguishing the two (Doolin and McLeod, 2005). One can probably argue that the approach often called 'critical realism' is a similar amalgamation of critical and positivist views. This raises the question of which aspects of a research approach can be mixed with others, on what grounds mixing may be permissible and how it is to be evaluated. Or is it possible, perhaps even desirable, to allow a free-for-all in which researchers can pick and choose for themselves what they want to use without any regard to paradigms, ontologies, epistemologies, etc?

Philosophical syncretism in information systems research

Syncretism is the 'combination of different beliefs, the attempted combination of different systems of philosophical or religious belief or practice' (*Encarta*,

1999, p. 1893). It is usually regarded with scepticism by adherents of a given philosophy or religion. The fundamental question concerning syncretism is always whether the combined belief systems are compatible. In the field of information systems one can observe frequent calls for the combination of methods, methodologies, epistemologies and paradigms. Calls for the abandonment of paradigms in general, as introduced earlier, can be read as implying that the mixing of the different components of the paradigms is admissible. Analysing examples of philosophical syncretism in IS research is made difficult by the fact that many scholars follow their own definitions of philosophical terms and that these are not always compatible. An added difficulty is that some concepts seem to imply a mixture of positivism and non-positivism, such as multi-method research (Hirschheim, 1985; Cavaye, 1996) or critical realism (Mingers, 2001a, b), but that the fundamental philosophical issues are rarely spelled out.

The typical form of philosophical syncretism in IS research is the assurance that positivism and non-positivism (usually interpretivism) can peacefully coexist and pose no threat to one another. One typical example is the interpretivist researcher who wants to promote understanding for his or her research approach but who is careful not to offend positivist researchers by insisting that both approaches are valuable. ('We must clearly state that it is not our intention to replace the positivist perspective with critical or interpretive ones' (Orlikowski and Baroudi, 1991, p. 24).) Others see a more complex relationship where positivist and non-positivist research enter into some kind of dialectical process whereby higher-level knowledge is produced (Klein *et al.*, 1991). There are few examples of actually mixing positivist and non-positivist research approaches and contrasting the results of doing research on the basis of different ontologies and their resulting choices of epistemology and methodology (see Trauth and Jessup, 2000). Nevertheless, most non-positivists seem to imply that positivism and non-positivism can coexist (Lee, 1991, 1994). Walsham (1995b) identifies four rhetorical figures used in the literature to justify the syncretistic approach.

Reasons for syncretism

If philosophical syncretism between positivism and non-positivism is widespread in IS research, then one can ask why researchers try to combine the two. There are several reasons. The most important ones are lack of clarity of the concepts, confusion of the levels, research interests, metaphysical convictions, and the history and politics of the IS discipline.

Probably the most important reason for mixing philosophical positions, particularly the paradigms of positivism and non-positivism, is the lack of clarity of the terms. I argued earlier that they are linked to ontological positions which are associated with epistemological, methodological and arguably other research-relevant aspects. One should concede, however, that there is no unanimity on the exact limits and definition of the concept of positivism, and less so on its alternatives.

The unclear use of the term 'paradigm' is partly responsible for the next reason for syncretism, namely the confusion of levels. I have argued here that the ontological assumptions of realism and anti-realism are mutually exclusive. However, the same is not necessarily true for the associated epistemologies and methodologies. Typical examples of this are given by Lee (1991, 1994) when he tries to integrate the positivist and interpretivist approaches to organisational research. A problem may arise when the methodological implications of paradigms are emphasised, where positivism stands for a certain methodology (usually quantitative methods) and interpretivism for non-quantitative methods (Benbasat and Weber, 1996; Cavaye, 1996; Landry and Banville, 1992; Eisenhardt, 1989; Weber, 2004). From this viewpoint there is no problem with a mixing of paradigms because quantitative and qualitative methods are not mutually exclusive.

The desire to mix paradigms or other philosophical underpinnings of research may partly be explained by the history and politics of the IS discipline, which determines the constraints and requirements that IS researchers are subject to. A look at the history of IS shows that the discipline has been established for 30 to 50 years (Hirschheim and Klein, 2003; Ward and Peppard, 1996). The established 'reference disciplines' (Keen, 1991), such as computer sciences, management sciences, organisation sciences or economics (Benbasat and Weber, 1996), tend to use positivist assumptions. Given the traditional strength of positivism in IS, researchers are under strong pressure to recognise it as valid in order to get their PhD recognised or their research published (Baskerville, 2001). Then there are the politics of the IS discipline, which has to survive among competing academic disciplines and which, according to some, lacks a recognisable core and definition (Benbasat and Zmud, 2003). It has been called a 'fragmented adhocracy' (Landry and Banville, 1992), which does not bode well if it wants to survive among the other positivist subjects. Independent of the truth and usefulness of such statements, they serve to exert pressure on academics not to be seen as divisive. As a result, the history and politics of the discipline combine to strongly pressure non-positivist researchers to accept positivist approaches.

Some scholars will even deny that there is a difference between positivism and non-positivism. This stance seems to be grounded in the lack of recognition that there are alternatives to a realist ontology. Weber (2004, p. v) exemplifies this position when he incredulously exclaims that 'surely some kind of reality exists beyond our perceptions of it!' and posits that it is inconceivable that anybody might contradict this statement. As proof, he offers the certain reality of death faced by everybody who jumps out of his office window. He neglects to see that, for the phenomenologist, death is always-mine (*jemeinig*, as Heidegger (1993) would have said) and thus the epitome of an idiosyncratic and thus non-objective experience. On a possibly more accessible level, the problem has also been discussed by Grint and Woolgar (1997) under the heading of 'What is social about being shot?'

There are also more sophisticated attempts to reconcile ontological differences. These can be based on post-positivism, postmodernism, critical realism,

Heglian dialectics, pragmatism or others (see Petter and Gallivan, 2004; Hirschheim, 1985; Varey *et al.*, 2002; Achterberg *et al.*, 1991; Goles and Hirschheim, 2000). There is no space here to discuss these in depth but, briefly, there seems to be no way they can avoid the dichotomy between an observer-independent and an observer-dependent reality. At best they open up a new meta-theoretical approach to reality, which typically depends on the observer and is thus anti-realist.

Consequences of syncretism

If the ontological foundations of positivism and non-positivism are not compatible and if, at the same time, IS researchers tend to mix them, then one should ask what the consequences of such syncretism may be. Are the differences between the paradigms impossible to bridge or is Weber (2004, p. vi) right when he says that it 'makes no difference to the fundamental goals' of researchers? This section will briefly look at implications in the area of research, politics and ethics.

Research implications

There is no algorithmic way of doing research according that follows from one's ontological position or paradigm. I do not support the thesis of the incommensurability of different methods (quantitative versus qualitative). However, the combination of different methods, epistemologies and ontologies needs to be justified in every single instance. It may be completely acceptable and logically stringent to use quantitative methods from an interpretivist viewpoint or to use semi-structured interviews from a positivist viewpoint. However, the same research method will mean different things depending on one's ontology. A positivist doing interviews will expect to find social reality as it is, whereas the constructionist will be part of the collective construction of the relevant reality. Two researchers using the exact same approach and getting the same results may thus come to opposing conclusions, based on the philosophical underpinnings of their work.

A related but more difficult question is that of the compatibility of epistemologies. Empiricist and hermeneutic or phenomenological approaches seem to be more difficult to combine than quantitative and qualitative methods. One problem of epistemology results from the fact that most interpretive IS research is based on the collection of empirical evidence. This means that anti-realist researchers doing empirical research need to spell out the nature of their findings: why they believe that this emphasis on empirical findings will help them. In the light of a anti-realist ontology and a non-empiricist epistemology it is not immediately obvious that empirical research is superior to other kinds, such as philosophical or conceptual research (Stahl, 2003).

A simple pick-and-choose approach to research philosophy guided by considerations of expediency is not acceptable, because it runs the risk of becoming self-contradictory. That means that the individual researcher should be clear about these questions and should address them in his or her research design. Collectively, the discipline, as represented by conferences or journals, chairs, reviewers, or editors, needs to make sure that these questions are properly and satisfactorily reflected.

A related aspect, leading us to the politics of IS research, is standards of research quality, validity, rigour or relevance. These much-debated problems will not be compatible for positivists and non-positivists. While they are in some instances related to specific methods, the underlying ontology determines whether a certain piece of research is acceptable. A central point here will be the truth theory used to assess these issues. These are very closely linked to the underlying ontology and they are currently rarely reflected in detail.

Political implications

Research does not take place in a vacuum (see Lee, 2001) but is embedded in social systems where politics play a great role. This should be quite obvious, particularly for critical researchers who recognise the social construction of reality. Yet non-positivist research politics are much less visible or successful than their positivist counterpart. Representatives of the positivist view are openly trying to set the agenda of IS research according to their ideas. They try to define legitimate research subjects like the IT artefact and to impose an 'identity' on the field (Benbasat and Zmud, 2003). They promote certain research methodologies and theories, favouring formal and mathematical methods, which are typically more useful to their ontology than to others (Weber, 2003).

While these attempts to promote the positivist agenda have created a lively debate (see the 'Core of IS' debate in the *Communications of the Association for Information Systems*), no concerted non-positivist action is visible. The reasons for this are manifold, but among the most important are the historical prevalence of positivism (Walsham, 1995b; Trauth, 2001) and the lack of coherence among non-positivists.

Ethical implications

A final important implication of recognising the incommensurability of positivism and non-positivism has to do with the ethics of research, and more specifically with how humans are perceived in research. Positivism requires ethical behaviour by the researcher (Hausman and McPherson, 1996), and it can even be described as an ethically motivated endeavour that promises to develop society (Wynn, 2001) and offer 'limitless progress' (Chomsky, 1998, p. 128). It would thus be wrong to see positivism as fundamentally 'unethical', but in effect it develops worrying ethical consequences. These are the result of the perceived possibility of distinguishing clearly between research object and subject and between objective description and subjective evaluation, which allows positivists to argue that they are detached observers and thus negates the necessity to become involved and therefore roots for the status quo (Orlikowski and Baroudi, 1991).

A realist ontology suggests that all things exist in some sort of objective universe, and this includes human beings. This, combined with methodological individualism, can create a disposition to treat humans as objects. Treating humans as objects means that one can treat them as means rather than ends, thus violating Kant's (1995, p. BA 67) famous version of the Categorical Imperative according to which humans should never be treated as means. Or to put it in more contemporary words: 'Such research may end up by recommending most people to be handled like billiard balls' (Nissen, 1985, p. 40).

A critical view of research philosophy

The chapter has argued that positivism and non-positivism are incompatible, owing to their ontological positions, but that other aspects of the paradigms can be combined. Given the philosophical and conceptual nature of the argument, it is impossible to 'prove' it wrong by using contradicting empirical data. Ontology is not subject to empirical investigation, because any empirical research must be based on an ontology which it cannot prove wrong because it determines which phenomena can be observed. The main area of contention will lie in the use of the concepts themselves. One potential weakness of the current argument is that the general use of the concepts such as positivism, interpretivism, empiricism, etc. does not always follow the definitions offered here. I have tried to show that these definitions are tenable and well grounded in the literature, but it is also true that some authors use them differently. The answer to such a claim would be that a different use of terms does not affect the content of the argument. A researcher must base his or her research on an understanding of the nature of reality. He or she will be faced with the dichotomous choice of an observer-independent or observer-dependent reality. The divide cannot be bridged, for logical reasons. As a result of, or at least affected by, the choice, the researcher will use certain epistemologies or methodologies.

Do IS researchers or practitioners need to worry about all this? Are there conclusions that need to be drawn or consequences that arise from it? In the light of the current debate about the core and definition of the field of information systems, the answer has to be affirmative. For many everyday purposes, researchers may be able to rely on their ontology in use and not worry about the underlying problems. At least, that is true for those who use the predominant approach of positivism. Researchers who prefer a different approach are put more often in a position where they have to justify their ontology. But in the overall climate of scarcity of resources (university chairs, research positions, studentships, funding, etc.) we need to consider which criteria constitute valuable work in IS, and these criteria are inherently dependent on the underlying ontology. If the current argument is right and positivism and non-positivism are not commensurable, then the discipline of IS should ask itself how it should view and possibly compare research from these two traditions.

Finally, there is the crucial question of the overall context of this discussion. This chapter has concentrated on philosophical arguments in the context of IS research. The question of ontology is by no means confined to research or to a specific discipline. On the contrary, it is a central assumption in our individual and collective world-views. It strongly influences questions of politics, social distribution, of war and peace. The problem of tolerance between positivist and non-positivist IS researchers would thus have to be viewed in the context of tolerance between positivists and non-positivists in general.

The final question is where critical research stands with regard to this debate. Critical research can have positivist or interpretivist attributes. Criticalists thus do not necessarily have to choose sides in the positivism–interpretivism debate. The history of critical research suggests that its practitioners will be sceptical of empiricism and thus the entire research approach is likely to differ from mainstream IS research. The critical perspective allows researchers to evaluate ongoing debates from a different perspective. The emphasis on domination and emancipation opens the view for the political implications of debates on research philosophy. Introna (2003a) gives the best published example of this when he uses a Foucauldian lens to analyse the power–knowledge relationship embedded in the positivist discourse on the identity of the field of IS. Critical scholars, with their broader understanding of the subject, have an ability to give better descriptions of it. One of these has to do with the purpose of research and the role of research in contemporary socio-economic structures. Much research in IS takes place in business schools. While these have moved far beyond being simple tools for the expansion of capitalism (Thrift, 2005), there is still a strong assumption of purposive rationality, and the idea of profit maximisation is upheld as an axiom of economic activity. In such an environment the discipline of information systems can be understood as a tool for the generation of profits. Much mainstream IS research can easily be read this way. Critical research can point to this and provide alternative interpretations of what IS can and should be. Criticalists should be able to use existing discourses and engage in them to influence the development of the field in directions which are more conducive to emancipation. Such ideas are present in much interpretive work as well, but critical research, with its interest in intervention, should be better placed to achieve such aims.

Part III

Application

I have spent the first two parts of the book describing the theoretical and philosophical foundations of critical research in information systems. This extensive attention to detail is justified by the fact that the conceptual underpinnings of CRIS are important in order to understand its position with regard to alternative research approaches but also to understand its claims, aims and results. A conceptual interest is a necessary precondition for scholars to engage in critical work. How is a scholar to understand the importance of language in research if she has not considered the ontological positions that are linked to her work? How can a critical researcher position his work in the current academic debates if concepts of paradigms, epistemology, methodology, etc. are not considered?

However, it can also be seen as a weakness of critical research that it emphasises conceptual work and seems to do little else. As Marx famously said in his comments on Feuerbach, philosophy has only interpreted the world, whereas it is important to change it (Marx, 1964 I, p. 141). This seems to imply that critical work must go beyond conceptual analysis and do something that will have an impact on social realities. How exactly this can be done in the context of academic research is a difficult question, and one that I will return to in Part IV, which will deal with reflections on critical research. At this stage I will present a range of topics that represent possible ways of doing critical research in information systems. Each of the chapters in this part of the book will explore critical views of some aspect or other of the use of ICT in organisations and society. They will show that different methodological approaches are possible and that topics for critical research can be found in many different areas. Critical research in information systems can be used to critique individual aspects of mainstream IS research but it can also be used to go beyond this and identify areas of domination and oppression that involve ICT and that traditional IS research mainly ignores.

9 Information systems as means of (dis)empowerment

The information society and decision support systems in local authorities in Egypt

I will start my description of possible applications of CRIS with a discussion of the use of ICT in development. The reason for this choice is that it renders the critical aspects of technology highly visible. International inequalities and injustices are hard to deny. ICT is frequently promoted as a means by which to address such problems. Governments and international agencies spend huge amounts of money on projects aimed at promoting the use of information and communication technology (ICT) in so-called developing countries (Mejias *et al.*, 1999; Montealegre, 1998). The immediate aim of such investment is typically economic growth (Klenow and Rodríguez-Clare, 1997). It is usually recognised, however, that economic growth is no end in itself. Economic growth is meant to produce employment, create welfare and improve the lot of all members of society. Its purpose is to allow people to live a fulfilled life according to their own design. Briefly, the final aim of the promotion of ICT in developing countries is the empowerment of the members of society.

This chapter will shed doubt on the empowering effect of ICT. It will do so by examining two major applications, namely the information society policy and the use of decision support systems at the local level in Egypt. In order to determine whether empowerment is indeed the aim of ICT use, I will look at the accompanying rhetoric and assumptions. These will be contrasted with social reality on the national level of the information society policy and on the local level of the organisational use of DSS. I will present evidence on both the macro and the micro level that ICT does not have the promised empowering effects. Instead, it is often actively disempowering. This discrepancy between message and reality is no coincidence. I will argue that the disempowering faculties of ICT lie at the heart of the design, plan and use of the technology.

I will use a Habermasian framework to carry out a critical discourse analysis of the Egyptian Information Society Policy at the macro level. This will be complemented by a Foucault-inspired investigation of the organisational practice of using DSS in local authorities. I will use these approaches to focus on two important areas of possible empowerment: democratic participation and education. The result of the empirical findings will be that in both areas ICT has disempowering effects which are known to the agents involved and arguably intended from the outset. The chapter will end with a reflection on the findings and the methods and approaches employed.

Critique of the use of ICT in Egypt

The starting point of this research was the apparent empowering properties of the use of ICT in the 'developing' world. When choosing the methodological approach I thus considered which aspects of these claims would be open to critical scrutiny and how to conduct such critical analyses. One characteristic of the use of ICT for developmental purposes is that it tends to be highly centralised. It is often driven by external agencies and organised by national governments. It was therefore essential to extend the scope of the study to explicitly include the national political level. At the same time, I wanted to explore whether ICT use has an empowering effect at the individual and organisational level. I also assumed that there would be a relationship between a political view of empowerment and organisational practice. The challenge was thus to find a research approach that allowed me to study the level of national politics and organisational reality. Furthermore, a methodology was needed that would allow me to question the status quo and to open discursive closures. I addressed these challenges by applying a Habermasian view at the macro level of national politics and following up the issues found there with a Foucauldian analysis at the micro level. These two approaches, which I shall now discuss in more detail, were used to identify claims to empowerment and contrast these with social reality.

Habermasian analysis: critical discourse analysis on the macro level

In order to identify contradictions between rhetoric and reality in the Egyptian ICT policy, I decided to do a critical discourse analysis (CDA) (see Fairclough, 1993; Chouliaraki and Fairclough, 1999; Schultze and Leidner, 2002; Fairclough, 2003) using a Habermasian framework. Examples of CDA in the literature (see Forester, 1992 and Thompson, 2003) demonstrate a central problem of the method, namely that it requires extensive discussions of the text. Because I intended to analyse a whole policy framework, it would not have been feasible to limit the discussion to a single book chapter.

I therefore decided to follow a novel way of doing critical discourse analysis, pioneered by Cukier *et al.*, (2003, 2004). This method is based on Habermas's validity claims (Lyytinen, 1992). It aims to identify such claims using quantitative and qualitative measures and thereby explicate the hidden assumptions of texts and discourses. Validity claims are discovered and coded by using a set of guiding questions for each of four claims: truth, legitimacy, sincerity and clarity. To help identify claims, I followed the guiding questions put forward by Cukier *et al.* (see Appendix A1). Drawing on these questions, texts were coded and validity claims in each text were determined. During the coding, several individual claims were noted as frequent and worthy of their own category or subcategory. (For a full list of claims identified during the discourse analysis, see

Appendix A2.) The main advantage of this approach to critical discourse analysis over traditional methods is that it allows the analysis of a larger body of texts.

The method was applied to the Egyptian Information Society Policy. The policy documents can be accessed from the homepage of the Ministry of Communication and Information Technology (MCIT) (www.mcit.gov.eg/index.asp) under the link 'E-Bridges'.[1] MCIT is the government department responsible for ICT. It is also the trendsetter among the Egyptian ministries and the organisation primarily responsible for policy and implementation of ICT in Egypt. The ICT policy is of great importance in Egypt and is supported by President Mubarak. The document has importance beyond Egypt because it was presented at the 2003 World Summit on the Information Society and has become the model according to which a range of other African states are developing their ICT policies. MCIT was set up in 1999 to realise the National Project for Technology Development (El Sayed and Westrup, 2003). External business observers view MCIT as a reliable partner and a forerunner of reform in the Egyptian administration (anonymous, 2004a). A clear sign of the internal importance of MCIT and its aim of furthering ICT use in Egypt is the fact that its first minister, Dr Ahmed Nazif, was promoted to the position of Prime Minister in August 2004.

The online version of the policy consists of 43 web pages with a length varying from half a page to 10 pages when printed out. It gives an overview of the intended use of ICT in Egypt and its contribution to the information society in general. The seven most important policy areas, including e-business and e-government, are outlined in five web pages each, which discuss the intention, principles, implementation, current state and planned action for each. I identified a total number of 1,248 validity claims (see Appendix A2).

Foucauldian analysis: power, surveillance and self-surveillance at the micro level

Corresponding to the Habermasian methodology at the macro level, a Foucauldian view was used at the organisational level. Foucault's theories lend themselves to a micro-level analysis because he was interested in the individual rather than broader social structures. Change and resistance are anchored on the local level (Chan, 2000). Power is exercised within the social body, rather than from above. It structures possible fields of action (Doolin, 2004). Specific aspects that allow micro-level power to be analysed from the Foucauldian angle are bodily discipline, surveillance and self-surveillance. The questions thus were: are there aspects of bodily behaviour that are linked to ICT use and that indicate power relationships? Are people observed by ICT, do they use ICT to observe others? And do they observe themselves with regard to the systems in such a way that power relationships become clear (Deetz, 1992; Doolin, 2004)? A related useful aspect of Foucault's writings is the idea of a regime of truth. Regimes of truth are the social constellations that allow the designation of true statements. They are affected by the mechanisms that allow the distinction between true and false, the means of sanctioning truth, or the states of those who sanction truth (Introna and Whittaker, 2004).

Since it was deemed desirable to use the Foucauldian lens to explore the empowering effect of ICT on the organisational level, an application was chosen that is widely spread throughout Egypt and linked to government structures. This application, the decision support units of the local governorates, is probably the most widely researched one concerning ICT in Egypt (Shoib and Jones, 2003). It is a public-sector project that has been developed across Egypt. The project has established information and decision support centres in each of the country's 27 governorates. Part of the aim of this project was to diffuse the use of IT to administrators outside Cairo and Alexandria (Nidumolu *et al.*, 1996). The first Information and Decision Support Centre (IDSC) was established by the cabinet to develop decision support systems for the Cabinet and top policy makers (El Sherif and El Sawy, 1988).

From 1987 onwards, IDSCs modelled on the Cabinet IDSC were established in each of the 27 governorates. Each IDSC consists of statistics, computer resource, decision support, library and publication units. The statistics unit collects information at the governorate level by collating information from many district-level IDSCs modelled on the governorate IDSC. This information is collected for sectoral databases looking at population, health and housing. By 1998 there were 1,202 district-level DSCs employing 7,300 staff (Elbeltagi *et al.*, 2005).

In order to establish the organisational reality of empowerment and to view it through a Foucauldian lens, face-to-face interviews were conducted with individuals involved in the DSCs.[2] The majority of the interviewees were either CEOs or managers of the DSC. The interviews were conducted in two stages: one set of 13 interviews were conducted from April to June 2000 and aimed to establish a general understanding of the work of the units. The second set of 12 interviews were conducted between June 2004 and March 2005. During this second set of interviews the question of empowerment was emphasised.

The (dis)empowering effects of ICT in Egypt

In this section I will present and discuss the findings of our research. I will start by identifying claims to empowerment through the use of ICT. These will then be contrasted by observations of social reality. The aim is to see whether the claims to empowerment are matched by empowering practices. During the research, two salient areas were identified where empowering claims and reality came into obvious tension, namely democratic participation and education.

A final caveat is in order at this point: the following narrative will attempt to draw a convincing picture of the lack of empowerment through ICT in Egypt that was encountered during the research. It was therefore decided to concentrate on those aspects that will allow for a linear story that renders the arguments plausible. The price to be paid for this is a diminishing of the complexity of the realities that were encountered. This is justified, because all research can be seen as an attempt to reduce complexity and create order out of chaos (Weizenbaum, 1976). Critical researchers are sceptical about the possibility of giving an 'objective' account of reality. It is clear that other narratives would have been possible, and there are good examples of ICT use in less developed countries that had planned or accidental consequences that proved to be highly empowering (see, for example, Wheeler, 2006). So, rather than try to be objective, I prefer to clearly signal my viewpoint for the reader to contextualise it with his or her experiences and perceptions.

Claims to empowerment through democracy and participation

In one of the central speeches promoting the ICT effort in Egypt, the Egyptian President, Hosni Mubarak (1999), said that the purpose of information technology is to facilitate a 'better living to all the Egyptians'. A similar reference to 'enhancing the quality of life for each and every Egyptian' was repeated by the President (Mubarak, 2000). Empowerment of the information society is the explicit aim of the Information Society Development Office, an organisation charged by the MCIT with promoting the information society (ISDO, 2005). All this suggests that empowerment is indeed a central aim of the use of ICT.

This idea of empowering people is repeated throughout the policy document. The information society, which is the centre of attention of the ICT policy, is said to be a society where 'citizens are empowered' [2]. Different aspects of the policy empower different stakeholders, such as the Egyptian IT community [17]. The empowerment includes participation, and explicitly mentions that ICT will allow 'genuine participation of citizens, including traditionally marginalized segments of the population' [2]. Two groups discussed specifically are women, where ICT training is meant to 'close the gender gap' [17] and 'enhance the role of women in managing commercial activities' [27] as well as that of disabled people [13], specifically those who are visually impaired [47].

The development of participation will lead to 'greater opportunities for all' [3]. Part of the process will be increased transparency, for example in the banking industry [27], as well as national and international solidarity [54]. A particular emphasis is given to freedom, especially the market freedom to do business and be successful, thereby overcoming the problem of poverty. Participation is to be supported by e-government, which will 'bring the benefits of the emerging global information society to the largest possible segment of the population' [19] and allow for 'community participation' [20]. Best of all, the potential of ICT is not something we will have to wait for much longer. 'A fully functioning, effective Egyptian Information Society is now just around the corner' [53].

Part of this empowering information society is to be realised through the local use of the DSC. The DSC is a project whose central mission is to diffuse the use of IT away from central administrations and give local managers support in making their own decisions through the use of a DSS. It should thus be emancipatory and empowering. The DSS should be a tool for gathering local information and enabling the users to make informed decisions concerning the local distribution of resources.

Macro-level critique

The emancipatory rhetoric of ICT and the information society contrasts starkly with the social realities. Political participation as an expression of empowerment is highly limited. Egypt officially claims to be a democratic system (Egypt, 2004), but the implementation of a 'presidential republic' where the main power holder is nominated by the People's Assembly and then confirmed by referendum leaves little space for political freedom. Compared to those of other countries, Egypt's political system may be relatively liberal and allow for limited opposition activities (Nidumolu *et al.*, 1996). Egypt also seems set for a further course of political liberalisation with the recent creation of a National Council for Human Rights, the appointment of the first female judge and the cancellation of state security courts (anonymous, 2004b). Also, Egypt has traditionally allowed greater openness and accountability in political decisions than other countries (El Sherif and El Sawy, 1988). President Mubarak was re-elected in 2005 in the first presidential election that allowed multiple candidates. The election was suspected of mass rigging, inappropriate use of government resources and vote buying (http://en.wikipedia.org/wiki/Mubarak, accessed 16 August 2007). No independent observers were allowed at the election, and the runner-up in the election, Ayman Nour, was imprisoned, arguably for political purposes (http://en.wikipedia.org/wiki/Ayman_Nour, accessed 16 August 2007). Also, Egypt has been ruled under Emergency Law since Sadat's assassination in 1981.

While the external political environment does not appear to be conducive to personal empowerment, a closer look at the policy itself shows that the empowering claims are not taken seriously and not followed through. The general gist of the policy document is one of top-down development of ICT applications, most of which are geared for specific stakeholder groups. Of 256 claims which identify a stakeholder, 156 refer to the government itself. The large majority of the remaining stakeholder claims (71) refer to businesses. Citizens are identified as stakeholders only 20 times. And where they are recognised as stakeholders they are invariably seen as passive recipients of government services. In the 16 of the 17 cases where an omission of relevant stakeholders was identified, these missing stakeholders were the citizens. No input from citizens to the development of the information society is sought.

A strong example for this exclusion of citizens from empowering participation is the 'e-government' section of the policy [19–23]. The focus of e-government is the efficient provision of services to citizens and, more importantly, to investors. Citizen input or even e-democratic participative models are not considered. Where decisions have to be made about which stakeholders will be served first, business invariably wins the day over citizens [23]. The analysis of the text allows the conclusion that e-government does not involve any influence on political decisions. Also, e-government is very much seen in terms of e-commerce, with one of the case studies and success stories of e-government [22] describing an online billing system. The problems of equating citizens and consumers are generally ignored.

Micro-level critique

The lack of empowering structures at the macro level is reflected on the organisational level of the DSS. The DSS has become a tool for reinforcing existing power structures through the support of an information flow directed towards the centre, symbolic support of power structures and encouragement to conformity. Staff in the IDSCs were aware of the inconsistency between the way the DSS was being used and the ideal goal of a DSS in the organisation. For example, a manager in the DSS unit of the El Monofia governorate said;

> these type of systems will enable managers in the lower level to be on the same level of importance to the senior managers which is not accepted either by the manager in the top level or even the managers in the lower level who is not prepared yet for this.

One of the managers in the information centre in the governorate of Aswan said that

> the role of DSS unit in making strategic decisions is very minimal if there is any role at all. The unit's only purpose is for collecting, saving data and sending it to the IDSC in the central government. The data is inaccurate because they are not able to get it from the right source.

He added that generally 'more than 85 per cent of the decisions are made without taking in considerations of information technology in general and DSS in particular'.

Although there is an understanding of the rationale for implementing a decision support system to enable more objective decisions, particularly concerning resource allocation, to be made on the basis of concrete statistics, this is largely ignored. A manager in the El Monofia governorate said, 'we make strategic decisions at the local level in meetings where the governor takes most of the responsibility and we are there to give our opinion if he asks us.' Governors tend to ignore the DSC and make decisions based on what they think central government will expect, decisions that will reinforce existing hierarchical structures. Data provided by the DSC and the possible decisions which may be inferred from the data are explicitly ignored. In the Domyat governorate a DSC unit manager said that he had not seen a strategic decision made on the basis of information he provided in 14 years. For example, where the information collected by the DSS unit suggested that a certain street should be paved, this was ignored. Instead, a different street was paved because the Member of Parliament lived there. We came across a number of similar examples.

At a micro level the functions and roles of the DSS are established in line with cultural expectations. The culture of Egyptian society and public-sector management depends on position and hierarchical power. Hierarchies are to be obeyed, rules are to be followed, seniority matters and decisions from above should not be questioned regardless of the implementer's view of whether they make sense. In the Elmenia governorate, a manager said

> The local authority has a very military culture to the extent that if you enter the door of the head of the city or one of the managers you need to go through a lot of people and you are not allowed to sit or talk until he gives you permission. If the manager passes by you should leave what you're doing and immediately stand.

Such a culture in the public sector is reinforced by the approved recruitment of senior public-sector officers from senior positions in the security forces. Said one governorate manager:

> The reason is that these people will be trained through their career to listen to instructions and not to make decisions. The government does not need to control anything more than what they are doing because they make sure only the people who will follow their policy and guidelines are appointed to key positions.

Such obedience to hierarchical power is arguably part of the Egyptian tradition of civil service.

While these observations represent a rather traditional view of power as top-down hierarchy, they can be supported from a Foucauldian point of view. The cultural and military aspects can be seen as part of the genealogy of power that explains the stabilisation of current power relationships. There is a strong undercurrent of surveillance and self-surveillance with regard to the use of DSSs. The technology is sometimes overtly used to observe data input and thus individual behaviour. More importantly, it has created a culture of pre-emptive obedience based on self-surveillance. This means that users know which data is required and which decisions are desired, and they strive to provide the data that will serve the purpose. At the same time, they make sure that they are perceived as fulfilling the expected wishes of their superiors. This act of self-surveillance is usually done subconsciously, but in some cases it became explicit. For example, in one city the DSS manager, who had described the lack of resources for using the DSS, expressed different views once he realised that his boss would also be interviewed. He asked us to tell the boss only the good things and to assure the boss that the system was being used 100 per cent.

Another Foucauldian angle is that of bodily discipline. Such bodily discipline is reflected in some of the above questions, which indicate that certain physical behaviour is required to express power relationships, such as standing up in the presence of superiors. The bodily discipline is closely linked to the military background of many of the managers and governors. Indeed, the military is one of Foucault's recurring examples of the creation of bodily discipline. We would argue that the Egyptian DSSs (and administration in general) use bodily discipline as a means of strengthening power structures. They do so by relying on individuals who are socialised to this type of discipline in the military.

As a final Foucauldian angle, one can see the system of national and local DSS as part of the creation of a regime of truth. Any information system encodes a business process or a set of activities. The use of a DSS requires structured data collection. It encodes a set of tasks. These involve collecting specific kinds of data from the social environment and entering them into the system. The DSS will constrain users to a certain structure of data collection. That structure is defined by central government who design the system. Some data is given importance, some is excluded. This structure of legitimate problems is enforced by the more or less subtle use of the DSS as a means to ensure compliance. An important aspect of this is that the local DSS provide employment and status for 7,500 well-educated employees, who are thus bound to be compliant and who will serve as multipliers of the established regime of truth, rather than question it.

Claims to empowerment through education

Another salient aspect of the Egyptian ICT policy that lends itself to a critical review is that of education. It has become conventional wisdom that in order to participate in society and lead a fulfilled life, one needs a certain amount of education. The Egyptian ICT policy reflects this standpoint and uses ICT as a lever for improving the provision of education to its citizens. The e-learning initiative aims to provide equal opportunities for learning 'regardless of age, gender, class, or geographical location' [15]. ICT is meant to improve all levels of education. On the most basic level it will 'strengthen attempts to eradicate illiteracy' [17] and 'encourage people to overcome illiteracy' [18]. At the same time, the provision of ICT facilities in schools and universities will improve the quality of learning. It will provide higher education with a much-related improvement in capacity and increase the 'competitiveness of [Egypt's] graduates' [13]. Teaching technology will also allow continuing education and lifelong learning. A specific emphasis is placed on teaching ICT skills, as these are seen as important for the job market and for international competitiveness [11].

The policy concedes that there are problems, most notably those of access, usage and skills [4], but also the general level of literacy and overcrowding of the educational system. However, the very use of ICT is seen as the solution to these, and the correct usage of technology in education will take care of them. In order to persuade students to learn ICT skills, the government has set up a Basic Skills Training Program which is available free of charge to every young Egyptian and is even linked to a stipend [17]. Additionally, the government has initiated several programmes which are aimed at spreading ICT around the country in a manner that will guarantee access to technology for everyone interested

[11]. International co-operation, for example with UK universities, will help overcome the shortage problem of higher education [17].

Macro-level critique

The Egyptian education system faces serious problems. The level of illiteracy in the Egyptian population is close to 30 per cent. Literacy is a concept that is hard to define, but literacy as a condition of participation in an information society is a multi-faceted competence that requires intensive educational effort. It seems to be an unrealistic assumption that the mere provision of technology will solve the problem of illiteracy. Furthermore, it stands to reason that the introduction of ICT will produce more need for traditional education rather than alleviate pressure.

The Egyptian educational system is not well equipped to deal with the challenges of the information society. It performs poorly when compared to other developing countries, partly because of its bureaucratic structure and its outdated pedagogical model (Warschauer, 2003). On top of this there is the demographic development with the number of secondary school graduates doubling from 375,000 to 650,000 from 2003 to 2005 alone and a further expected increase to 800,000 in 2007 and 1,200,000 by 2017 [13]. Even a perfect system would find it extremely hard to deal with this sort of challenge.

The solution outlined in the government policy, namely to leverage technology to solve the problem, will most probably not solve it. It is insensitive to contextual, political and pedagogic issues. It concentrates on technical matters, most notably on the provision of equipment and technical access, which, at best, will be preconditions for a successful use of ICT. In the document on e-readiness entitled 'The Way Forward' [12], the government concentrates on technicalities of access provision that are so advanced that they would have little relevance even in the most developed societies. The concentration on technology allows the more difficult social issues behind the education problem to be sidestepped (Warschauer, 2003). Solutions are suggested, such as the use of schools as publicly accessible internet cafés [15, 17], which go counter to the established local use of ICT. Finally, the literature on e-teaching and e-learning which suggests that the introduction of technology into education may introduce new problems is ignored.

ICT education, which is praised as a solution, is organised so that it is impossible for students to fail. Owing to the lack of equipment, ICT education is often done theoretically without access to technology. And even where technology is available, it is often not made accessible to students because it is perceived as being too valuable (Warschauer, 2003). The policy itself demonstrates that the government is not following through on its emancipatory promises. If education is to lead to empowerment, then one would expect that teachers and students, as main stakeholders, would have a say in its provision. However, rather than students being seen as active participants of education, they are passive recipients. Where stakeholders of education are explicitly named, we find the names of major corporations [17]. Education is seen not as an end in itself or as a means of empowerment but rather as a way to produce 'human capital' and make Egypt attractive to foreign investment. Literacy or education are named relatively frequently as benefits of ICT (37 times), but this number pales in comparison to economic benefits, which are cited 110 times.

In general, the use of ICT is promoted as a way of solving the very serious problem Egypt is facing with regard to the education of its rapidly growing population. However, the discourse concentrates on technical matters, thus leaving unexplored the more important underlying questions such as the purpose of education (see Sahay, 2004), the pedagogical fit of technology, and the wider social issues, including illiteracy.

Micro-level critique

Education is a central area where Foucauldian ideas of the generation and per-petuation of power structures gain importance (Foucault, 1975). Regarding the local DSS, there is a lack of education and training on the part of the employees and users. In the DSS unit of the El Qalubiya Governorate one employee sat quietly at his desk watching a film on the PC, another played solitaire. They turned to see the arrival of the researcher. 'I've come to do an interview with one of the managers.' 'Do you know about DSS?' an employee asked. 'Can you give us information to help us use the system properly?' At the Dakhlia Gover-norate the researcher was warmly welcomed as a source of wisdom about DSSs. Far from increasing computer literacy and encouraging learning, the DSS in the local governorates tends to act as a block to learning, another black box to which the privileged have some access.

Hence, the implementation of the DSS may be interpreted as a disempower-ing act because it establishes a new symbol of exclusion. Those who are not trained may look on it as a barrier to their empowerment, while those who are trained may see it as a privilege which increases their submissiveness and obedi-ence within the social structures and encourages self-surveillance.

That is not to say training wasn't available. But training in computer skills and problem analyses was centralised in Cairo (Nidumolu *et al.*, 1996). Travel to such training was difficult and involved staying away in Cairo, which caused problems for employees with supplementary jobs and family responsibilities.

The reason for the centralisation of DSS training in Cairo was a lack of train-ers and equipment. However, since equipment was available locally, it could have been envisaged that the trainers would tour governorates, and local trainers could have been appointed. It is likely that the centralisation of the training enabled centralised control over what employees learned and how they used the system. However, the perception of DSS as a power artefact for the privileged few also led to a situation where

> some people who even travel to IDSC in Cairo and get this training are not willing to share their experience when they come back, otherwise they will

lose a source of power they have if most of the rest of the people know what they know.

In the Egyptian context, the status of the trainers needs to be considered. Because of the hierarchical system, training of DSS managers could be culturally acceptable only if done by a very senior manager. One DSS manager in a city in the El Gharbia governorate said, 'If anybody is going to train me in the use of DSS, it had better be an experienced head of a city council who has used the system.'

The shortcomings of the educational systems and their effect on the use of systems such as the DSS were a recurring theme in the interviews. At the micro level there was a perception that there was a lack of resources in education. One manager in the Aswan governorate said:

> If we are to sort out the problems of using IT in local authorities, we need to start with the root of the problem, which is in the education system. We lack teachers and resources like PC labs and even up-to-date textbooks not only at a basic level, but also in the universities as well.

This perception of the inadequacy of the Egyptian education system is only reinforced by the view of its cultural shortcomings. An education system based on the learning of facts provided by teachers and excluding critical thinking inhibits the ability to use IT in a creative and critical way. A manager in the Domyat Governorate said, 'The employees graduate mainly from the universities of Egypt. So they have most of the education system's diseases like lack of innovation and poor skills usage.'

Even when Egyptian nationals are trained abroad and pick up more liberal educational values, the impact on Egyptian educational culture is minimal:

> A big problem we have in Egypt on the macro level which has an effect on the micro level here in local authorities, is the brain drain. There are about 750,000 immigrants to Europe from Egypt and those people have Master's and PhDs. This costs the central budget billions of dollars investment. We end up with a lack of human resources and even qualified people here lose motivation because of their financial problems.
>
> (DSS Unit Manager, El Sharkia Governorate)

People who may have the intellectual capacity and cultural awareness to challenge and change the culture of education often do not return to the Egyptian education system.

Such a prevalent perception, at the micro level, of the inherent inadequacy of education in Egypt catalyses a sense of helplessness and disempowerment. There seems to be nothing the manager can do when faced with an overwhelming ingrained problem at the macro level.

These observations are again amenable to a Foucauldian interpretation. Foucault emphasises the relationship between power and knowledge, both of which are affected by education. The DSS are objects of power in a traditional sense because they help make political decisions. More importantly, they define valid knowledge and are thus an important constitutive element of a regime of truth. They are part of the network that defines power relationships. The bodily aspect pervades through the management culture, which is influenced by the military background of many managers. There is also an aspect of bodily power in the fact that training is offered only in Cairo, which, for most users, requires physical relocation. The dual aspect of education as a precondition of the use of DSS in the governorates and education/training for the specific application thus offers a number of Foucauldian angles which explain how power relationships are created and solidified though the use of ICT.

Summary of findings

The above description of our research findings supports the conclusion that the use of ICT in Egypt, on the national level of the Information Society Policy, as well as on the organisational level of the local authorities' use of DSCs, is actively disempowering. There is a strong empowering rhetoric on both levels. This can easily be seen in the wording of the policy documents, but it is also obvious in the promises made at the micro level. This empowering rhetoric is an important aspect of the promotion of ICT because it lends legitimacy to the endeavour.

This empowering promise of ICT is not kept. The very different theoretical frameworks of Habermas and Foucault allowed the identification of contradictions between the rhetoric and the underlying intention. The critical discourse analysis demonstrated that the rhetorical validity claims are contradicted within the policy itself. The general gist of the policy document is one of one-sided economic liberalism that is fundamentally unconcerned with the empowerment of the individual.

Similarly, on the local level users and managers of the DSCs are aware of the empowering potential of the technology but they are equally aware that empowerment is not intended. The Foucauldian viewpoint allowed for the identification of instances of surveillance, self-surveillance and active construction of power/knowledge that ran counter to emancipatory ideals. This could consistently be shown in the areas of political participation and education, both of which could play a central role in the realisation of empowerment, were it taken seriously. The chapter achieved what I indicated in the introduction, namely to provide evidence for the disempowering faculties of ICT in Egypt.

Reflections

Critical research claims to be reflective, and the final chapter of the book will be dedicated to reflection. In order to live up to this standard, it needs to reflect on itself. Weaknesses, biases, alternatives and assumptions must be subject to critical reflection. This goes beyond the usual discussion of limitations and must question the heart of the research. I will thus offer some reflections specific to this chapter on the Egyptian use of ICT, which indicates how reflexivity in critical IS research can been developed.

Theory and methodology

There are a number of questions one could raise about the use of concepts, theory and methodology in this chapter. A noticeable omission of the chapter is the lack of a definition of 'development'. The term is contentious and divisive (Escobar, 1995), and a prolonged discussion would add little to the argument. Egypt is a developing country by most standards, and the use of ICT is linked to efforts of development, however defined.

Another problematic aspect might be the use of theory. Did I do justice to Habermas and Foucault? And is the attempt to combine these two very different thinkers viable? I believe that one can answer both questions in the affirmative and have made this argument earlier. However, the question is arguably of limited relevance for critical research. For critical research it is more important to follow the 'emancipatory spirit than ... the authoritative letter of any particular Critical Theorist' (Alvesson and Willmott, 1992, p. 3). Critical research is a matter not of applying a theory correctly but of using theoretical guidance to promote the critical intention (Avgerou, 2005; Walsham, 2005a).

An important part of the critical reflection is the clarification of assumptions and biases the research is based on. The most important bias in this chapter is that I developed the argument in the western tradition of thought, whose applicability to Egypt is not obvious. This raises the difficult problem of the transferability of thoughts between cultures (see Walsham, 2001; Stahl and Elbeltagi, 2004). As I argued earlier, the aim of emancipating and empowering people is universal and can be applied to non-western environments as well as to western ones. I concede that empowerment may take a different form in the Arab world as compared with in the West.

Exclusion of other stories

By developing the present narrative I had to choose which aspects to discuss and which to neglect. This story therefore hides a multitude of other possible stories which may also be worth exploring. There are a few obvious candidates for alternative critical narratives of ICT use in Egypt. One of them is the international political order with its important influence on Egyptian politics. Western democracies seem to agree that peace and quiet in the Middle East (again, a western description) is a political aim of high importance and they therefore stabilise the Egyptian government as best as they can. One can easily draw a line from Egyptian politics to the struggle of Israel and the Palestinians but also to other political developments in the Middle East, particularly the unstable situation in Iraq. This in turn is linked with questions of the desirability of certain types of government over others. There is an important connection to religious matters and the West's attempt to limit the political power of Islam. This in turn is linked to the world-wide paranoia over terrorism, which influences western policies.

Another issue is that I have attempted to present the narrative in as linear and unequivocal a fashion as possible in order to make it more accessible to the reader. While I hope that I was successful in so doing, I realise that I may have neglected some important aspects. One of these is the concept of resistance. In the attempt to show that ICT is used for disempowerment we did not pay attention to the idea of resistance. Any Foucauldian scholar will know that for Foucault there is no power without resistance. Similarly, there were examples of resistance to the government's approach and the normalising power in the vicinity of local DSSs. Critical research is never finished and always needs to be contextualised. I therefore believe that the omission of resistance and other observations counter to our narrative is justified by the fact that this chapter is only one contribution to a larger discourse. Like any other research, critical research has to draw the limits of the phenomena it describes.

I nevertheless believe that our investigation succeeded in realising the critical intention to make a difference, because it facilitated one of the main aims of critical research, namely the exposure of reifications and the opening of discursive closures. This chapter has exposed the emancipatory ideals of Egyptian top officials, including the President, as false or, at best, misleading. As a result of the research, further work using the empowering rhetoric will lose legitimacy. The chapter will thus contribute to a discourse on how ICT can be used to promote empowerment, and this discourse itself will be an empowering success. It will be harder for western consultants to promote their agendas without interacting with local participants.

I do not claim to know how emancipating and empowering use of ICT in Egypt should be achieved. But I believe that finding out will require greater participation by everybody involved, including the citizens of the country. Currently the political system and local culture militate against such an approach. It is therefore safe to assume that the achievement of empowerment and emancipation will take some time and that it will require considerable social changes. It will not be easy and will require a realignment of power relationships. Empowerment and emancipation will also most likely go far beyond the question of ICT use and affect large parts of the society and the political establishment.

10 Responsible and heroic management of workplace privacy
A critical view of ICT management

The first example of the application of CRIS in the previous chapter took a novel approach by combining a Habermasian and a Foucauldian analysis and by using different types of data for the investigation of emancipatory faculties of ICT in a particular developing country, namely Egypt. This chapter takes a very different approach. It takes a conceptual approach and concentrates on some of the salient topics of critical work: rationality and management. Using the link between ethics and critical research, I will argue that traditional management is not capable of discharging responsibility for morally relevant issues, such as employee surveillance. The chapter thus offers a critique of some of the implicit tenets of mainstream IS research such as the desirability of management and the possibility of improving it by technical means.

It is generally recognised that the managing of information systems is a task that requires responsibility. IS can raise and be jeopardised by a number of different issues ranging from financial and organisational to legal and ethical ones. Responsible management is meant to address these problems and to facilitate the success of IS and consequently of the organisation. Using the example of employee privacy, this chapter questions whether this apparently simple and linear relationship between management, information systems and responsibility is helpful. Simple accounts of management are often based on a straightforward view of managers as competent and reliable agents of the organisation who, given their superior knowledge and experience, can address most problems arising in the normal course of organisational activity, acting as 'heroic' individuals turning round difficult business situations, sometimes apparently single-handedly. The idea of such heroic management has held considerable popular appeal. I argue that when applied to normative issues such as employee privacy and surveillance, heroic management creates paradoxes that it cannot overcome. Therefore, a more reflective, connected style of management is called for as a more appropriate and ethically defensible approach rather than the rugged individualism seemingly implied by heroic management.

In this chapter, I concentrate on two problems created by heroic management when applied to the ethically and legally complex area of employee privacy, as an example of a major management problem area. One argument is that management is part of the construction of the problem and therefore lacks the objectivity to find rational and objective solutions. The other argument holds that the very concept of responsibility is based on a participative view of social inter-action which goes counter to the individual and top-down theory of heroic man-agement. So the question is: What form of management is appropriate for taking a responsible approach towards employee privacy?

Heroic responsible management appears to raise conceptual problems. This raises the question of how responsible managers can address normative issues such as employee privacy, which leads us to the concept of reflective respons-ibility to be developed as a response to the challenges of heroic management.

In order to develop this critique of responsible management of employee privacy, I will start with a short introduction to the concept of heroic manage-ment. I shall then revisit the most important issues raised by employee privacy and surveillance, concentrating on ethical and legal questions. On this basis I shall analyse the contradictions arising from the attempt to manage employee privacy concerns. The conclusion will reflect on the implications of this self-contradictory nature of responsible management in IS. I will argue that respons-ible management of IS is possible after all, namely as reflectively responsible management, but that, in order to allow for the ascription of responsibility, man-agement must be reconceptualised away from the heroic model.

A critique of (heroic) management

The term 'management' has connotations that result from its context and general usage in everyday language. These reflect the position of managers in the eco-nomic system, which, in turn, reflects general societal beliefs and assumptions. The resulting understanding of management, often conceptualised in individual-istic, even dramatic, terms, which I label 'heroic', can lead to conflicts with the term 'responsibility', which is grounded in ethics and morality. I will briefly outline the concept of heroic management and then offer a critical review of the term. This will then lead to the discussion of the application of this critique in the difficult field of employee surveillance.

Heroic management

I aim to explore whether and how normative problems such as employee privacy can be managed responsibly. The answer to this question depends on the defini-tion of the terms. The main argument will be that the term 'management' has the connotation of hierarchical power exertion and purposive rationality, which can create the very normative problems that responsibility is meant to address. Heroic management relates to the exertion of power. It should be clear that this does not imply that all managers are one-dimensional tyrants. In practice, man-agers always have other roles to play simultaneously, they have aspirations that go beyond their organisational role and they have to reconcile multiple aims and objectives. Furthermore, most managers have the desire to be 'good' managers, which refers to wider social and ethical goals as well as their immediate tasks. I am thus not aiming to vilify managers individually or collectively but rather to explore connotations of the ideal type of the concept of management. Furthermore, in order to render the argument clear, I will concentrate on a particular understanding of management, namely the hierarchical and top-down approach to organisational problem solving. In using the term 'heroic management' I describe an ideal-typical view of management which strongly influences how management is perceived from the outside (general public, business students) but also from the inside, from managers themselves. The critique aims to expose conceptual problems of the ideal type rather than imply that managers are bad people or doing their job badly.

Current management literature does not unequivocally support this heroic style of leadership. Nevertheless, heroic management has considerable appeal in the public eye. Much has been written about alternative management approaches, and there are whole streams of research such as critical management studies that aim to provide alternative accounts of management. The mainstream view of management and its underlying view of individual purposive rationality has long been recognised as problematic (Argyris, 1971; Mumford and Ward, 1968). McGregor (1985), in his critique of 'Theory X' (top-down hierarchical management, comparable to our 'heroic management'), developed the alternative 'Theory Y', which aims at participation and employee empowerment. In the area of management of information systems, alternative views of management are reflected in Mumford's (2003) ETHICS methodology or in Boehm and Ross's (1989) 'Theory W', which strives to overcome conflicts and power struggles by making everyone a winner. Despite this long-standing critique of the foundations of rational scientific management, I contend that there is still a widely shared perception among the general public, but also among business and management students, which builds on a dominant research tradition that sees management as 'heroic'. It is often reflected in the management of IS literature and practice, and it has been identified as a problem when it comes to handling privacy issues in IS (Culnan, 1993; Greenaway and Chan, 2005).

Etymologically, the verb 'to manage' (originally probably derived from the Latin *manus*, the hand) comes from the Italian *maneggiare* – to handle, to be able to use skilfully – and originally referred to the handling of horses. Today it means 'to conduct, carry on, supervise, or control', according to the *Oxford English Dictionary* in 2004. While 'management' thus has a wide meaning compatible with different problem-solving styles, it often aims to convey a more specific meaning, which might be termed 'heroic management' (Gosling and Mintzberg, 2003). Heroic management stands for the type of management taught in many business schools and propagated by management magazines. It depicts the manager as the individual who is personally responsible for success or failure of organisational activities. Heroic management is based on a particular view of an appropriate rationality, which, following Max Weber, is often called purposive rationality. This heroic rationality is not confined to management and can be found in other professions such as engineering (Adam, 2001c).

The purposive rationality on which heroic management is based is not a new concept. It was famously brought to bear on management by F.W. Taylor in his *Principles of Scientific Management* (1911) and applied by Ford in the assembly line production of the first mass-produced automobiles. As the name suggests, it aims to transfer methods and approaches from the natural sciences to social situations. The possibility of such a transfer has been debated intensively over the past century. This refers to the management literature but needs to be understood as just one aspect of a larger philosophical debate on the appropriateness of certain world-views as discussed earlier in the book. An important stream of this ongoing debate is the contribution of critical theorists. These have long recognised the deficiency of the one-dimensional rationality represented by the scientific approach. Its applicability to social settings has been described as functionally misleading and ethically problematic. As Feenberg (1991, p. 166) puts it, 'Critical Theory attacks capitalism by attacking its forms of rationality'.

The orthodox business school view of heroic management is supported by a relatively standardised and coherent body of knowledge comparable to that of other academic disciplines such as law or medicine (Knights and Willmott, 1999). Management takes place in most levels of organisations, but the main interest lies in top-level management where the strategy of companies is decided (Bourlakis and Bourlakis, 2003). Indeed, conventional management wisdom suggests that every organisation must have a strategy and that the organisation will be lost in the turbulent business environment if it does not have one (Knights and Morgan, 1991). Managers are in charge of creating the strategy and aligning organisational efforts with it. A considerable amount of effort is therefore spent describing the qualities and characteristics of the manager. The manager is a role model for employees (and for students of management). He (rarely she) is 'seen as someone who represents what society believes in and whose behaviour is regarded to be, in principle, morally correct' (Introna, 1997, p. 23). Examples of the managerial virtues are rationality (Newell *et al.*, 2001), motivation, effectiveness and efficiency. But there are also less tangible virtues. The manager is reliable and keeps his calm in the storm. He is a leader but also reassuring and helpful. The fact that few, if any, individuals actually combine all of these characteristics does not diminish their importance as an ideal type. It is justified to call this understanding of management 'heroic management' because the individual manager is depicted as a hero, the saviour of the organisation. And just as the term 'heroic' has the connotation of good and desirable, the same is true of the term 'management' (Lawler, 2004).

Mintzberg (2004) has characterised the 'heroic manager', although, as I have described, the concept's roots lie in older views of scientific management. Drawing on his earlier and widely influential work (Mintzberg, 1973) where he identified the 'Great Man School' as one of the main types of management style, Mintzberg has become increasingly critical of 'heroic management' or, more specifically, 'heroic leadership'. Indeed, 'heroic leadership' is an apt term as it denotes a style of heroic management where 'the CEO is the company, a heroic leader who single-handedly steers the business to success' (Simons *et al.*, 2002).

One thinks of heroic, larger-than-life CEOs who might be attractive to the media. Simons *et al.* (2002) criticise such a style of leadership, as it is disconnected from the people who make organisations work.

> Real leadership is connected, involved and engaged. It's often more quiet than heroic. Real leadership is about teamwork, about taking a long-term view, about building an organization slowly, carefully and collectively. As CEOs, your job is to set an example of energizing others, no, not to take dramatic actions that let you take the lion's share of the spoils.

Other popular critiques of heroic management (Coyote, 2006) emphasise the way the hero myth spotlights the individual hero. Heroes are never team players.

A brief review of the hero myth shows why the concept of the hero has such a tenacious grip in western thought. From storytelling and folklore the idea of the heroic story has grown. One thinks of Homer's *Iliad* and *Odyssey*, Virgil's *Aeneid* and Bunyan's *Pilgrim's Progress*. Importantly for our argument, the notion of the hero has always been linked to ethics. For instance, MacIntyre (1998, p. 6) notes that the initial function of the Homeric epic hero tale was to show the qualities that men should have: to be a brave and skilful warrior, to know one's place in the moral order so as to perform one's social function according to an idealised view of society. The hero is, therefore, a moral hero.

The hero is meant to stand apart from the rest of society, acting alone, often undertaking an epic journey, leaving family and loved ones behind. The hero is rational in that the rationality of the heroic approach is never questioned. It is compulsive.

In modern organisations, whistleblowers can be seen as moral heroes. Whether the heroic manager can be seen as a moral hero is another matter. Following Simons *et al.* (2002), the heroic manager may work long hours for the company, but much of that effort may be directed towards the self-interest of a large pay packet.

The problems with heroic management

Despite the fact that it is probably the predominant view of management, heroic management also runs into problems. Not surprisingly, critical management studies is interested in the downside and weaknesses of heroic management (Alvesson and Deetz, 2000). The problems of heroic management can be divided into practical, theoretical and ethical ones.

The main practical problem is that heroic management often does not work. The heroic approach to project management, for example, does not seem to affect the outcome of projects (Couillard, 1995). Managers are caught up in webs of relationships which make it hard for them to establish their heroic leadership, and even if they do, there are conflicts with other managers holding similar positions as well as internal conflicts regarding other roles managers may play (Knights and Willmott, 1999). So even if a manager tries to act in the heroic mould, he (or she) is inevitably dependent on a network of relationships within the organisation. Any attempt to move away from a traditional bureaucratic structure towards a flatter, more democratic structure hardly supports the notion of heroic management.

There are theoretical problems concerning the fundamental reasons why heroic management tends to fail. It is not at all clear under what circumstances a heroic approach would be useful. This means that the acceptability of heroic management is not in the hands of the manager, which diminishes his control of success or failure. Another theoretical argument against the concept of heroic management is that it overlooks the fundamental determinants of humans who act as managers. Managers are not the abstract rational *homines economici* described in parts of the management literature, but they are being-in-the-world in a Heideggerian sense (Heidegger, 1993; Introna, 1997; Ciborra, 2002). They are incapable of leaving their bodily restrictions, the fact that they are always caught up in situations (Lawler, 2004) as well as the ideologies and discursive webs surrounding them (Levy *et al*, 2003). The myth of rationality, on which heroic management is built, is thus exposed as untenable. Rational decisions in a decision-theoretic model are the rare exception for managers who have to make do in bounded rationality, and for whom emotions are often more important than 'objective' information (Fineman, 2001; McGrath, 2006). Managers have to make sense of an uncertain and changing world (Ciborra, 2000; Newell *et al.*, 2001; Hughes *et al.*, 2002; Thomas, 1999).

There are a number of ethical problems associated with the notion of heroic management. The one which I explore in this chapter relates to the question of responsibility. The moral hero has an ambivalent relationship to the notion of responsibility. This will be demonstrated using the morally complex issue of employee privacy and surveillance.

Employee privacy and workplace surveillance

Privacy and surveillance are probably the most important and most widely discussed normative issues in computing and information systems. The following discussion draws upon empirical research in the area (Stahl *et al.*, 2005), but it is aimed at showing that responsible management of normative issues of privacy is a conceptual problem, not an empirical one.

Reasons for employee surveillance

Even though it is not always clear what exactly constitutes surveillance and how it works (Lyon, 2002), an everyday understanding of it as the observation (directly or using technical means) of someone, independent of that person's agreement to being observed, is sufficient for our argument. One of the reasons why surveillance is often seen as problematic is that it is perceived as an infringement of privacy. It is a contentious issue because it seems to embody a direct collision between organisational and employee interests (Beu and

Buckley, 2001). Despite this contentious character, surveillance in general and surveillance of employees is widespread in most Western societies (Schulman, 2000; Hartman, 2001; Ball, 2003; Stanton and Stam, 2003).

While individuals may monitor others' behaviour for reasons of personal curiosity and states may do so because of an interest in security or crime prevention, private organisations usually give economic reasons for doing so. It is often said that companies lose huge amounts of money because of non-work-related use of company resources (Boncella, 2001; Siau *et al.*, 2002). This seems to be such an important problem that scholars have seen a need to come up with terms such as 'cyberslacking' (Block, 2001), 'cyberslouching' (Urbaczewski and Jessup, 2002), or 'cyberloafing' (Tapia, 2004). The use of surveillance technologies is supposed to limit such personal use of technology and thereby increase worker productivity and company profits.

A related problem is that of legal liability for employee behaviour. Companies fear that staff may abuse their systems and that the company may be held liable for their actions. Possible problems range from harassment (Spinello, 2000) thought negligence in hiring, retention, supervision (Brown, 2000; Panko and Beh, 2002) to cyberstalking and child pornography (Catudal, 2001; Adam, 2002). The solution to all this seems to be to install some sort of technology that will allow managers to know what exactly employees are doing – in brief, surveillance. However, not everybody agrees that surveillance can or should be the answer to these problems.

Moral problems of surveillance

There are many arguments against surveillance. One can distinguish moral, ethical and legal ones. Moral problems are those that result from a conflict with the accepted norms (morality) of a society, whereas ethical problems are those that result from the theoretical justification of morality. Moral problems of surveillance are often discussed in conjunction with the concept of privacy.

Privacy is another concept that most scholars agree is valuable but that is quite difficult to define (Weckert and Adeney, 1997). It can mean different things in different situations. It can be seen as a right, a claim, a form of control, a value (Gavison, 1995). The most widely used definition is probably the one put forward by Warren and Brandeis (1890) as the 'right to be let alone'. This right is often understood to mean that individuals have a right to control information about themselves (Tavani and Moor, 2001). This has been extended to a right to informational self-determination, which is generally accepted in Europe (Stalder, 2002).

Surveillance is a threat to privacy and it is therefore seen as a moral problem. To understand why this is so, one can take a look at the assumed consequences for the individual of breaches of privacy. Breaching someone's privacy can be seen as an expression of disrespect (Elgesem, 1996). Privacy is often seen as a prerequisite for developing individual identity and autonomy (Severson, 1997; Nye, 2002). A lack of privacy can prevent individuals from developing their personality to its full potential (Brown, 2000) and threaten their mental health (Nissenbaum, 2001). This type of argument is usually linked to the concept of autonomy, which is central in much of post-Kantian ethics (van den Hoeven, 2001).

This leads to a second group of moral issues with surveillance, namely the consequences it has for social interaction. If individuals become deficient in their personality development then they are not good candidates for successful social interaction (Rachels, 1995; Introna, 2000). However, there are reasons why surveillance can be bad for groups and societies that go beyond individual effects. These typically concentrate on power relationships. Surveillance can be seen as an expression of power. While all human interactions are laced with power, the increase of surveillance can be interpreted as an increase of power of one group over another. From a Marxist point of view one could thus see the increase of employee surveillance as an advantage of capital over labour. But even if one does not share the Marxist view, it is plain to see that surveillance changes power balances in organisations (Forester and Morrison, 1994). IS also lend themselves to an interpretation as Panopticons (Foucault, 1975; Yoon, 1996; Goold, 2003).

Finally, there are economic arguments against surveillance. It can hurt labour relations, decrease motivation, create problems of data transfer and international jurisdiction, raise intellectual property issues and decrease trust (Soule, 1998). All of these have at least a moral aspect to them. But the problems do not stop here.

Ethical problems of surveillance

When something is a moral problem, that means that a relevant number of individuals will react to it by saying, 'this is bad' or 'this is wrong'. The ethical question remains why something is perceived to be immoral or what moral behaviour would look like. Raising ethical problems of surveillance in our context means that the manager who decides about the use of surveillance technology not needs to be aware not only of the moral problems but also of their ethical evaluation and justification. Without this awareness it is impossible to weigh different claims and arrive at a reasoned decision. We have seen that there are legitimate reasons for surveillance but that there are also legitimate reasons to avoid it. In order to discuss these meaningfully, the manager must understand ethical reasoning. This is problematic, however, because there is no universally accepted ethical theory. Furthermore, the individuals involved in the moral dilemmas of employee surveillance are usually not philosophers and therefore not aware of the potential breadth of ethical debate.

There might, for example, be an employee who thinks that surveillance is acceptable because employees are paid for their time and thus should only work for the company during working hours. This is a moral stance which requires a complex ethical underpinning. It takes for granted concepts of property and ownership. Power relationships between employers and employees are seen as justified. The right of one person to tell another what to do on the basis of eco-nomic inequality is not questioned. The entire scenario is probably underpinned by an implicit utilitarian belief that the capitalist system is justified and that effi-cient work is a moral value because it creates wealth and employment. On the other hand, there might be an employee who docs not want to be observed, who wants to be left alone even during work. This might imply a strong valuing of autonomy and a belief that there are individual rights in the workplace that cannot be overwritten by economic considerations. It follows from this view that contractual obligations are subject to interpretation and that the conditions of entering into contracts in capitalism are too unequal to view their results as auto-matically justified.

This description of ethical considerations could easily be extended. It is important to note that most of these ethical thoughts are implicit. Even profes-sional philosophers would be very hard pressed to extract all the ethical assump-tions implied in such positions. Managers and employees will usually find it even more difficult because they lack the conceptual apparatus. This is deeply problematic for heroic management, which requires a sufficient understanding of a given situation. But it is not only ethics that complicates matters; there is also the legal situation.

Legal problems of surveillance

The normative muddle surrounding employee surveillance becomes even worse when one includes legal considerations. Let us take a look at the example of the United Kingdom. The most obvious legal regulation concerning privacy and sur-veillance is the Data Protection Act 1998. The Act regulates the duties of data controllers, in our case the employer wanting to use surveillance technology. It also states who can have access to which type of data and which exemptions from data protection are admissible. In order to contextualise the Act one needs to know that it is the national legislation required by the European Directive 95/46/EC. That means that case law pertaining to data protection can be British or European. Additionally, there are other acts and European Directives which can affect the legal situation. These include the Telecommunications Regulation 1999, giving effect to the EU Directive 97/66/EC, as well as the Privacy and Electronic Communications (EC Directive) Regulations 2003. Then there is the Freedom of Information Act 2000, which was fully implemented in 2005. Because of all the new regulations, case law has yet to be established. Addition-ally, the entire European approach to data protection is guided by article 8 of the European Convention on Human Rights, which is legally binding in European signatory countries (including all EU member states).

As if this were not sufficiently complex, there are international problems regarding different data protection regimes and jurisdictions. One of these is that European data protection legislation forbids export of personal information to countries where data protection is less strict, including the United States. That means that if our surveillance manager wants to use a server located at company head office in the United States to store some of the surveillance data, he or she may be in breach of UK law.

Responsibility: the solution?

Managers can have good reasons for introducing employee surveillance techno-logy, but such activity is also problematic. Why can responsibility be seen as a solution to the problem? First, responsibility is a normative concept that can be used to convey moral, ethical, legal or other normative content. When I say that I am responsible for my child, then this implies all of these aspects. Second, responsibility is a well-recognised concept in business organisations, where it again implies different normative aspects and expectations. Third, responsibility seems to be geared towards practical solutions and is not necessarily confined to specific ethical theories. The concept of responsibility has consequentially been used to address a range of normative issues in IS, including moral and ethical questions (Bechtel, 1985) but also related issues such as security (Backhouse and Dhillon, 1996).

The concept of responsibility

Like all widely used terms, the word 'responsibility' is applied in different ways with different meanings. A good way to introduce the term is to take a look at the etymology of the concept. At the root of responsibility there is the response, the answer. Lewis (1972, pp. 124–125) therefore concludes that it means 'liabil-ity to answer'. This same etymological root, the answer, can be found in other languages such as the French *responsabilité* (Ricoeur, 1990) or the German *Verantwortung* (Lenk and Maring, 1995). Responsibility is thus closely linked to communication.

The defining feature of the different uses of the concept is that they describe a social construct of ascription (Hart, 1948). The term 'responsibility' establishes a link between an object and a subject. The subject is the entity that is respons-ible and the object is the fact or action that the subject is responsible for. While this describes the essence of responsibility, one should note that every single example of responsibility ascriptions involves a host of other aspects which can be of importance. Among those there is an additional dimension apart from subject and object, namely the authority which determines the success and results of the ascription. Other aspects are the type of responsibility (legal, moral, role, etc.), the temporal horizon (*ex ante* versus *ex post*), the normative background, etc. A complete description of any instance of responsibility would have to consider all of these (see Stahl, 2004a).

There are three aspects that most, if not all, ascriptions of responsibility share. These aspects are openness, an affinity to action and a teleological orien-tation. Openness means that responsibility ascriptions are dynamic social events which need to allow the participation of those involved and which are therefore not predictable. Affinity to action describes the fact that the very use of the word 'responsibility' implies that something will happen (Staddon, 1999). When we hold someone responsible, this means that that person will have to do something, will be rewarded or punished. Finally, there is the aspect of teleology. This means that, on the one hand, responsibility ascriptions aim to improve life, to get closer to the 'good life', whatever that means in a particular situation (French, 1992). At the same time, responsibility ascriptions are based on consequences, be they manifest and in the past or only expected in the future. These three general characteristics will become important later on for the development of a sustainable use of the concept.

Why could this concept seem like a possible solution to the normative problems of IS? The reason is that its formal and communicative nature allows the discussion of complex normative questions without an a-priori definition of their nature as moral, ethical, legal, economic, etc. That means that questions of privacy and data protection that might be raised by a surveillance system can be addressed from different angles simultaneously. Another advantage of responsibility is that it does not require an immediate choice of ethical theory. While it could be argued that responsibility is closer to some ethical theories, such as ethics of communication or consequentialist approaches, than others, such as deontological or virtue-based theories, this does not necessarily hold true.[1] During the process of ascription, moral problems can be described in terms of different ethical theories, and there is no fundamental reason why responsibility cannot correspond closely with duty (De George, 1999).

The concept of responsibility is of great interest to critical researchers. I have argued throughout this book that critical research is based upon ethical intuitions and I will continue to argue that critical scholars need to find a way to make their ethical beliefs explicit in order to be able to link them with their critical work. At the same time, ethics and morality are often central problems for critical research because they can be used to cement oppressive social structures and to legitimise suppression and alienation. I shall shortly give examples of the misuse of moral concepts for such purposes. This leaves the critical scholar in the dilemma of having to come to grips with ethics in an environment where ethics is simultaneously central to the critical approach but also a possible impediment to the achievement of the aim of emancipation. The solution to this dilemma, as I have indicated during the discussion of the problem of emancipation, is likely to be a procedural approach. Such a procedural approach leaves questions of material morality (i.e. what is good or bad) open and concentrates on the creation of the condition under which moral conflicts can be addressed equitably. The concept of responsibility is one possibility for framing such a procedural approach to ethics. Responsibility is open to all sorts of ascriptions. It thus does not prejudice the description of moral problems or possible solutions. At the same time, the concept of responsibility provides a framework that can be used to arbitrate competing ascriptions and competing moral claims. Its use in such a way, however, requires that responsibility ascriptions are open to discussion and possible revision and that those who are affected have a fair chance in raising their points. Such conditions are not always given in hierarchical relationships, which leads us back the problem of responsibility under conditions of heroic management.

Heroic responsibility

If the concept of responsibility does indeed offer an avenue to address normative issues of employee surveillance, then it stands to reason that managers who see themselves in the heroic tradition of management should assume and assign responsibility. In that case, responsibility would be a relatively static and objective ascription. The task of introducing and conducting employee surveillance would be divided into a number of responsibility objects to which subjects would be assigned. Such objects might be the design or procurement of a suitable system, the introduction of the technology, the installation of procedures to undertake surveillance, or the development of processes that determine the outcome of different observation events.

The logic of heroic responsibility would require the individual ascriptions to conform to the logic of the greater responsibility structures of the organisation. Thus, the top manager involved in the surveillance project, say the Chief Information Officer, would assume overall responsibility for the success of the project. She or he would assign sub-tasks to lower-level managers, who in turn could delegate tasks and responsibilities to other employees. The entire chain of responsibility would need to be designed in such a way that it was integrated in the strategy of the organisation and thus was conducive to the official responsibility framework of the organisation. The heroic activity of the manager would in all likelihood have to rely on supporting bureaucratic activities that would facilitate the heroic ascription.

Such heroic management will need to define the outcomes, measures of accountability, and sanctions of ascription. If all this happens in the mindset of heroic management, it will be considered desirable that the outcomes and intermediate objectives will be clearly described and, if possible, quantifiable. The sanctions, be they punishments or rewards, will be directly linked to the achievement of the quantitative goals. Managers observe the different processes, and when they notice deviance from planned protocols, will take appropriate measures to bring processes back under control. This brief sketch should have given a plausible outline of responsible heroic management in general and has hinted at the general structure such an approach could take with regard to employee surveillance. It is clear that this is not a complete description of real management, nor does it exhaust the possibilities of managerial action. The description relies on the heroic properties of the manager but it is also underpinned by the bureaucratic approach to management. Heroic and purposive rationality are intermingled, and the following critique will address both.

Problem I: detached rationality and objective reality – the problem of self-awareness

Responsibility ascriptions are complex social processes that can raise problems for a large variety of reasons. There are structural problems of responsible heroic management that cannot be overcome in the traditional top-down objectivist mindset. Some of these become obvious when we compare the description of heroic responsibility and the normative problems of employee privacy and surveillance. Employee surveillance raises a number of moral, ethical and legal questions. Some of these can be identified in advance and subsequently be addressed by traditional management methods. Indeed, a compliance approach to responsibility often tries to address specific legal questions. However, the fundamental issue is that the problems created by employee surveillance are not objectively given. Rather, they are based on individual and social experiences and develop over time. They are culturally variable and depend on a number of unmeasurable factors. A heroic top-down approach will be unable to identify all of these, not because of a lack of effort but because they have no objective context-independent reality that would allow them to be described in an algorithmic way.

An important aspect of this problem is that management is not a detached entity with a privileged observer position with regard to surveillance but is an involved agent that constitutes part of the problem. For example, whether employees find it objectionable to have their internet access monitored will in large part depend on the relationship between the employees and the managers. If employees feel that they are not well treated or not trusted by management, then they are likely to interpret surveillance as an expression of mistrust, and thus as objectionable. Alternatively, employees may see surveillance as a measure for their protection. Furthermore, management making decisions about surveillance base these on their moral ideals, based in turn on their (often implicit) ethical convictions. These will rarely be identical to those of the employees who are affected by surveillance. Management thus introduces and privileges a certain morality, which in itself will usually constitute an ethical problem.

I should clarify that these problems are not caused by bad managers or bad management practices. Rather, they are intrinsic in traditional and heroic management that takes an objective reality for granted and believes that problems can be addressed from a detached and rational point of view. A resulting fundamental problem is that legitimate concerns of employees based on their moral or ethical views cannot be accommodated in such an objectivist world. Where employees raise concerns, these will typically be considered resistance to change, resistance that management must overcome. Since employees see their objections as justified, management will have to make use of formal powers to overcome the perceived resistance. This will often work in the sense that management's ideas are realised, but it will not solve the underlying problem. Instead, it will create another moral problem by forcing people to work under conditions they see as not justified.

These observations of the clash between heroic management and responsibility can be extended to cover the very concept of responsibility and its relationship to management. Since management is part of the normative problems of employee surveillance and in many cases their root cause, the heroically responsible management approach is structurally blind to some of the central problems.

Problem II: the concept of responsibility – heroic and reflective responsibility

The second problem of the attempt to manage responsibly within the mindset of heroic management refers to the concept of responsibility itself. I have argued earlier that there are three fundamental characteristics of responsibility: openness, affinity to action, and teleology. I have elsewhere developed in more depth the concept of 'reflective responsibility' (Stahl, 2004a). The basic idea of such reflective responsibility is that a normative idea such as responsibility should be applicable to itself without contradiction. That means that the use of the concept of responsibility should be a responsible action. Or, to break this down to the main characteristics, an ascription of responsibility should be open, lead to action, and support the intended *telos*, the aim of responsibility. Reflective use of responsibility should thus determine whether an ascription is, indeed, viable and whether it can achieve its aims.

Considering this question will require attention to detail in every single case. There are nevertheless a number of issues that can be discussed in general terms. These can be divided according to the main dimensions involved: subject, object and authority. If any of these dimensions is lacking or opaque, then the responsibility ascription in question will not be open, it will not be successful (thus not lead to action), or will not achieve the desired aim. I will briefly describe some of the problems of each of the dimensions with regard to a heroic management approach to employee surveillance.

The subject is the entity who is responsible. In heroic management this will usually be a manager. The higher up in the hierarchy, the more responsibility one will expect. This exclusive focus on individual responsibility is problematic, however, because in complex modern organisations it is usually not trivial to draw a direct line between individuals and certain actions or decisions. Many decisions are taken by collectives or emerge from the history of the organisation without being attributable to a single person. Moreover, individuals in organisations do not meet all the conditions that need to be fulfilled in order for responsibility to be acceptable, such as freedom, knowledge and power (Fischer, 1999; Goldman, 1999). Individuals higher up the hierarchy will often have more freedom and power, but they lack the local knowledge of pertinent problems. Those individuals who have the local knowledge typically have no power to change things. With regard to surveillance this means that it is not clear who should be held responsible. The individualistic heroic approach precludes the consideration of important factors such as the history or working culture of the organisation, which may have huge influence on surveillance decisions but cannot be represented by individuals. One could argue against this, however, that there are hierarchies of responsibility and delegation that allow these questions to be addressed. To some degree this is certainly true, but it overlooks the fact that some of the problems are structural rather than issues of scope. Heroic management is intrinsically individualistic and therefore needs to blend out issues that do not fit an individualist world-view. Furthermore, such an argument overlooks the next problem, the problem of determining the object of responsibility.

The object is that which the subject is responsible for. A traditional approach would define the objects at the outset. In a surveillance situation these might be employee compliance with regulations, or an increase in productivity. These would be measured by variables such as the reduced time spent by employees doing personal business or the overall hours of employees monitored. One main problem is that of side effects. Side effects are those consequences of actions that are caused but not intended. In surveillance, the entire area of moral issues can be described as a side effect. The original aim of surveillance has little moral significance, and it can even be described as morally desirable because it prevents the free rider problem. However, as outlined above in the description of privacy, moral considerations are likely to enter the picture. Employees can feel threatened or mistrusted. Surveillance can undermine company morale. It can cause individual psychological problems and hurt communication and intellectual exchange. It can be considered morally 'bad' for a variety of reasons, and even intrinsically bad (Introna, 2003b). Any of these will jeopardise the acceptance and thus the success of the technology. Employees who do not agree with a technology will resist it and find ways around it (Attias, 2004; Doolin, 2004). The main problem of the object of ascription is thus that a top-down objectivist approach is likely to miss a considerable number of the most relevant issues, including most moral questions. Again, this is not because managers do a bad job, but because moral problems are context dependent and emerge as side effects that management as the subject of responsibility by definition cannot foresee.

The last main dimension is that of the authority. It determines sanctions for objects. For this purpose the authority must be able to recur to a set of accepted norms, which allow the attribution of rewards or punishments. We are thus looking in part at a problem of power and in part at a problem of ethics. Ethics as the theory and justification of morality helps evaluate the severity of moral issues and is thus intimately linked to responsibility ascriptions. The problem is that there is no generally accepted ethical theory. Employee surveillance may be a moral good from the point of view of a utility-based theory, which emphasises the economic gain to be expected, but it may be a moral problem from a duty-based theory, which emphasises respect for the other's autonomy.

The main problem with heroic management here is that it privileges a particular viewpoint, namely that of management, in the process of establishing and sanctioning responsibility. Most ethical theory is based on the idea that ethical evaluations must be impartial. A heroic and detached approach to surveillance cannot by definition be impartial because, even when considering other stakeholders' views, it determines outcomes on the basis of management's view of the world.

A traditional approach to responsible management of employee surveillance thus falls short of the requirements of responsibility with regard to all three major dimensions. It finds it difficult to identify the right subject, it will miss some of the relevant objects and it will not be based on an acceptable set of norms and thus not produce viable sanctions. To reiterate the point: this is not because managers are bad people or because management does not do its job well. The problems are structural and conceptual. They are based on the intrinsic contradiction between a traditional and heroic approach to management and the requirements of responsibility.

Reflective responsibility: the way forward?

So far I have argued that there are substantial conceptual problems related to the attempt to manage responsibly the normative problems raised by employee surveillance. Responsible management of information systems seems to be conceptually problematic, at least in so far as management is understood in the traditional top-down scientifically rational way, which I have termed heroic management. What conclusions can be drawn from this? Heroic management that concentrates on organisational imperatives and neglects the wider context can still be promoted. It will have blind spots and not be sensitive to the moral and ethical issues discussed in this chapter, but it can be used to further organisational ends. Anecdotal evidence suggests that this is the solution that the majority of IS managers choose. Such an approach has two major disadvantages: an ethical and an organisational one. The ethical disadvantage is that responsibility understood in a top-down strategic manner will fail to pick up on many moral problems raised by surveillance. Furthermore, it does not have the ethical breadth to deal with those it does pick up. It will thus ignore relevant and legitimate concerns or will try to suppress them as unjustified resistance to change. The organisational problem with the approach is that its insensitivity to moral and ethical questions can lead to organisational problems. Employees who find their moral expectations violated by surveillance or who do not agree with its ethical justifications by management are likely to resent the use of such technology; they will resist it and, often, neutralise its effects. The heroic approach can therefore hurt working relations as well as decrease productivity by forcing employees to devise ways of deceiving surveillance technology.

The alternative to this unsatisfactory approach would be to understand the concept of management in a different way: in a way that is compatible with the concept of responsibility. This is where we come back to the idea of reflective responsibility introduced earlier. Reflective responsibility stands for the attempt to realise the ascription of responsibility in such a way as to render it a responsible activity. This means that responsibility is ascribed in such a way that it will be open (in terms of process and outcome), that it will have manifest results and that it furthers the original intention of the ascription. It goes far beyond the confines of this chapter to describe the details of reflective responsibility (for an in-depth discussion, see Stahl, 2004a). Suffice it to say that reflective responsibility will require participative processes that define all steps and dimensions of responsibility in an interdependent way. That means that an instance of responsibility needs to be defined in terms of subject, object and norms or sanctions. The subjects need to be chosen so that they can affect the outcomes and so that they adhere to the norms and react to the sanctions. In terms of employee surveillance this will mean that there is no one single ascription of responsibility but rather a web of interlinking responsibilities which will refer to one another. Subjects will most likely include individual managers but they will not be confined to these. It is possible that individual employees may become subjects of responsibility, or collectives, such as work groups, or whole organisations. The objects will again include the traditional organisational-centred ones (profit, productivity, compliance, etc.) but they will go beyond these, covering questions of respect, working climate, individual perceptions, issues of particular technologies, and whatever else the affected parties find worth ascribing responsibility for. The relationship between subject and object will be defined on the basis of acceptable norms, which can be economic ones (profit maximisation), but which can also be explicitly ethical (autonomy, freedom, justice, etc.) or of a different nature (tradition, local culture, etc.).

Such a web of responsibility requires a fundamentally different type of interaction between managers and other stakeholders from the one implied in heroic management. In practice the process of responsibility ascription will look more like Habermasian discourse (Habermas, 1981) or a stakeholder debate in the sense of stakeholder management (Donaldson and Preston, 1995). The main advantage of this reflective approach to responsible management of normative issues of IS is that it allows the identification and consideration of the wide range of moral and ethical issues that are potentially raised by surveillance. It faces neither of the two main problems of heroic management discussed here. Since it is not one-sided, top-down and power-based responsibility, management does not have the most important place. Managers are of course legitimate stakeholders in the process of ascription and they can argue for their desired objectives. However, they need to take into consideration the viewpoints of other stakeholders. Doin so allows a definition of the problems (objects of responsibility) that overcomes the partial interests of management. The ascription is therefore not fraught with the problem of self-awareness. By considering questions of realisability and desirable outcomes, the process of ascription also addresses the second main objection raised earlier. The simultaneous definition of subject, object and authority allows the development of viable ascriptions. Finally, the web of responsibility created in this way needs to remain open to revision and thus is not a static construct. It can react to changes by adding or modifying ascriptions.

Another advantage of this reflectively responsible approach is that it overcomes the pathologies of heroic and purposive rationality. In Habermasian terms this reflects the move from purposive to communicative rationality. However, a similar change of rationality is not limited to explicitly critical approaches but has been expressed as desirable in the mainstream IS literature as well. Kumar *et al.* (1998), for example, provide evidence of the shortcoming of purposive rationality and promote a new, trust-based rationality.

One can raise a number of objections to the model of reflective responsibility. The main ones are that it is a hugely complex undertaking, particularly when applied to large organisations and processes, and that it does not offer a guarantee of success. These points of critique are valid but can be countered from the point of view of reflective responsibility. It is an intrinsic characteristic of reflective responsibility that it is modest in its goals, that it aims to further the moral objectives of the community of discourse without claiming to achieve perfection. The counter-argument would thus be that the reflective approach at least offers the possibility of overcoming the shortcomings of heroic responsibility and that such an attempt should be worth the cost – first, because it can help overcome organisational problems; and second, because it is a morally acceptable way to deal with the other, in this case the employee privacy and surveillance.

There is, however, another reason why this approach, as well as related attempts to redescribe the role of management in information systems, finds it difficult to be accepted, namely that the role of the manager changes drastically. The manager is no longer the lone and rational hero who brings salvation to the organisation. Instead, he or she becomes an involved member of a community and, at best, a facilitator of discourses. In terms of established management theories one can restate this as saying that the Fordist understanding of management needs to be overcome and replaced with a more inclusive and participative management theory and style. I am not the first to make this argument, which is consistent with critical theory and its scepticism regarding established capitalist forms of organisation. What I have added to the debate, however, is a stronger conceptual foundation that takes the critical concerns and supports them with a conceptual argument pointing out the weaknesses of heroic management. These are particularly obvious where management must deal with complex normative issues such as employee privacy and surveillance. The current argument will thus raise resistance from those who have an interest in the status quo, including managers and some parts of the business education industry. I believe, however, that the critical arguments are sound and deserve to be heard. To be accepted, they will require a more far-reaching discourse on the theory and reality of management in organisations. I hope that this book will contribute to this discourse. Without such a discourse and a change of our understanding of the role of management, the heroic approach to managing normative issues such as privacy is likely to prevail despite its problematic nature.

11 Trust as fetish

A critical theory perspective on research on trust in e-commerce

The third example of an application of critical research in information systems aims at problematic aspects of mainstream IS research. The example of empowerment through ICT in Egypt underlined the social relevance of the critical perspective, whereas the example of responsibility and heroic management was meant to show the importance of conceptual work in critical research. This chapter uses the critical instruments to analyse and critique the traditional understanding of research. It builds directly on much of what I outlined in Part II on the philosophy of critical research, particularly epistemology and ontology. The chapter goes beyond such general elaborations and develops a critique of mainstream IS research by investigating research on trust in e-commerce. It continues the ongoing themes of the book by emphasising the question of ethics and morality and arguing that these require more explicit recognition in traditional as well as critical research. Moreover, it develops a concept that forms part of the classical Marxist critique of capitalism, namely the concept of fetishism, and applies this to e-commerce trust research.

Research on trust in e-commerce has become a veritable industry. The reason for this is that e-commerce, despite its many advantages, is still not living up to its full potential. This is apparently caused by the lack of trust that end users have in technology and technology-enabled exchange of goods. Since lack of trust is a major obstacle for the success of e-commerce, research concentrates on understanding trust and its components in order to facilitate the development of trust. This should lead to approaches and mechanisms that will facilitate more and better economic exchange.

I will argue that such instrumental use of the concept of trust is problematic and unlikely to lead to the desired outcome. The chapter will begin with a review of the concept of trust which will argue that moral views and their ethical justifications are integral to trusting relationships. The use of the ethical concept of trust for the promotion of commercial activities is self-contradictory. Critical theory has coined the term 'fetish' to describe the heart of the problem. Trust becomes a fetish when it is no longer desired for its own sake but becomes an exchangeable commodity independent of human relationships. Such fetishised trust loses its ethical properties and therefore its binding nature that it requires to further exchange.

This main argument will be supported by a critical discourse analysis. The analysis of a number of the leading publications in the area of e-commerce trust will demonstrate that, despite a considerable breadth of understanding and theoretical underpinning, trust is generally treated as a fetish. If this is correct, then research on trust in e-commerce faces a serious problem. Independent of the quality of the research, it will not be capable of fulfilling the self-declared aim of establishing trust. At the conclusion of the chapter I will discuss what this means for future research and how critical theory can further our understanding and contribute to emancipation in e-commerce.

Trust in e-commerce

The argument will require a working definition of the concept of trust. Since there is a wealth of literature on trust, the following review cannot be comprehensive. I will concentrate on trust in e-commerce, and here particularly on trust in business-to-consumer (B2C) relationships. This leaves a range of other potential online trust relationships such as managerial trust (Soule, 1998; Stanton and Stam, 2003), trust in virtual teams (Jones and Bowie, 1998; Gallivan, 2001; Brown *et al.*, 2004; Pauleen, 2003), trust in supply chains (Welty and Becerra-Fernandez, 2001) and others. There are related areas such as trust in the economic system in general (Castells, 2000a) or trust in e-government (Yee *et al.*, 2005) that the argument cannot include.

In the following review of the literature on trust, I will distinguish between two perspectives, which I will call the positive and the critical. The positive perspective is characterised by the assumption that trust is static, objective, measurable and rational. It serves as the base of positivist and quantitative research that aims to prove or disprove hypotheses. The critical perspective (this is a generally critical view that does not necessarily rely on critical theory or critical research as defined in Part I of this book) sheds doubt on the positive view and outlines facets of trust that are difficult if not impossible to capture from the positive viewpoint.

The positive view is the root cause of the treatment of trust as a fetish. It is therefore necessary to discuss it in some depth. To do so, I will first discuss some definitions of trust. These are linked to its functions as well as different classifications and types. Trust research typically investigates the conditions of trust, which will subsequently be introduced. Finally, I will discuss the consequences of the positive view for research and practice in e-commerce.

Definitions of trust

As is the case for most frequently used concepts, there is no generally agreed-upon definition of trust (Rousseau *et al.*, 1998). One reason for this is that trust covers a range of issues and problems that are not necessarily identical. Speaking of 'trust' can thus mean different things for different speakers. In the positive view, trust tends to be endowed with a purpose. That purpose is usually to facilitate interaction or exchange. This is the crucial point in research on trust in e-commerce (Hoffman *et al.*, 1999; Cheskin/Studio Archetype, 1999).

A central aspect of trust is that it has to do with a psychological state of the trusting person, the trustor (Rousseau *et al.*, 1998). It is an attitude (Alpern, 1997) that is typically based upon a belief (Egger, 2001) linked to an expectation (Mui *et al.*, 2002) and often accompanied by certain feelings (Solomon and Flores, 2001). All these aspects are only relevant in a relationship. Trust can only arise in a relationship between a trustor and a trustee (Reagle, 1996) and possibly other entities (Viega *et al.*, 2001). A trusting relationship can arise in situations where the trustor does not have complete control over the trustee. The trustor relies on the trustee (Jones *et al.*, 2000) and therefore needs to accept a certain amount of vulnerability (Brenkert, 1998; Hosmeh, 1995). Willingness to accept vulnerability has therefore been suggested as a definition of trust (Mayer *et al.*, 1995, p. 712; Gallivan and Depledge, 2003, p. 162; Pennington *et al.*, 2004, p. 202). Agents are likely to accept vulnerability if they have a positive view of the person to whom they make themselves vulnerable; if they expect benevolence (Bhattacherjee, 2002).

Positive reviews of trust often emphasise its functions. Possibly the most important one is the reduction of uncertainty. Many scholars refer to the sociologist Niklas Luhmann, who emphasised the human need for the reduction of uncertainty and who identified trust as one central way of achieving this aim (Gefen, 2000; Gefen *et al.*, 2003; Grabner-Kräuter, 2002). Uncertainty in a situation of economic exchange is closely related to risk. Trust is therefore often described as relevant in risky situations (Mayer *et al.*, 1995) or as a risk management approach. Trust seems to be most valuable in situations where control is lacking and future interactions are difficult to predict (Lane and Bachmann, 1996). Accordingly, trust is highly relevant in e-commerce transactions because customers often have little knowledge of vendors and must deal with ambiguity, uncertainty and risks outside of their control. Higher levels of trust should thus lead to more transactions (Bhattacherjee, 2002). Trust, then, can also be seen as a form of social capital (Preece, 2002) or an asset of a firm.

Table 11.1 summarises the most important characteristics and functions of trust.

Types and conditions of trust

In order for trust to develop, many conditions need to be fulfilled. These are not universal but depend on the type of trust. There are many different ways of classifying trust. Koehn (2003, p. 5) distinguishes between goal-based, calculative, knowledge-based and respect-based trust. Gefen *et al.* (2003, p. 62) identify knowledge-based, institution-based, calculative-based, cognition-based and personality-based trust. This reflects a similar but shorter list by Berg and Kalish (1997), who distinguish between calculus-based, knowledge-based and identification-based trust. Lane and Bachmann (1996, p. 371), drawing on Zucker (1986), list process-based, characteristic-based and institutionally based

Table 11.1 Characteristics and functions of trust

Characteristic/function of trust	Explanation
Belief/psychological state/expectation	Trust is rooted in the individual whose psychological predisposition influence her expectations and beliefs
Trust as relationship	Trust can only arise in a relationship between a trustor and a trustee
Acceptance of vulnerability	Trust is only necessary in situations where the trustor does not have full control and needs to rely on the trustee
Reduction of uncertainty/complexity	The function of trust is to reduce uncertainty and complexity, thus facilitating action for the trustor
Social capital	From an organisational perspective, being perceived as trustworthy is a form of social capital that can be translated into economic capital through the reduction of transaction costs

trust. According to Rousseau *et al.* (1998, p. 393), definitions of trust can be distinguished according to the academic discipline in which they are used. For Dribben (2004, p. 27), trust can be divided according to the 'layer' in which it is active, helping him to distinguish between dispositional trust, learned trust and situational trust. Furthermore, there are different stages of trust, with initial trust clearly differing from trust that is well established (McKnight *et al.*, 2002, p. 335). The schema of trust development can be more complex, as for example for Flores and Solomon (1998) and Solomon and Flores (2001), who distinguish between simple trust; naïve trust; trust as yet unchallenged; unquestioned (the faith of a well-brought-up child), blind trust; obstinate, possibly even self-deluding, basic trust; and authentic trust.

Not all types of trust are always of the same importance. There seems to be general agreement that trust in situations of economic exchange requires or is built upon reliable institutions (McKnight and Chervany, 2000; Pavlou and Gefen, 2004; Rousseau *et al.*, 1998). The nature of economic interaction also implies the existence of rational economic actors who are able and willing to maximise their expected utility, which gives a central role to calculative trust (Ba and Pavlou, 2001; Lewicki and Stevenson, 1997).

In order for trust to arise, many conditions have to be fulfilled. Not all of them are necessary for each type of trust. One can distinguish between conditions referring to the structure and environment, the personality of trustor and trustee and the relationship between them. Structure and environment are important because they shape actors' perceptions and assumptions about other actors and ways of interacting with them. In order to successfully reduce complexity by trusting, trustors will rely on their background knowledge of the

situation. In modern impersonal economic transactions such background knowledge is highly important (Lane and Bachmann, 1996). The relevant situational
background ranges from national culture to the details of the planned interaction
(Gallivan and Depledge, 2003). Of importance is the legal system and the
agent's awareness of its functions, because it provides deterrence for misuse and
thus helps in calculating the utilities of the trustee (Rousseau *et al.*, 1998).
Particularly with regard to online interactions, the issues of privacy (Fukuyama,
1998; Hoffman *et al.*, 1999; Johnson, 2001) and security (Salam *et al.*, 2005,
Viega *et al.*, 2001) are determining factors of situational knowledge that can
influence trust.

Even perfect institutions are no guarantee of trust, if the characteristics of
trustor and trustee are not conducive to it (De George, 2003a). The trustor must
be endowed with the ability and the willingness to trust. This disposition to trust
is linked to the personality of the trustor and is shaped by his or her socialisation
and personal experience (Salam *et al.*, 2005). It is sometimes called a 'trusting
stance' (McKnight *et al.*, 2002) or a disposition to trust (Pavlou and Gefen,
2004) and is linked with a willingness to depend on others (McKnight and Chervany, 2000). The trustor's willingness to trust must be matched with corresponding characteristics of the trustee, which are often summarised as
'trustworthiness'. Trustworthiness is a concept that needs to be understood from
the trustor's perspective. It is thus somewhat idiosyncratic. There is nevertheless
much literature that attempts to pin down constituent aspects of trustworthiness.
Mayer *et al.* (1995) suggest ability, benevolence and integrity as necessary
characteristics of the trustee.

Bews and Rossouw (2002) add openness, competency, personal characteristics and a history of interactions as further requirements of trustworthiness. A
complete list of trustworthy characteristics, while desirable for commercial purposes (Cheskin/Studio Archetype, 1999), is impossible to achieve, because trustworthiness, like beauty, is at least partly in the eye of the beholder.

Apart from the individual characteristics, the final set of conditions of trust
are found in the relationship between trustor and trustee (McRobb and Rogerson, 2004). It is not enough for the trustee to be trustworthy; he or she also must
be perceived as being trustworthy by a trustor who has the propensity to then
engage in a trusting relationship. One important way of ensuring a fit between
trustworthiness and perception is a history of favourable interactions (Preece,
2002). Trust is most likely to develop in stable long-term relationships which are
mutually beneficial (MacDonald, 1997). Previous interactions are important
because they allow the trustor to develop confidence in his or her positive expectations (Gefen, 2000); this can create reassuring interdependence (Rousseau *et
al.*, 1998) – in brief, because it creates familiarity (Gefen, 2000).

Consequences of the positive view of trust

Thus, trust is conducive to interactions that contain an aspect of uncertainty, which
includes business transactions. A conclusion that is therefore drawn frequently

Table 11.2 Conditions of trust

Condition	Explanation
Structural	Institutions, particularly the legal system, culture, specific rules as in security or privacy
Personal	Trustor: propensity, disposition to trust Trustee: trustworthiness, depends on trustor but includes ability, benevolence, integrity, openness, competency, personal characteristics
Relationship	Positive history, long-term stability, familiarity

from discussions of trust is that it can be put to functional use in creating, establishing and maintaining commercial relationships (Dirks and Ferrin, 2001; Hosmeh, 1995; Flores and Solomon, 1998; Solomon, 1992). This is particularly true for online relationships because many of the traditional mechanisms for developing trust are missing there (Pavlou and Gefen, 2004; Ba and Pavlou, 2001). Since commercial exchange is usually predicated to serve the goal of profit maximisation, trust is often described as a tool for the generation of profits (Ba and Pavlou, 2001; Gefen, 2004; Moores, 2005; Salam *et al.*, 2005; Tarantino, 1994). Using economic theory, it can be argued that trust promotes efficiency (Donaldson and Dunfee, 1999; Hausman and McPherson, 1996). The most important mechanism for generating profit through trust is the reduction of transaction costs (Ba *et al.*, 1998; Gefen, 2000; Koehn, 1997). Trust can thus be seen as a form of social capital that a company should strive to possess (MacDoand *et al.*, 2002).

The high value of trust and the lacking traditional mechanisms of establishing it have led scholars to seek ways of using technology to promote and create trust in e-commerce. Much detail about trust-conducive design of technology, particularly websites, has been published (Cheskin/Studio Archetype, 1999; Olson and Olson, 2000). Another avenue of such research focuses on improving the security of online systems (Rutter, 2001), for example by strengthening encryption (Khare and Rifkin, 1998) or trust in operating systems (Faldetta, 2002). The computing industry has reflected these considerations by promoting new technology under the title of 'trusted computing' or 'trustworthy computing' (Anderson, 2004; Kursawe and Wolf, 2006). In the area of e-commerce, much effort has been spent on investigating how perceptions can be affected by good web design (Cantrell, 2000) or how structures such as feedback mechanisms can be created that could provide proxies for trustworthiness (Ba *et al.*, 1998; Pavlou and Gefen, 2004).

Limitations of the positive view of trust

My review of trust in e-commerce may not be complete, but I am prepared to argue that it reflects the mainstream understanding of trust as presupposed in much research in the field of information systems. It is important to note that not everyone agrees with it and many scholars argue that it is flawed for a variety of reasons. In this section I will outline the reasons for such disagreement. I will briefly summarise general problems of the positive view, its implied conditions and the downsides of trust. The heart of this critique will be a discussion of the moral and ethical nature of trust.

Positive accounts generally portray trust as an unambiguous good that needs to be striven for (Jarvenpaa *et al.*, 2004). They neglect the fact that in many cases trust fails, which raises new problems. Trust is a concept that was developed in direct personal relationships. It is not uncontested whether the concept can be used at all for technically mediated relationships (Introna, 2000; Mui *et al.*, 2002), particularly since e-commerce transaction typically do not allow for the negotiations that are typical of offline trust development (Koehn, 1997). One fundamental flaw of the positive view is that it neglects the bodily and existential aspects of humanity, which may render the transfer of the concept of trust to the disembodied space of e-commerce void (Solomon and Flores, 2001). Furthermore, trust is a dynamic and continually changing property of human relationships. Another problem is that the positive view is strongly based on economic theory of utility maximisation and corresponding, albeit possibly bounded, rationality. Apart from the theoretical problems this axiom of economics raises, empirical evidence seems to suggest that online consumers simply do not act rationally in an economic sense (Berendt *et al.*, 2005; Moores, 2005). The lack of rationality also renders the concept of trust as a mechanism of risk management deeply problematic (Ciborra, 2004).

The positive view of trust tends to see technology as well as the regulatory environment as objectively given and suitable objects of research. It thereby neglects the richer conceptualisation of technology, such as that offered by science and technology studies (Howcroft *et al.*, 2004). It also neglects the close relationship of regulations and technology (Reagle, 1996) as well as the uncertainty surrounding much of the current institutional context of e-commerce (Berleur and Poullet, 2006).

Moreover, it implies that it is possible and permissible to create trust using technical means. This may simply be a conceptual misunderstanding, because trust as characteristic of human relationships cannot be digitised, transmitted or displayed (Fukuyama, 1998; Rutter, 2001; Grabner-Kräuter, 2002). Indeed, some of the technical means of trust creation, such as enhancement of security, may have the opposite effect of disabling trust (Nissenbaum, 1999). And even the proponents of trust creation admit that perfect adherence to their proposals will not guarantee the development of trust (Ba and Pavlou, 2001; Mayer *et al.*, 1995).

The simplified concept of trust underlying positive research pays little attention to the negative sides of the term. As Flores and Solomon (1997, p. 69) put it, 'being trusted [...] can be an awful burden, unwanted, undeserved, manipulative or coercive'. Trust can have a range of detrimental effects. Husted (1998) argues that trust can be used for the exclusion of groups such as women, misallocation of capital, nepotism, corruption and the promotion of illegal behaviour. The reason for this is that trust is a strong mechanism for social control (Alpern,

1997; Kumar *et al.*, 1998; Gallivan and Depledge, 2003), which can lead to oppression. Trusting can thus be a problem, and the disposition to trust can be likened to naïveté (Gefen, 2000). In many instances, consumers may be better served by distrusting vendors, rather than trusting them. This poses a problem for trust research, which emphasises the possibilities of increasing trust because 'increasing trust between buyer and seller in business exchanges may not be altogether a noble quest' (Browne and Blank, 1997, p. 156).

The ethical nature of trust

One aspect of trust that the positive view cannot do justice to is the area of ethics and morality. A central and usually unexamined assumption of positive work on trust is that it is 'good', which arguably includes moral goodness (Nissenbaum, 1999; Brenkert, 1997). The recognition of the moral nature of trust can be explicit or implicit (Bews and Rossouw, 2002). This moral quality of trust exists independent of its faculty of improving economic interaction (Harris *et al.*, 2004). At the same time, the ethical aspect of trust is arguably a necessary precondition for its economic benefits to materialise (Jones and Bowie, 1998). Furthermore, trust can be described in terms of many of the traditional ethical theories. It is based on and expresses a duty (Hosmeh, 1995), which reflects the importance of obligations in a functioning society (Hollis, 1994). It can be described in terms of values, which again is a frequently used concept in moral philosophy (Brenkert, 1998; Donaldson and Dunfee, 1999). Trust can be seen as either a virtue in itself (Koehn, 1997; Flores and Solomon, 1997; Solomon and Flores, 2001) or an expression of traditional virtues such as friendship (Koehn, 1997; Browne and Blank, 1997), honesty (Lewicki and Stevenson, 1997), benevolence (McKnight *et al.*, 2002) or authenticity (Solomon and Flores, 2001). Trust is defined by the fact that it concerns a human relationship, and all relationships affect others and thus have an ethical quality (Alpern, 1997; Johnson, 2001; Harris *et al.*, 2004). Relationships are based on communication, and it has been argued that communication of any kind necessarily carries ethical connotations (Habermas, 1983, 1991). Finally, some of the conditions of trust as discussed in the e-commerce literature, notably security (Giddens, 1984) and privacy (Introna, 2000), are not just technicalities but touch on fundamental human needs and are preconditions for the development of autonomous moral humans.

I have emphasised the moral and ethical quality of trust in this critique of the positive view because it demonstrates the complexity of the concept, which a positive approach arguably cannot capture. Moral norms must be reflected ethically in order to avoid becoming hardened and sedimented into pure domination. For this, a flexible and dynamic understanding of the moral issue in question is required. A purely observational and behaviourist approach is not capable of understanding the internal states of agents and thus of capturing their view of trust. Furthermore, the issue of ethics is linked to the critical approach, which provides the theoretical grounding of my main critique of the positive view of trust.

A critical view of trust

In this section I will first introduce some of the concept of critical theory and then discuss the findings of a critical discourse analysis of some of the leading texts of the positive view of trust in e-commerce.

Some further critical concepts

In my earlier introduction of critical research in IS I did not cover the history of all critical concepts. There are several of these concepts that are closely linked to critical theory, in particular to its Marxist stream. The concepts in question are those of commodification, reification and ideology. A term used in critical research that captures all these is 'fetish'. Fetish, as I will use the term here, goes back to Marx's 'Capital' (1998), to his description of economic exchange during the development of capitalism. Marx distinguishes between the exchange value and the use value of items. In capitalism, because of the importance of private property, things become commodities, which means that their value is measured in money. Exchange value and use value consequentially become independent of one another. The originally social nature of the exchange of goods turns into a depersonalised process, which is facilitated by commodities. People desire commodities despite the fact that they have little use for them. All aspects of society are increasingly commodified, including the most intimate personal characteristics, such as the employee's working power. Commodities acquire the status held by fetishes in indigenous cultures because they represent powers and are accepted by individuals without regard to their actual usefulness.

This concept of fetishism is closely linked to the concepts of reification and ideology. Reification is the process whereby social structures become solid, become things (*res* is Latin for 'thing'), which then cease to be the subject of social negotiation (Feenberg, 1991). Reification is one aspect of ideology, which is often understood to be the collection of generally accepted but one-sided beliefs. Ideology in the critical tradition stands for the way power relations influence beliefs and perceptions in such a way as to promote particular interests and stabilise one-sided and alienating relationships.[1] This leads us to the last concept of importance here, namely rationality. Commodity fetishism and the related ideology and reification are a direct result of a particular way of viewing the world, which is based on a specific type of rationality.

Evidence of fetishism in e-commerce trust research

In order to provide evidence to support my claim that current e-commerce trust research displays characteristics of fetishism, I used the Habermas-inspired type of critical discourse analysis (CDA) introduced in Chapter 9 concerning ICT and empowerment in Egypt. To repeat my caution concerning this way of collecting data: critical discourse analysis is based on the hermeneutic circle, which means that there is a circular interaction between speaker (or writer) and audience (Gadamer, 1990). Listeners' (or readers') understanding depends on their prior

Table 11.3 Critical concepts relating to e-commerce trust

Critical concept	Explanation
Reification	Trust becomes a thing, separate from its social contexts and history
Commodification	Trust becomes a good that can be traded like any other commodity
Ideology	A particular world-view that privileges certain interests and hides this fact by making the current state of affairs appear natural
Fetishism	Trust acquires the status of an independent entity that interacts with humans of its own accord

knowledge, which helps them understand the speaker and further their understanding. The meaning of a text is therefore not objectively given but depends on the understanding of the listener or reader. CDA therefore does not claim to be able to unearth objective truth about a discourse but opens new avenues for the understanding and interpreting of texts. The results of the CDA that I will now introduce are thus not objective findings in the way traditional IS methodologies seem to promise, but subjective perceptions that are made explicit. They thus promise to facilitate the expansion of knowledge by enabling new avenues of discussion.

I chose seven academic papers dealing with e-commerce trust from the most prominent IS journals: *MIS Quarterly, Information Systems Research* and the *Journal of Management Information Systems*. The papers (Ba and Pavlou, 2001; Bhattacherjee, 2002; Gefen *et al.*, 2003; Gefen, 2004; McKnight *et al.*, 2002; Pavlou and Gefen, 2004; Pennington *et al.*, 2004) were chosen on the basis of their topic, namely issues of trust of individual consumers in e-commerce. Other papers on trust, such as trust in virtual teams or trust between businesses, were excluded because they might have given rise to different issues and be based on a different understanding of trust. The practical approach to evidence collection was that I made a list of terms and ideas based on the literature review, which indicated what claims about trust were likely to be made. In addition, there were claims that I expected to be able to shed light on the role of ideology, reification and fetishism in trust research. I then coded the papers, noting the occurrence of different claims as well as the wording in a database. An overview of all claims identified and collected can be found in Appendix B. I will now discuss the most pertinent claims within this stream of e-commerce trust discourse, divided by types of claim.

Truth claims in e-commerce trust research

The vast majority, namely 438 of 685 of the claims identified during the CDA were truth claims. This is probably not surprising, given that all papers analysed were academic research papers. The majority of the truth claims were descriptive of trust. All the aspects of trust discussed so far were mentioned. However, trust as a means of risk management or uncertainty reduction was mentioned 62 times and the nature of trust as a belief or expectation 56 times. Another salient aspect was that the benefits of trust were strongly emphasised. There were 78 instances that emphasised that trust can facilitate economic exchange and 30 which clearly stated that trust leads to financial benefits. Another important aspect was that there were 25 instances of economic rationality and express utility maximisation being imputed to market participants.

The need for trust was supported by 22 claims about the disadvantages of e-commerce, most of which could presumably be overcome by installing trust. There were a fair number of omissions in the claims. These were mostly taken from the 'limitation' sections of the paper, where the authors discussed the shortcomings of their approaches. Finally, the papers also mentioned problems of trust frequently, with references to the conceptual confusion concerning the concept of trust being mentioned 21 times.

Legitimacy claims in e-commerce trust research

The second biggest group of claims identified during the CDA were claims concerning the legitimacy of the texts. Fourteen claims referred to the way research was legitimated, namely academic theories and mathematical or statistical validity. In fact, claims of mathematics and statistics as source of legitimacy pervaded all papers. I will return to them in the next subsection as a 'meta-claim'. The texts included a range of assumptions about trust and about research in general. The biggest group of implied assumptions (71) concerned the idea that it was possible to create trust in some way. This was linked to the idea that trust can be measured and, more specifically, quantified (22). Of further interest were assumptions about research. Of the 51 claims identified here, the majority claimed that it was the purpose of research to increase understanding. However, these were often directly linked to practical applicability of the knowledge found. A further interesting aspect concerned assumptions about appropriate treatment of research subjects. Finally, there were 29 claims that clarified the limitations of the research undertaken.

Other claims in e-commerce trust research

The CDA did not find any clear and unambiguous sincerity or authenticity claims. These are problematic in the best of circumstances because sincerity of the speaker can never be observed directly. All that can be observed is a certain use of language that may suggest that the author does not fully believe or support his or her statements. Since all the papers were academic texts, they did not contain any clearly misleading metaphors or false assurances. Similarly, there were few claims concerning the clarity of the texts. They were all written competently, following academic standards. Where there was lack of clarity, this referred to the mathematical jargon used, and this clearly depends on the prior knowledge of the reader.

This leads to the last types of claims which emerged during the CDA. When I was undertaking the CDA, it became increasingly clear to me that the texts contained a number of claims which seemed to be obvious to the authors but which could not be linked to individual statements. I call these claims meta-claims. The first meta-claim concerns the audience. In order to be able to follow the texts, the reader must have a high level of competence in at least the areas of economics, game theory, and statistical methods in social sciences. Without these, the main narrative is impossible to understand, and the way the hypotheses are supported or rejected cannot be followed. Another meta-claim concerns the objectivity of research. All the texts in question clearly imply that research is there to give a true description of an objectively existing world. Social sciences can use the methods of natural sciences to increase our understanding of the world. Finally, there is a related meta-claim of quantifiability. This means that all papers implicitly agree that social phenomena can usefully be measured and quantified. Of course, these are some of the basic tenets of positive research, but it is interesting that they are so ingrained that there seems to be no need even to mention them.

Critique of e-commerce trust

The CDA supported my contention that current mainstream e-commerce trust research treats trust as a fetish. Critical theory can help us see the reasons for this as well as the mechanisms that facilitate it. One of these mechanism is the positivist world-view. As this issue has been discussed in depth already, I will not elaborate on it here. The only remark I would like to make here is that the positive research does not even seem to be able to fulfil its self-professed purpose of providing general knowledge for practical applications. The empirical findings are always limited to a very specific subset of subjects and have to contend with all sorts of limitations (students as subject, self-selection bias, omission of disappointed customers, etc.) such that they simply could not be generalised, even if generalisability were unproblematic, which is arguably not the case (see Lee and Baskerville, 2003). The authors tend to be frank about this in their discussion of limitations, which, however, does not stop them from making sweeping recommendations. Furthermore, the research will be difficult to apply because it is clearly not written for practitioners, who for the greater part would find it highly difficult to follow the narratives.

The value of the CDA is that it allows the researcher to understand the beliefs and assumptions that underpin a social reality. It is thus worthwhile to extract shared assumptions of the analysed texts in order to see how they relate to issues of ideology, reification and fetishism. The best starting point for the analysis of assumptions is probably a look at shared assumptions about the concept of trust. The texts under consideration all provided a lengthy and quite comprehensive review of the literature on trust. At the same time, there was almost unanimous recognition that trust is a deeply complex concept that is impossible to capture in full during positive research. All the papers therefore chose one or several aspects of trust that they deemed to be of central interest and researched this in depth. The underlying assumption clearly is that complex social relationships can be split up into parts without significant loss of the overall phenomenon. This explains why conventional trust research can investigate particular aspects of trust, such as calculative trust or institutional influences, while at the same time ignoring other important aspects such as the ethical and moral nature of trust. The pragmatic explanation of this is that calculative properties of trust are easily measured whereas the internal view of subjects, including their moral norms and ethical reasoning, is not. This is nevertheless problematic, even from the positive point of view, because a purely rational and calculative view of trust is not capable of explaining how trust can function (Dasgupta, 2000).

The concept of trust that underlies traditional e-commerce trust research is thus impoverished. The rational and calculative faculties of economic subjects are emphasised to the detriment of aspects that are difficult or impossible to measure. On the grounds of such an impoverished view of trust it can be explained why there is no debate about the merits of quantifying trust measures. It also explains why the concept of risk and risk management, which are often described in statistical terms, appeals to positive scholars. This view of trust illuminates the underlying tenets and indicates how critical theory can help understand traditional e-commerce trust research

Reification and commodification of trust

It is thus clear that trust in e-commerce is treated as a thing, as an object. The relational aspects of trust are undervalued for the sake of better scientific measurement. Another indicator of the reification of trust is the unquestioned belief in quantification. If trust is an object, then it can be measured and quantified. Reification thus takes place literally, in that a complex social construct becomes a thing. At the same time, traditional e-commerce trust research also contributes to the reification of this approach by presenting it as natural. Questions and concerns about the underlying ontology and epistemology are simply not asked, and it is presented as natural that one can do research on trust this way. At the danger of stating the obvious, I would like to remind the reader that this is by no means natural. It is arguably possible to measure and quantify trust only by removing much of its phenomenological content. An analogy that may enlighten this is the concept of love, which arguably is similar to trust in many respects. One could no doubt undertake similar studies using 'love' instead of 'trust', but few people would agree that the results would have much to do with what we typically mean when we say 'love'. Some might even go so far as to say that it is not permissible to objectify, reify and quantify love because that would change its character. It would lead from love to prostitution.

The objectification of trust goes hand in hand with its commodification. Because trust has become an object that can be measured, one can also give it a price tag. The studies analysed here do not go so far as to quantify the financial value of trust, but it is not fundamentally difficult to imagine its being done. Commodification thus leads to trust being something that can be bought and sold and that is subject to market mechanisms.

Ideology of e-commerce trust research

Ideologies have been defined as shared views of the world that promote particular interests. The CDA in this analysis produced evidence of several shared ideological beliefs. One set of ideological beliefs can be summarised under the heading of 'methodological individualism'. This stands for the assumption that actions are fundamentally based on individuals who are endowed with a (possibly bounded) economic rationality. That means the individual actor will act in such a way as to maximise his or her expected utility. This view leaves little room for considerations of the history of interaction or for any sort of collective action. Most of the papers reviewed here clearly concentrated on the individual and his perceptions. The only exception, the paper by Pavlou and Gefen (2004), which looks at trust in a collective of sellers, still does so from the point of view of the individual buyer.

Methodological individualism is based on economic rationality. This comprises a set of characteristics that neo-classical economics supposes subjects to have. It culminates in the already mentioned maximisation of expected utility. There has been much debate about this and many attempts to enrich the idea from within and from outside economics. The problem is that it is based on unrealistic beliefs (complete information, complete utility preferences, high information processing speed, etc.). Beyond the criticism that the assumptions are unrealistic, there is also a lively debate as to whether they are admissible and desirable. The economically rational subject is fundamentally egotistical. That does not mean that it is immoral, since it can have moral preferences. However, it has been argued that promoting this type of rationality as a descriptive tool can have undesirable social consequences and render individuals more self-centred.

The ideological beliefs linked to economic rationality and methodological individualism are directly linked to the theoretical and practical bases of capitalism. From *The Wealth of Nations*, first published in 1776 (Smith, 1986), onwards, capitalist theory has emphasised the role and capabilities of the individual. Marx's contribution was to show the limits of this individualistic approach and point out the importance of economic structures and the power they exert on the individuals. Capitalist ideology hides such power structures and ascribes responsibility to individuals. A good example of this in the current research is the complete lack of attention to socio-economic class.

Even though e-commerce is open only to individuals who fulfil a number of conditions that typically locate them in the western middle class (literacy, some above-basic education, access to IT, financial wealth, ability to use payment mechanisms, etc.), the studies in question do not touch upon issues of class. E-commerce has an impact on digital divides because it can reduce transaction costs, but only for those who are in the privileged position of being able to participate in it in the first place. Such classical critical concerns with economic structure and power relationships are systematically ignored in positive trust research.

Finally, e-commerce trust research caters mostly to the holders of power. Even though all the studies investigated consumer perceptions, none of them takes the consumer seriously. The stakeholders to whom the research caters are fellow academics and e-commerce businesses and their managers. The overarching purpose of the research is to identify trust mechanisms in order to facilitate the creation of trust with the aim of enabling transactions, which will lead to corporate profits. There is an implicit belief in the congruence of the interests of businesses and consumers that is never explained or justified.

Overall, one can conclude that trust is indeed treated as a fetish in positive e-commerce trust research. The concept of trust is impoverished, objectified and made a commodity. The commodity is being consumed for the purpose of consuming it, not because anyone has any intrinsic need for it. It becomes independent of its creators. The research is built on a number of ideologies and hides this fact by treating contentious choices and assumptions as natural and not in need of explication.

Should we trust positive e-commerce trust research?

Positive researchers might counter the critical arguments by pointing out that e-commerce transactions are highly artificial and particular types of interaction. As such, they do not involve the rich texture of face-to-face trust. The concentration on particular aspects of trust can thus be justified. To further this debate, one can apply the considerations of trust research to the outputs of the research itself. Trust research has functions similar to those of trust itself, namely to reduce complexity, help manage risks and promote transactions. The crucial question now is whether trust research can fulfil its self-professed goal of contributing to the building of trust and contributing to overall utility and convince its audience that it is trustworthy.

The answer to me seems to be negative. There are several reasons for this. First, it seems doubtful whether the results of positive trust research can support its aims even from within the positive perspective. The research contains too many caveats and limitations to produce general conclusions. The concept of trust is reduced to the point where it does not reflect consumers' perception. Positive trust research can thus at best offer anecdotal evidence which may or may not be useful to practitioners. Finally, the alleged intended audience – businesses and managers – will hardly be able to understand the published output of the research. These internal problems of the positive approach are well known and some of them have been discussed in the 'rigour versus relevance' debate in IS (Benbasat and Weber, 1996; Benbasat and Zmud, 1999; Ives *et al.*, 2004), so I do not have to elaborate on them.

However, there are even more serious problems linked to the approach. On a very basic level, one can argue that the attempt to engender trust is a performative self-contradiction. Saying 'trust me' implies that the other does not trust me and may have good reasons for not trusting me. By asking people for trust one thus reveals that one may not deserve it (Brenkert, 1997). A similar phenomenon has been described as the self-promoter's paradox in the management of legitimacy (Suchman, 1995). With regard to positive trust research, this is exacerbated by the narrowing of the concept of trust. If one treats humans as economically rationally *homines economici*, then one must assume that they will attempt to free-ride if possible (Koehn, 1997). Monitoring and enforcement costs will go up and trust will thus lead to higher costs, rather than the lower ones expected. Some authors have indeed noticed the problem of creating a 'market of lemons' by promoting trust (Pavlou and Gefen, 2004, p. 54).

The main contribution of this chapter, however, is the reading of trust from the viewpoint of critical theory. Using these findings explains even more clearly why positive trust research is not trustworthy. The CDA has found evidence of ideology, reification, commodification and thus of the fetishisation of trust. That means that positive e-commerce trust research first impoverishes the concept of trust to the point where it has little to do with the ordinary usage of the word. It furthermore hides this transformation of the concept by treating it as natural, and proving this by empirically and quantitatively measuring it. This serves to hide the ideological assumptions and the particular interests hidden in the approach. Trust becomes a commodity that can be traded. This hides the fact that the main interests promoted are those of commercial businesses. The problems of trust are downplayed and trust misuse is ignored. The fact that trust is a form of social control is generally not mentioned.

The most salient aspect missing from positive trust research is that of ethics and morality. While there are numerous references to the fact that trust is related to ethics, the actual treatment of the term rarely touches upon it. Furthermore, where moral behaviour is included, it leaves no space for an adequate understanding of ethical reasoning. This, however, renders trust lifeless and unconvincing. When I trust you, then this says something of importance about our relationship. If trust is limited to calculations of utility maximisation in commercial exchange, then most of the moral underpinnings of the mechanisms of trust become redundant. Trust changes its nature and loses the binding moral quality that it has in face-to-face interaction. Critical research thus provides us with further reasons why the question in the heading of this section should be answered in the negative. There are good reasons not to trust positive e-commerce trust research.

The argument of course does not stop here. An interesting question could be why the positive view is propagated despite its shortcomings. Critical theory is able to shed light on the mechanisms that lead to this particular approach and the way it sustains itself. Another interesting area for further exploration is trust in environments similar to e-commerce and trust beyond electronic interaction. Finally, the current chapter leads to questions about the assumptions and research approaches in other areas of information systems.

12 The ideological use of privacy and security

In the previous chapter I argued that trust, a deeply moral notion, could become reified, commodified and fetishised, partly because its moral content (as well as its additional social connotations) has been ignored by positive IS research. This does not mean, however, that a consideration of ethics will solve all problems that the positive view raises. In this chapter I will give a counter-example, one based on the recognition of the moral content of privacy and security. These concepts are used for ideological purposes precisely because they are morally relevant.

As I have already indicated in Chapter 10, which concerns management issues of privacy, privacy and data protection are among the prime problems of the information society. Many of us are concerned by the fact that electronic data about us can be used for purposes beyond our control. Privacy therefore has a close relationship with security. If data about us is not secure, then this lack of security can threaten privacy. This line of argument suggests that privacy requires security. A somewhat contradictory argument would be that in order for security to be guaranteed, we need to limit privacy. If all information about everyone were known, then security threats would be much easier to address and sanction. In this scenario, privacy and security seem to be mutually exclusive. One aspect of this problematic relationship between privacy and security is that there is no generally agreed-upon definition of either term. There is also no agreement on how privacy and security are to be protected or enforced (by ethics, the law, markets or other mechanisms) or who should assume responsibility for them (the state, the individual, organisations, etc.) (see Stahl, 2004).

Briefly, the intersection of privacy and security is a conceptual muddle and consequently characterised by policy vacuums (Moor, 1985, 2000a, 2004). Both concepts have ethical relevance. At the same time, they attract a considerable amount of attention from the commercial sector because of their potential to determine the success or failure of many business ventures, most obviously e-commerce activities. Both are closely related to the issue of trust discussed in the preceding chapter. The location of privacy and security on the fault line of a variety of discourses is one of the reasons for some of the problematic use of the concepts that this chapter will discuss.

The ethics of privacy and security

The main argument of this chapter is that there are discourses concerning privacy and security that focus on the ethical quality of the concepts and that the resulting ethical connotation of the terms is used to promote particular interests. I have detailed the ethical nature of privacy in Chapter 10 and will therefore concentrate on the argument why security is of ethical value.

Security, at least with regard to computing, seems to be a more straight-forward concept than privacy. There are different areas and topics of security ranging from national and military security to the security of one's personal belongings. The topic of this chapter, computer or information systems security, can have an influence on many of these. There are general definitions, such as the classical one by Landwehr *et al.* (2001, p. 2), which states that a system is secure 'if it adequately protects information that it processes against unautho-rized disclosure, unauthorized modification, and unauthorized withholding (also called denial of service)'. Unfortunately, the text goes on to say that no practical system can achieve these goals simultaneously and that security is inherently relative. In an earlier paper, Landwehr (1981) points out that even in strictly structured social systems such as the American military, security is never unam-biguous.

Security is thus similar to privacy in that most people think that it is import-ant but they find it more difficult to agree on what actually constitutes security (Anderson, 2004) and why it is important. Security has an economic aspect (Camp and Lewis, 2004), but its importance goes far beyond financial consider-ations. Security is important for all of us individually but, given the lack of agreement on the concept of security, there is no generally accepted behaviour that would express security concerns and it has been argued that people act inconsistently or self-contradictorily with regard to security. Berendt *et al.* (2005), for example, discuss a study which seems to indicate that users voice different preferences with regard to security and privacy from the ones they actually act upon.

The main question of interest here is whether and in what way security can be seen as an ethical concept. One main argument for the moral quality of security is that it seems to be a psychological need, which Giddens (1984, p. 50) terms 'ontological security'. Security is thus important for the ability to interact with others in a self-confident manner. It is also required to develop relationships of trust with others (Viega *et al.*, 2001).

A main argument for the moral quality of security is thus based on individual needs and perceptions as well as the impact of security on interaction. However, there are also aggregate issues of security that have a moral side. Security in computing is a major cost factor, with estimates of overall cost of security (or lack thereof) varying widely but always of the order of billions of dollars, euros, pounds, etc. Such costs are of course a moral issue from a utilitarian point of view and they also prevent society from investing these resources in other worthy causes. Security issues also play a large role in computer crime and digital forensics. The ubiquity of computing in modern society renders it an important ingredient of many types of crime (Wall and Paroff, 2005). Hacking and viruses are a major concern. Apart from the economic issues they raise, they are also related to criminal activities, and breaches of criminal law are generally viewed as being morally problematic. Another moral issue on the social level is that security can be seen as an externality (Camp and Wolfram, 2004). Externalities (and public goods) have long been recognised as being important ethical issues of markets (Gauthier, 1986).

On a more general level, the question of the moral quality of security can be described in terms of the harms that its infringements would constitute (Nissenbaum, 2005). This leads her to an interesting discussion of two types of security related to computing: technical or individual security and political or social security. Nissenbaum argues that these two are often conflated even though they are fundamentally different and require different technical or political solutions. Drawing on the Copenhagen School, she discusses the concept of 'securitisation'. Securitisation stands for the depiction of a possible risk in terms of a fundamental threat to an important entity, such as the nation-state. The securitisation of a risk means that it becomes a moral imperative to protect the entity in question. This implies a strong moral standing of security that overrides opposing concerns. Nissenbaum argues that computer security has been securitised in particular following the 2001 terrorist attacks on New York and Washington. Such securitisation leads to possible solutions that are arguably not relevant for individual computer risks such as hacking, viruses, etc. Nissenbaum's considerations are of relevance to this argument because the process of securitisation of computers and ICT contribute to the high moral standing of security that makes it a suitable tool for ideological misuse, as I shall discuss.

Privacy and security

Having established that privacy and security are notions with moral content and ethical justification, I will use this section to briefly discuss their relationship. When we look at the use of the concepts in a commercial environment, it will be important to know how they relate to each other.

Given the complexity and multi-faceted nature of both concepts involved, there is no clear and unambiguous description of their relationship. The literature shows examples of different conceptualisations of the link between privacy and security. In some respects, most notably from a law enforcement view, they are contradictory. Individual privacy preferences, where they involve criminal activity, will run counter to security needs. There is a wide variety of legal activity on both sides of the Atlantic, ranging from the US Patriot Act to the European Convention on Cybercrime, which bears testimony to this. Governments everywhere are tempted to limit privacy rights in order to promote security considerations (Forester and Morrison, 1994).

At the same time, one can argue that privacy and security overlap and reinforce each other. On the level of the individual user, security can be seen as a precondition of privacy because a lack of security may allow unauthorised access to data, which in turn, will jeopardise privacy. But even in the field of criminal activity it has been pointed out that decreased privacy can lead to a decrease in security because guarding privacy via anonymity allows some individuals to interact with the police and give tip-offs, which they might not do if their identity were known (Shostack and Syverson, 2004). Another reason for overlap of the concepts is that they both have to do with control, with strong control of personal data apparently equating to privacy as well as security (Camp, 2001). There are several technologies which can be used in this sense and which support privacy as well as security. These include encryption (Tavani, 2000) and so-called privacy-enhancing technologies (PET) (Tavani and Moor, 2001) or anonymising technologies (Camp, 2001).

This technical overlap of security and privacy can be explained at least partially by the fact that they serve the same moral ends. Both cater to the individual psychological need to feel protected from outside interference. They are part of the 'protective cocoon' which facilitates the building of identity (Brown, 2000). Both are required to build trust (Rutter, 2001) and therefore for the establishment of sound relationships (Hoffman *et al.*, 1999). Trust and security are thus mutually enforcing moral goods for the individual, even though an overemphasis on security can also create problems of trust (Nissenbaum, 1999). They also lead to social well-being and the creation of general utility. Respecting them is a sign of respecting individuals and their autonomy. It is also a sign of a morally good character disposition. The moral value of privacy as well as security can thus be explained by the most important ethical theories from Kantian deontology to utilitarianism and virtue ethics. Having established this much, we can now proceed to look at ways in which the concepts of trust and security are used, which do not necessarily conform to their moral nature.

Ideology and its critique

I have very briefly touched on the concept of ideology in the preceding chapter, where ideology was described as one aspect of the commodification and reification of trust. In this chapter I will elaborate on the concept in more depth. This will lead to a discussion of ideological issues likely to be involved in debates on privacy and security as identified by the literature.

Ideology

Ideology is a central concept of critical research in information systems as well as critical research in general (Freeden, 2003; Hawkes, 2003; McLellan, 1995). Ideologies limit the ability of the individual to perceive the world and they are therefore opposed to the main aim of critical research, namely emancipation. Within critical research the concept of 'ideology' plays a central role. Fairclough (2003, p. 9) suggests that ideologies be defined as 'representations of aspects of the world which can be shown to contribute to establishing, maintaining and changing social relations of power, domination and exploitation'. It is important to see that ideologies are not necessarily falsehoods or based on bad faith (Schumpeter, 1994). Instead, ideologies are taken-for-granted, shared conceptualisations or constructions of (social) reality. The problem is that such constructions will often become reified and taken for absolute truth (McAulay *et al.*, 2002). These objectified constructions typically hide vested interests and power relationships (Hirschheim and Klein, 1994). Such hidden agendas are problematic when they can no longer be discussed, which is the case when they become recognised as natural 'facts'. Ideology therefore makes it harder, or even impossible, for individuals to reach their full potential. It thus precludes emancipation (Hirschheim *et al.*, 1995).

Ideology in ICT

How can we identify instances of ideology in ICT? If the kind of ideology we are concerned with is the reification of social constructions for the benefit of particular groups, then we need to pay attention to situations where certain groups or individuals are advantaged to the detriment of others. Of particular concern for this chapter are such instances where the moral nature of privacy and security is used to limit discourses, with the aim of facilitating gains for certain groups or individuals.

One could thus speak of ideology in cases where one can identify the promotion of, say, security as a moral and thereby universal good in such a way that it privileges certain groups. This is often the case in ICT security, which is frequently designed specifically to protect certain interests, typically those of the vendors and their customers, with little regard to other possible stakeholders. Furthermore, it can be used even more specifically to protect the interests of vendors to the detriment even of their customers, who can be economically locked in (Anderson, 2004).

One could argue that such situations are not particularly serious because, in a functioning market, customers could seek different suppliers. They can do so, however, only if they are aware of the problem. This is where ideology as reification plays a role. If the state of affairs is perceived as natural and unchangeable, as the result of developments which cannot be influenced, then those who are privileged no longer need to justify themselves for their advantages. Such technologies are then removed from democratic scrutiny (Feenberg, 1999) and they can be promoted using moral arguments including arguments relating to privacy and security. Pertinent examples of this might be the assumption that the introduction of surveillance technology such as CCTV cameras will lead to a reduction of crime (Lyon, 2003) or that the use of ICT in teaching will lead to better educational outcomes (Sahay, 2004). While there is a long tradition of criticising the idea of technological determinism, it can still be found as a powerful aspect of governing ideologies.

Ideologies are generally accepted social constructions and as such they are based on a shared use of language. Indeed, language is not only the vehicle of ideology, but its essence. When one thinks about the relationship of ideology and ICT it is thus important to concentrate on linguistic aspects. Proponents of certain ideological interests often use rhetorical devices to promote their view. A frequently used one is the use of metaphors. Such metaphors, if used successfully, will take on a life of their own and render the originating interest invisible. They can be turned into reifications when they shape the generally accepted definition of technology or its properties. I will return to the use of metaphors and their relevance to critical research in the following chapter.

These uses of ideology have many manifest implications. They lead to the hardening of social practices, for example in the intellectual property area. By withdrawing technology from discourse, ideology establishes precedents that become self-reinforcing. One example of this would be a hierarchical information systems development process. There is much literature suggesting that participative development projects have a variety of advantages from an ethical as well as a business perspective. However, if ICT is seen as fundamentally determined, then there is no need to have users or other stakeholders participate in design decisions. Emancipation cannot become part of the agenda.

Ideologies are not 'false' and cannot be proved wrong. It is arguably impossible to overcome ideologies. The appropriate way of dealing with ideologies is to expose them as what they are. By exposing them, they lose their naturalised character and become open to debate. If it can be shown that a certain group profits from ideological constructs, then the exposure of the ideology can force this group to seek new justifications of the status quo. One way of achieving this is to undertake a critical discourse analysis. For the purposes of this argument, I have done this, using the Habermas-inspired approach that I have used in several of the preceding chapters.

The ideology of privacy and security: some evidence

The main purpose of this argument is conceptual. It aims to show that the moral and ethical nature of privacy and security can lead to their misuse as ideological tools. If I left it with this conceptual argument, however, there is a high probability that the argument would be accused of 'armchair philosophising' that is, of having no bearing on the 'real world'. This raises the issue of remaining able to communicate with the wider IS community and beyond. Some readers might find it easier to accept the argument if it were provided with some external validity or examples. The critical discourse analysis (CDA) described in this section therefore provides evidence of the link or links between ideology and privacy/security.

For this purpose, the CDA needed to investigate texts emanating from organisations that have an interest in security and privacy but at the same time have vested interests in promoting a particular ideological view. A first task was thus to consider which organisation or organisations to investigate. The potential population included all commercial organisations involved in software or hardware. An obvious choice was therefore to look at Microsoft, which as the biggest software company in the world has developed a broad range of activities in the areas of privacy and security. Microsoft is the market leader in operating systems, and therefore its statements can be seen as representative of vendors to the end-user consumer market. Furthermore, Microsoft has often been criticised for its business practices and is seen by its detractors as a bad example of market dominance and misuse. It was therefore a reasonable starting point of the CDA to assume that Microsoft will use ideological devices to further its causes.

The next question was to decide which texts created by Microsoft to analyse. First, it was decided to use parts of the Microsoft website because they are easily accessible and, more importantly, because they represent the official views of the organisation. Such statements are therefore more suitable for a discourse analysis than, say, interview data, which has a more idiosyncratic character. It then had to be decided which part of the website was to be analysed. Two sections were chosen for detailed analysis: the 'Trustworthy Computing' and the 'Microsoft Vista' sites.

Validity claims in Microsoft's 'Trustworthy Computing' and 'Vista'

Windows Vista (www.microsoft.com/windowsvista) is the latest generation of Microsoft's operating system MS Windows. It is partly based on and closely linked with the considerations expressed in Microsoft's 'Trustworthy Computing' (TC) policy website (www.microsoft.com/mscorp/twc/default.mspx). The websites were downloaded and analysed in spring 2006, before the commercial launch of the Vista software. They have since changed their appearance and will thus be discussed using the past tense. Both websites outline the most important aspects of TC and Vista respectively to promote acceptance of these developments by potential users. It is the nature of websites to be dynamic and to contain links to other websites, so that limiting a discourse analysis to a website is necessarily a somewhat arbitrary endeavour. This is not overly problematic for the current research because its aim is to support the contention that moral concepts such as privacy and security can be used to promote ideology, rather than to carry out a comprehensive analysis of a certain text or organisation.

For this chapter, I analysed the two websites with regards to the validity claims concerning privacy and security they contained. The TC site was structured in an overview page which links to the five main components of TC: security, privacy, reliability, business practices and building momentum. Each of these (except 'building momentum') was broken down into three subsections titled 'overview', 'progress' and 'resources'. The TC introductory page summarised the aim of the TC initiative: 'Trustworthy Computing is a long-term, collaborative effort to provide more secure, private, and reliable computing experiences for everyone. This is a core company tenet at Microsoft and guides virtually everything we do.' This summary indicated the different validity claims raised by the site. The central truth claim was that MS takes TC seriously and was trying to promote and develop its components, including security and privacy. At the same time, it conceded that there 'is no single solution to resolve computer security issues', which was the reason for MS to explore all possible avenues to improve it.

In the rightness claims there was no overt reference to ethics or morality, but the website stated clearly that it was in compliance with 'global privacy laws'. Rightness also covers legitimacy, the assurance that one's claims are acceptable. MS promoted this by portraying itself as a responsible leader, with the term 'responsible leadership' being repeated in several different contexts. However, it was emphasised that MS does not act in isolation but collaborates closely with 'industry, law enforcement, and academia'.

The authenticity/sincerity claims portray MS as a diligent organisation trying hard to help and support customers. The TC website stated that MS is 'hard at work every day', that it 'shares [...] knowledge [and] learn[s] from others' and subscribes to the customers' 'right to control their personal information' and their right to be 'left alone' and have a trusted experience. Since authenticity claims can be explored by examining metaphors, the very concept of 'trustworthy computing' can be interpreted as a metaphor aimed to promote the image of sincerity.

The Vista website was structured in a similar way to the TC site but it was more clearly directed at end users and had a less formal and informational appearance. It was divided into three main areas: experience, features, and community. It contained a variety of claims regarding privacy and security, which are probably best summarised by the following quotation: 'At Microsoft, we recognize that privacy is a critical element of a secure computing experience.' Privacy was thus subsumed into security, which is recognised as a central aspect of Windows. Vista was meant to be 'the most secure version of Windows yet'. There were many instances where the document underlines the centrality of security for Vista from the perspective of private users, businesses and developers. Security features were integrated into the software and could be controlled and managed centrally.

The normative claims mirrored the emphasis on security. They underlined how increased security would render the tasks of systems administrators easier while allowing end users to engage in (apparently legitimate) activities such as enjoying television and music on their PC. Probably the strongest claim to legitimacy was linked to the protection of children. A centralised control function allowed children to be protected from innocently installing malware. Another function ('family safety settings') allowed parents to designate what children could do on the computer, including controlling their access to programs and websites, and keeping a log of all activity.

The authenticity/sincerity claims support the implication that MS was serious about helping its customers. The website used emotive images such as a lonely figure on a mountaintop in the twilight to express feelings of independence and strength. The 'features' part of the website started by displaying a young tattooed man of presumably African background holding a guitar, which expresses a connection to younger consumers and their wish for freedom. Another interesting sincerity claim was the metaphor of the word 'vista' itself. According to the *Oxford English Dictionary*, 'vista' can mean '[1] mental view or vision of a far-reaching nature'. This can be interpreted as implying that MS had recognised customers' needs (particularly for security) and had integrated them into its long-range vision.

Ideology in Microsoft's 'Trustworthy Computing' and 'Vista'

The discussion of the validity claims contained in MS's two websites under investigation will probably not surprise anyone. They project the image of a corporation interested in its customers' well-being and therefore sensitive to their moral concerns, including concerns relating to security and privacy. The interesting question therefore is whether there is evidence of instances of ideology and what the consequences of the promotion of such ideology might be.

One such instance is the use of rhetorical devices to cloak underlying problems. An example of such a device is the use of the term 'trustworthy computing', which MS adopted recently, having changed it from 'trusted computing' (Anderson, 2004). It is probably fair to say that MS is not trusted by a considerable part of the computer science and programming community. Trust is a complex social construct, but, as I have argued in depth in the preceding chapter, it is not something that can simply be created. There clearly seems to be a lack of trust in computing by users, largely due to a perceived lack of security and privacy (Cavusoglu, 2004). Microsoft uses a rather technical view of trust (Anderson, 2004) but does not elaborate on this concept in its websites. The emphasis on trustworthy computing is therefore misleading because it is an open question whether Microsoft's and its customers' understanding of trust are compatible. A similar issue arises with regard to the functionality of Vista. The website frequently cites issues of control and implies that it will give control to users ('Windows Vista puts you in control of what you want to do'). It is meant to create confidence in customers and improve their 'computing experience'. These are very problematic assertions, as I shall show.

Both websites privilege particular interests, most notably those of Microsoft and its paying customers. This goes counter to the nature of security problems, which are collective issues and cannot be solved by individual or sectoral activities. Among customers, corporate interests are privileged. Despite some of the emancipatory rhetoric, the website makes it clear that, internally, MS relies on hierarchical power structures to enforce its policies, including privacy policies. The validity claims raised on the website also use one of the most powerful instruments of ideology, that of reification. Most importantly, the website reifies both security and privacy. In practice this means that these two concepts become things – things which are still morally relevant but no longer open to debate and scrutiny. The way this is done is to present privacy and security as technical features which can be addressed in a technical way. The best example of this reification of a social construct is that MS aims to 'engineer privacy into [its] products during the product life cycle'. It thus becomes a matter of technical expertise, which MS has without doubt, to deal with this issue. This reification also allows a simplification of the complex relationship of privacy and security by subsuming privacy as an aspect of security.

This leads us to another ideological device, the hiding of contentious relationships. The equation or subsumption of privacy under security hides the fact that there is no simple law stating that more privacy will create more security or vice versa. In the 'privacy progress' part of the TC site, MS stated that it is committed to working with the police to deter hacking and other 'software sabotage' through proactive security practices. It ignores the fact that there may be good reasons for hacking. The law enforcement attitude leaves no room for legitimate expressions such as 'hacktivism'. By complying with laws on security and privacy without ethical reflection, MS promotes a one-sided understanding of complex issues. This recently backfired when Microsoft was criticised for complying with the Chinese government's request to curtail free speech on the internet. The one-dimensional narrative on the website, while serving corporate purposes, leaves no opening for dissenting voices and hides legitimate conflicts. It also camouflages the fact that many of the problems current developments are supposed to address, such as lack of security, are home-grown problems that have been caused by Microsoft's long-time lack of attention.

Another instance where the claims on the website hide an important moral issue has to do with control. MS Vista offers an unprecedented amount of control over user activities. This is described in positive terms as ease of administration and supervision of children. It is quite obvious, however, that the same technologies can be used to control employees and keep them under surveillance. I have earlier discussed the moral issues of workplace surveillance, but the reification of privacy hides these. Another completely hidden issue is the question of digital rights management (DRM). DRM raises a host of moral and legal challenges and, according to the literature, will be linked to MS Vista. The website does not discuss any of these issues, presumably because of the simplistic approach that MS will comply with legal requirements (which it often shapes) and thereby discharge its moral responsibilities.

Critical reflections on ideology in ICT

To pre-empt unnecessary criticism of the argument, I should clarify some points. The argument does not suggest that ideology can be overcome once and for all. Ideology is part of the pre-judgements that we require in order to function as social beings. It does suggest, however, that ideologies can be exposed and thereby put into perspective. Furthermore, this chapter should not be misread as merely another example of helpless Microsoft-bashing. Microsoft's websites were used because of the overwhelming market power of the corporation and because it exemplifies the issues raised here. A similar exercise could most probably be undertaken for the majority of ICT suppliers.

Another point of criticism might be that the argument does nothing more than state the obvious. Microsoft is a commercial entity and as such attempts to promote itself and its causes. While this is true, the interesting aspect of the chapter is that it demonstrates how official publications of corporations use and thereby reproduce ideological views. A statement to the effect that we should not believe promotional commercial publications would only show that communicative action seems to be impossible in our society, which, if true, should give us pause to consider whether this is what we as a society desire.

Where I hope the argument will promote the debate most clearly is in the relationship between ethics, technology and ideology. The unique angle elaborated by the chapter is that it is exactly the moral connotation of notions such as privacy and security that allows them to be used to uphold ideology. It is the moral recognition of privacy and the protection of children that allows Microsoft to promote a strict system of control which, if exposed as such, would be much more difficult to market. Similarly, security has now become such an obviously desirable goal that it can be used to override other legitimate democratic and moral concerns.

The argument, by its very nature, does not offer any solutions to these problems. It can only aim to raise attention and awareness and to promote discourse. In the tradition of critical research, its main aim is to provide a dissenting voice and to caution users not to take concepts at face value. This is particularly important for value-laden concepts because these values, positive as they may be, hold the potential to curtail debate and thereby allow for the promotion of ideology. In this sense, the argument should have an emancipatory effect. It will allow individuals to question the meaning of privacy and security and to require contextualisation of the terms. Doing so can help free us from false preconceptions and thus allow us to move, albeit incrementally, towards more freedom and autonomy.

13 The metaphor of evolution in e-commerce

A critical evaluation

Now that we have discussed the ideological use of concepts central to ICT and its management, in the previous chapter, this chapter will develop a similar argument, albeit one with regard to the influence of general discourses in ICT. I will analyse the influence of the use of the concept of evolution on discourses surrounding electronic commerce or e-commerce. This is one example of the use of concepts from non-related fields, in this case from biology, where the purpose of importing the concept is to come to a better understanding in IS. Such a use of non-related terms is not necessarily a problem and it can have positive consequences. What is often overlooked, however, is that there are negative sides to be considered. This is particularly true for concepts and ideas from the natural sciences and their application to social constructs such as e-commerce. E-commerce has driven technical as well as regulatory developments in the area of ICT. It has changed the nature of many commercial interactions and has offered new opportunities to many consumers. E-commerce has changed our understanding of important concepts as well as the nature of many industries. These changes are likely to continue and intensify.

E-commerce, like all human interaction, relies on properties of humankind that are a result of evolution. If humans had not evolved visual sight, then the use of screens on computers would not be useful. If humans could not reason abstractly, then they would not be able to link an electronic order with an expected delivery and the resulting utility. Some of the evolution that e-commerce relies on is of a cultural nature. Cultures evolve, and only successful cultures survive. One of the important cultural evolutions that e-commerce relies on is a widespread ability to read and write and do basic calculations. There is thus no denying the importance of our shared evolutionary background in e-commerce. Furthermore, e-commerce in its current form can itself be seen as the result of evolutionary processes that favoured certain business models or processes. The concept of evolution thus appears to be useful for comprehending different aspects of e-commerce.

However, I will argue that the evolution of e-commerce can also be understood as a metaphor. The use of this metaphor is not value neutral. It is not a purely descriptive category. Metaphors are carriers of accepted meaning. The use of metaphors implies certain contexts and understandings. I argue that the metaphor of e-commerce can be used as a device that favours particular interests.

The chapter begins with a discussion of the concepts and develops the relationship between e-commerce and evolution. The subsequent section concentrates on the use of metaphors in e-commerce. I briefly explore the use and effects of other metaphors in the area of e-commerce and information systems. By concentrating on ethical issues raised by e-commerce, I will then develop a critique of the use of the metaphor of evolution in e-commerce. The main argument is that evolution is a biological concept and as such can raise problems with regard to normative ethics. By choosing to depict e-commerce in Darwinian terms, a speaker can imply that it is a natural process that is not in need of intervention and regulation. Acceptance of this view can favour some market participants to the detriment of others.

Evolution and e-commerce

In this section I shall discuss the concepts of evolution as well as e-commerce and explore in what way it may be justifiable to speak of e-commerce as a phenomenon that is the product of evolution. It is important to note that I am not aiming to make strong claims on the truth of evolution of e-commerce. I am not saying that one cannot speak of evolution of e-commerce or that Darwinian concepts lead to false conclusions in this context. The main interest of this chapter is to explore how the concept of evolution can be used and is used.

Evolution

Etymologically, the term 'evolution' is derived from Latin *e* (out of) and *volatus* (rolled). Its original meaning referred to the unrolling of parchment books. It was only in the seventeenth century that its meaning changed to 'change', passing through discernible stages (see Giddens, 1984, p. 229). Until the middle of the nineteenth century, evolution referred primarily to embryological development. In its current meaning, the term describes the 'theory of the change of organic species over time' (Sloan, 2005). The current use of the term has been influenced by a number of authors but it is most closely associated with Charles Darwin's *Origin of Species*, published in 1859. Darwin's unique contribution was to link the concept of evolution with that of natural selection. Drawing on the observation that variations within species occur, he was able to explain the development of species over time as a reaction to the environment. This idea was revolutionary because it replaced, with a relatively simple mechanism, a natural teleology needed to explain the development of different species. Darwin later borrowed the term 'survival of the fittest' from Herbert Spencer, which further emphasised the mechanical nature of natural selection and evolution.

Darwin's concept of evolution was deeply contentious at the time because of its religious connotations. Most importantly, it no longer required the assumption of a supreme divine being to explain the way the world is. Darwin's idea has been interpreted as an attack on Christianity and other religious narratives that posit a Creator. A hundred and fifty years after their introduction, these debates are still not resolved, and are now enmeshed in disputes about creationism and intelligent design. Darwinian evolution has to contend with other critique as well (see Bringsjord, 2001) However, I will not follow these streams of criticism and instead take Darwinian evolution as the generally accepted theoretical basis for the explanation of the development of biological species.

Despite this general acceptance of evolution, I want to point out that there are limits to its use. Evolution is meant to describe the natural world and explain why there are different species. Since humans are an evolved species, it also applies to humanity. However, evolutionary theory is just that, namely a theory. Like all theories, it is a partial description of reality. As such, it is constitutive of our perception of reality, and arguably of reality itself. One needs to note, however, that no theory can claim to be comprehensive. This means that there are aspects of reality that a theory does not cover. Exclusive concentration on a theory blends out aspects of reality. In most cases this is to be desired. Theories help scholars describe phenomena, and they do this by providing a limited view of reality. Theories concentrate our attention. If, for example, a physicist is interested in the interactions between stellar bodies, he or she will use theories of gravitation, and maybe relativity, to describe these and possibly predict them. The physicist will accept that most aspects of the phenomena are made invisible in this approach (for example, the colour of the bodies, the question of whether alien intelligence exists on them, and the romantic view of them when seen from Earth). Such concentration on particular aspects is widely accepted and usually completely legitimate. It is nevertheless important to realise that it occurs, because in some cases it may become problematic.

E-commerce

In order to understand the relevance of e-commerce in this chapter, we need to briefly consider its advantages. The use of ICT in commercial transactions is usually held to decrease cost (Shin, 2003). This, in turn, is based on the perception that ICT moves markets closer to the models of neo-classical economics (see Zerdick *et al.*, 2001). ICT, and particularly the internet, allow suppliers and customers to find each other as well as information about products, prices and markets. In other words, the use of technology lowers transaction costs, including search costs, information costs, bargaining costs, decision costs, policing costs and enforcement costs. (see Welty and Becerra-Fernandez, 2001; Castells, 2000a). Transaction costs decrease, while the quality of markets increases (Spinello, 2000). Through to the use of technology, new economies of scale can be leveraged (Copeland and McKenney, 1988). Because of the acquisition of new customers, costs can be decreased, for example through disintermediation. Furthermore, the technology allows for network effects that increase the value of certain goods and services (Hanseth, 2000).

Despite these many advantages, e-commerce can also have downsides. These can be of a technical, financial, social or other nature. The one set of problems that I would like to emphasise here concerns ethics. Some of the ethical problems raised by e-commerce pertain to all capitalist exchange. There is a long history of debate of the relationship between ethics and commerce. Suffice it to say that commerce, as an example of human interaction, is of ethical relevance. That is not to say that ethics must rule every single action within a market. But one needs to recognise that the very idea of markets is based on (utilitarian) ethical ideas and that the purpose of markets is to contribute to the greater good of society. At the same time, ethics plays an important role in stabilising behaviour expectations and thereby facilitating successful interaction in the first place. I do not wish to be drawn into the details of the many debates that are being held in business ethics. The purpose of this paragraph is simply to underline that commerce in general, and hence, e-commerce is not an a-moral activity. There are good reasons for considering ethical implications of commercial relationships and to review and possibly regulate them for ethical reasons.

E-commerce as an evolved phenomenon

This review of the concepts of e-commerce and evolution shows that it is justifiable to speak of e-commerce as something that has evolved. Human characteristics that can be understood as the result of evolution strongly influence our use of technology and thus the development of e-commerce (Kock, 2005). Information is a central concept of evolution (Wiener, 1954), and it is therefore reasonable to assume that technology used to exchange information is of evolutionary relevance. Furthermore, markets can be likened to nature, and the process of biological evolution thus seems to play out in markets as well. One could thus say that liberal markets and societies mimic natural evolution (Rauch, 1993). Indeed, the relationship between markets and evolution goes even further. Darwin himself admitted that liberal economic theories of his time inspired his view of evolution (see Hawkes, 2003, p. 134).

At the same time, it should be clear that the concept and theory of evolution do not create a comprehensive description of e-commerce. Evolution is a macro-level descriptive theory that does not take into account the micro-level or individual view. From an evolutionary viewpoint the individual is of relatively little concern. Unless the individual carries a particular evolutionary advantage, he or she is not likely to make a difference to overall evolution of the species. An individual who is maladapted will simply not pass on his or her genes. For the theorist of evolution this is of little importance, but that clearly changes if we look at it from the point of view of the individual. Being able to interact successfully or pass on one's genes can be of the highest personal importance, irrespective of evolutionary theory. This is not an argument against evolution but an example that shows that evolution does not cover all aspects of social reality. Another such example, which is central to the current argument, is that focusing on evolution renders it impossible to develop a prescriptive ethics that would regulate contentious ethical issues arising from e-commerce, such as those indicated earlier. While morality can be described as a consequence of evolution, a theory of evolution is not capable of telling us what we should do – whether or how we should address ethical issues of e-commerce such as digital divides. The point I am making is that the evolutionary viewpoint is not the only one that can legitimately be applied to e-commerce. There are aspects of e-commerce that it cannot capture.

The conclusion to be drawn from this is that the use of the term 'evolution' in relation to e-commerce cannot provide a comprehensive and objective description of reality. In many cases it can better be understood as a metaphor. The use of metaphors with regard to technology, particularly ICT, is well researched and I will draw upon this research to further the argument that speaking of the evolution of e-commerce can have ideological roots and consequences.

Evolution of e-commerce as a metaphor

The *Encarta World English Dictionary* (1999, p. 1188) defines a metaphor as an 'implicit comparison; the application of a word or phrase to somebody or something that is not meant literally but to make a comparison'. This definition sounds inconspicuous, but metaphors can lead to problematic social consequences.

Since metaphors are an important use of language that facilitates understanding and interaction, metaphors play an important role in understanding technology. If research aims to promote emancipation, then it needs to be aware of the linguistic constructs that set the scene for the use of technology. This section will therefore look at why we use metaphors and then discuss examples of metaphors used with regards to technology.

Advantages of metaphors

We should be aware that everyday language is full of metaphors. The same is true, although maybe to a lesser degree, of much academic and scientific writing. It is therefore important to understand why this is so. The most fundamental reason for the use of metaphors seems to be the attempt to promote understanding by using a well-established point of reference. As Alveson and Deetz (2000) put it, the 'advantage of a metaphor is that it captures the imagination and provides a coherent image that one may stick to' (2000, p. 174). For researchers, a metaphor can provide a focus for empirical research but more generally it allows an audience to be enrolled into a particular view of the world.

Another important task of metaphors is the reduction of complexity. A well-established concept used as a metaphor can allow the audience easily to understand what aspects of a phenomenon are to be emphasised and which ones can be ignored. Like theories, metaphors are representations, but unlike theories they are easily understood (Weick, 1989). As an interesting twist on the current argument, it has been observed that our use of metaphors seems to be a consequence of evolution. Evolution has equipped our brains with the ability to quickly grasp certain concepts (concrete physical and spatial ones) that hunter–gatherers needed for survival. At the same time, we find it much more difficult to deal with abstract descriptions. Metaphors can help us bridge the gap and visualise complex situations (see Casacuberta, 2005).

Overall, it is important to understand the fundamental value of the use of metaphors. They allow us to communicate and achieve agreement where a purely abstract language would most likely fail. There is thus good reason to support the use of metaphors despite the knowledge that they are always misleading to some degree. Consequentially, Carnap (1980) argues for tolerance as regards metaphors. And it is therefore not surprising that metaphors are frequently used to explain the constituent phenomena of e-commerce, namely business and ICT.

Metaphors in e-commerce

The previous section has argued that metaphors have positive consequences and are an integral part of all communication, including professional communication. At the same time, it is important to note that metaphors are not value neutral. By focusing attention on known properties, they influence the way we perceive and deal with phenomena. Some scholars have paid close attention to the use of metaphors. Critical management studies researchers, for example, have investigated how metaphors influence the view of business. A good example of this is the use of military metaphors in management, which leads to preferences for aggressive behaviour (Levy *et al.*, 2003). Similar studies have been conducted in the area of ICT, IS and e-commerce. I will now discuss some examples of metaphors before I return to general disadvantages of their use.

Metaphors can be sources of information regarding the use of particular technologies, such as the internet (Wyatt *et al.*, 2002). Their function as sense-making tools can help bridge differences between technology and its social and organisational context in the field of information systems (McBride, 2005). Furthermore, they facilitate the 'translation' of organisational culture (Doorewaard and van Bijsterveld, 2001).

There are groups of metaphors that concentrate on a particular theme. Discussing these will make it easier to understand their function. One of them is the traditional machine/technology metaphor. This draws on our understanding of machinery from the industrial revolution onwards to make sense of ICT. In a machine culture, work has to be organised around the physical principles of the machines. Applying such understanding to ICT-based society and work will lead to structures and processes that may not be suited to new technology (Dahlbom, 2000). Another example is the metaphor of the 'information highway' or 'information superhighway' to describe the technical infrastructure of the internet. The metaphor of the highway implies individual travel and the commercialisation of interaction on the internet (Yoon, 2001). Particularly from a US perspective, the metaphor of a highway simultaneously raises romantic visions of freedom and individuality (Jones, 2001).

Another group of metaphors draw on biology to explain the use of ICT in society. Technology is described as an open system, comparable to living systems in biological systems theory. A telling example of a biological metaphor is the use of the word 'life' to describe information systems. A widespread application of this use is the 'Information Systems Life Cycle Development' methodology. The metaphor suggests that the technology is independent of humans and has a natural beginning and end (van der Blonk, 2003). While this metaphor has positive connotations, biological metaphors can equally be negative. The use of the term 'virus' for self-replicating programs immediately signals that they are not desirable. Like biological viruses, computer viruses are viewed as bad *per se*, and any action to eradicate them is seen as automatically justified (Klang, 2003). One could argue that from an evolutionary point of view, viruses are not always bad. Viruses can lead to fatal infections but they can also be used in medical therapy and have therapeutic value. But that is beside the point. In ordinary language viruses are associated with disease and thus perceived as bad. The use of the word 'virus' as a metaphor has connotations that have political implications, whether intended or not. There are plenty of further examples of the use of metaphors in e-commerce, but the above instances will suffice for the current argument.

Problems of metaphors

The problems of metaphors should have become clear from the description I have given. Metaphors by definition cannot be true or false, merely more or less appropriate. Their main problem is that they structure perceptions and consequently spaces of action in particular ways that may not be desirable. The metaphor of the information highway suggests certain ways of defining property rights and securing resources that may not be optimal for the internet. Speaking of viruses rules out a positive appreciation and thereby a range of possible uses. Such metaphors can translate into strong social norms or laws. Speaking of 'piracy', for example, has certainly lent support to stronger legal protection of intellectual property.

The downsides of metaphors need to be weighed against their advantages. In many cases this is no issue, because metaphors are easily recognisable as such. It becomes difficult to do a cost–benefit analysis, however, if it is not clear that a given term represents a metaphor rather than a factual description. In such cases, metaphors can take on a life of their own and lead to the closure of discourses and thus to the diminishing of spaces of action and solution. It is this problem that I will explore with regard to the metaphor of evolution when applied to e-commerce.

Before doing this, I will need to discuss the question of how we can distinguish between a metaphorical and a theoretical use of the term 'evolution' in e-commerce. I have said earlier that one can legitimately speak of evolution of e-commerce, but my case rests on the assumption that the term is often used as a metaphor. So how can we tell the difference? There is no easy answer to this.

There is probably overlap between the different uses, and the speaker will in many cases not be aware of it. As a rule of thumb, one might say that a term is being used metaphorically when the same content could be expressed without the use of the term. Again, applying this rule may be difficult in practice, and raises the question of who is to determine the difference. Despite this difficulty in drawing a clear dividing line, it is still plausible to assume that it is possible to use the term in a purely or predominantly metaphorical way. Some authors on evolution and e-commerce explicitly point out that the terms are best understood as metaphors (e.g. Singh, 2001).

E-commerce evolution as ideology

I will discuss the problem of evolution as a metaphor under the heading of ideology because the term 'ideology' provides a well-established framework that I have introduced earlier. My main argument, which I developed in the previous subsection, is that, as a biological metaphor, the concept of evolution deflects attention from normative ethical issues raised by e-commerce. By doing so it promotes particular interests and closes down possible solution spaces.

The evolutionary metaphor as ideology

From what I have said, it is easy to deduce that metaphors have at least the potential to promote ideologies or become ideological tools. There are many ways in which this can happen. Possibly the most important one has to do with naturalisation or reification. Examples of this type of reification-based ideology are legion. It is upheld by the privileging of the voices which are typically predominant in the first place (Mansell *et al.*, 1999).

One of the reasons why such reifications are supremely successful ideological tools is that they remove their topic from discourse; they lead to discursive closure. There is no need for debate, as it is an obvious waste of time to debate whether nature has political intentions. Apart from discursive closures, metaphors as (misleading) representations of social reality can also have manifest political and legal consequences. The metaphor of 'piracy' to support strong protection of intellectual property has already been mentioned. Another example would be the metaphor of e-'mail' as a letter, which suggests certain ways of dealing with the content of electronic communication.

These arguments are easily applied to the metaphor of evolution of e-commerce. If evolution is applied to the development of technology, then it becomes a matter of mechanistic progress. Only the most 'appropriate' ('fittest') technologies survive, and these will be the most advantageous and desirable. Human interference or even steering becomes impossible and useless, leaving us with a strong technological determinism (see Grint and Woolgar, 1997). A similar effect can be observed when Darwinian ideas are applied to social environments. Social Darwinism applies ideas of natural selection and evolution to humans in society with the consequence that inequality and injustices become results of natural developments. Such a state of affairs not only is beyond reproach, but, moreover, it can be seen as socially benign in improving the overall structure of society (Galbraith, 1998). Applied to e-commerce, this means that, whatever the current state of affairs is, the technology, as well as the related distribution of access, knowledge, and ability to use it, are removed from scrutiny. Only the best technology will survive, and those who profit from e-commerce are those who are most suited to survival. The implicit (albeit arguably fallacious) conclusion is that the current state of e-commerce is justified and not in need of any intervention.

One could counter that these views are fallacious because they do not represent the state of the art in the theory of evolution. Evolutionary theorists will be careful in making statements that could be perceived as supporting the above views. One principal reason for this is that the theory of evolution is descriptive and explains why the current state of affairs came about. It can say little about future states because the environment may change, and with it the outcome of selection. Furthermore, the theory of evolution cannot create normative statements, for reasons to be explored in the next section. Such considerations are not of relevance, however, if one uses evolution as a metaphor. The metaphorical use does not claim to be exact or represent theory correctly but rather is meant to create understanding and agreement. Where evolution is used for such metaphorical purposes, as for example in Nazi Germany, where social Darwinism was used to legitimate the killing of disabled persons, this was not so much a misunderstanding of the theory as its metaphorical use for political purposes.

Evolution and ethics in e-commerce

The previous subsection has shown that evolution as a metaphor can display characteristics of ideology. My main concern about this has to do with the ethical implications it entails. A Darwinist might argue that ethics is the result of social and cultural evolution. Only those societies with a suitable set of moral rules will survive. Furthermore, ethics relies on properties of humans that are evolved, such as the ability to communicate and think abstractly (Bedau, 1998). It has also been argued that evolution can serve as a model for systems designers to incorporate ethics (Mumford, 1996). All these statements are correct within the theory of evolution, but they overlook that there is more to ethics than the theory of evolution can tell us.

The theory of evolution can be quite useful in descriptive ethics when it explains why certain rules or moralities seem to be almost universals whereas others are very specific. What it cannot do is to create new moral rules or justify them. In terms of e-commerce, evolution can inform us why certain behaviours are accepted and lead to successful interactions and organisations. It cannot tell us, however, what rules future developments of e-commerce should follow. There are two reasons for this:

1 Following Hume (1948), philosophers have widely accepted that norms cannot be deduced from description. To do so would be what has been termed a naturalist fallacy. Evolution as a scientific theory of the natural world can tell us how present states of affairs came about but cannot tell us what future developments would be desirable.

2 The theory of evolution has little predictive value. It cannot tell which characteristics of organisms (or cultures, or societies) will prove beneficial and promote their propagation, because future environments are uncertain. That means that even if we knew what state of society will be desirable in the future, evolutionary theory could tell us little about how to get there.

In addition to these problems, there are inconsistencies between the evolutionary natural science view of the world and most ethical views of the world. Most ethical theories require the existence of autonomous individuals who are capable of making decisions and reflecting on these in a rational manner. While there are obvious empirical limits to this view, the underlying idea of freedom and autonomy is central to the constitution of modern industrialised democratic societies. Evolution as a biological concept has no room for such freedom and reflection. The subjects of evolution are endowed with desirable characteristics by the lottery of mutation and find themselves winners of the game of evolution without any way of contributing to this.

This does not mean that one conceptual framework is right or the other wrong. It just means that they describe different phenomena and that these descriptions are not always compatible. In most cases this is no problem. Neglecting ethical questions in the natural world is unproblematic, because ethics simply plays no role there. Similarly, neglecting evolution in social environments where ethics is relevant is usually unproblematic. An issue arises only if a certain use of language leads to the rendering of ethical questions invisible in cases where they are relevant, as for example when the use of metaphors of evolution leads speakers and listeners to overlook ethical issues.

Speaking of e-commerce in terms of evolution can render ethical issues invisible. There is neither the need nor the possibility to address questions of justice and digital divides. Changing power structures and their ethical implications are no longer open to scrutiny. Technology is given and determined. Attempts to regulate it turn into misguided (and ideologically motivated) political activism that cannot be justified and stand no chance of success. Overall, the ethical dimension of e-commerce becomes invisible and can no longer be discussed and criticised.

Overcoming the ideology of evolution?

It is clear from the tone of this argument that I believe this state of affairs to be problematic. E-commerce is a social practice based on social constructs and as such should be open to ethical debate. If the use of the metaphor of evolution precludes such debate, then it is an example of ideology. As in all cases of ideology, we can ask who benefits and who suffers. The beneficiaries of the exclusion of ethics from debate are the main technical and business stakeholders of e-commerce. This includes hardware and software vendors as well as the big established players in the market. Where ethical interventions are successful, they could lead to stronger regulation and the reduction of profits. The holders of market power thus have an important interest in avoiding attention to ethics. The use of biological metaphors therefore promotes their interest. On the other hand, those who would benefit from the inclusion of ethical issues are typically the less powerful stakeholders such as employees, consumers and the environment. They would profit from ethical debates because these would give their viewpoints more legitimacy and thus more chances of success.

One could counter this critique by suggesting that all I am doing is replacing one ideology with another one. The reflective side of critical theory means that critical scholars should apply their reasoning to their own arguments (Gouldner, 1976; Alvesson and Willmott, 1992). Doing so shows that, indeed, my argument has produced without justification some concepts that are at least as contentious as the ones I am attacking. Questions of freedom of will and action and human autonomy have a long history of being debated. If it is just a question of exchanging one set of ideological terms and reifications against another, then where is the added value of the argument? The answer to this question is that it will lead to a heightened awareness of one's constructs and their implications, and a willingness to question these. My main argument is that the use of the term and the ideas of evolution can preclude ethical debates in e-commerce despite the necessity for having such debates. This does not mean that I have a perfect solution or that my argument has no weaknesses.

What are we to do concerning e-commerce and evolution? One possibility would be to stop using the metaphor of evolution in connection with all social processes, including e-commerce. This is problematic for several reasons. First, one cannot change the use of language by decree. Second, and more important, metaphors have advantages, and these can be substantial. Speaking of the evolution of social constructs can promote understanding and communication, and thus be valuable. The solution should therefore be in a more reflected use of the metaphor. When we hear people speak of evolution, we should immediately ask: who is speaking, are they using the term as a metaphor, who benefits from the metaphor, what implications of the metaphor have been neglected? The ideological implications of the metaphor need to be understood. Once they have been, they can easily be debated. It is imperative that metaphors become visible as such and lose their reifying property. If this is given, then the advantages and disadvantages of the use of the metaphor can be weighed and justified.

The solution to the problem of ideology is thus to render it visible. Where speaking of evolution of e-commerce leads to discursive closure, the way out is to open new discourses. This is where critical research can help further debates and it is where this argument finds its use. I do not claim to be able to overcome ideology, and indeed some readers will point out that the entire book is itself based on ideological assumptions. Nevertheless, by opening the debate on ideology, this chapter can help in overcoming its effects and, more specifically, can allow the issues of ethics in e-commerce to re-enter the debate. This is important for reasons of intellectual honesty, but also for reasons of ethical authenticity.

14 Commercial colonisation
E-teaching and e-democracy

This final chapter of the application section builds on the figures of thought outlined earlier. It investigates the implication of the use of commercial thoughts and language in settings where these have not always been deemed appropriate. This concentration on commerce and its potentially problematic implications also builds on the traditional Marxist critique of capitalism. It is, however, less of a general critique of capitalism than the attempt to delineate the legitimate boundaries of capitalism. In some respects the chapter is inspired by Habermas's description of the colonisation of the life-world. While Habermas's argument focused on the rebuttal of systems theoretic critiques of his work, this idea that impersonal systems such as markets are replacing traditional ways of interacting is applicable to a variety of situations. The argument here will show why and how economic considerations have the potential to be detrimental to established positions or practices. As in most of the other applications of critical theory in IS considered so far, the concept of ethics will play a central role in the argument.

The ethics of education: e-teaching and commerce

Ethics is relevant to education. From the ancient Greeks to modern theories of development, ethics and morality are seen to be closely connected with the process of teaching and learning. Computers and information technology are increasingly used for educational purposes. If one accepts the relationship between ethics and education, it would seem that e-teaching has the potential to pose moral questions (see Stahl, 2002a, b). E-teaching not only offers a new approach to some of the conventional problems of education but is also a multi-billion-dollar business. Given this development, combined with the moral quality of education, it can be argued that the vested economic interests in e-teaching could become a threat to its moral legitimacy.

I will begin the argument by examining the relationship between ethics and e-teaching. The first step will be to demonstrate that education is an intrinsically moral process. In the second step, the impact that e-teaching will have on education will be outlined and the opportunities and drawbacks of e-teaching in general discussed. From this, the conclusion will be drawn that e-teaching has an ethical impact. The next section will then examine the relationship between e-teaching and business. Four reasons why e-teaching is likely to shape the educational process in favour of business interests will be discussed. I argue that businesses not only have a strong interest in e-teaching as a large market opportunity but are already in the process of changing the nature of education in the information society. The fourth section will then discuss in detail the reasons why and how business interests and e-teaching combine to produce an ethical problem in education. The moral character of education depends on its impartiality, and this feature is jeopardised if any special interest group dominates education. The conclusion will stress that such a development can endanger the legitimacy of education, thereby calling into question the educational system.

This argument should not be misunderstood as a polemic against e-teaching. As I shall discuss, e-teaching offers many new chances and opportunities. Nor should it be misconstrued as being anti-business in a simplistic sense; business interests have played an ever-increasing role in education since the industrial revolution. Instead, I argue that the introduction of computers and information technology into teaching can inadvertently strengthen business interests and that such a quantitative change can result in a qualitatively new situation which requires us to reconsider our basic assumptions.

Ethics and e-teaching

The argument hinges on the recognition that education and ethics are deeply intertwined. This is important because ethics provides a basis of legitimacy which, albeit often in the background, is of central importance for the role of educational institutions in society. The following subsection will therefore outline the relationship between ethics and education.

The ethical purpose of education

There are different tasks that are traditionally associated with education, most of which have an ethical dimension. First of all, education is supposed to support and guide individual development. This is important from an ethical point of view because we know that humans' ethical abilities are subject to development, and that this development depends, at least partially, on external stimulation (see Kohlberg, 1981). Even more important than the fact that ethical reflexivity depends on education is the role of moral practice. According to Weil (1998), education is moralisation; it is the acquisition of a *habitus* which allows the individual to act without self-contradiction. Ricoeur (1991) interprets this task of education as the integration of morality, work, tradition, and law, all of which we need for our social existence. One ethical tradition which stresses the importance of moral formation and education is virtue ethics. Aristotle emphasises that virtues do not develop by themselves, but that humans are by nature made to absorb and then perfect them through habituation (Aristotle, 1998, Maritain, 1960; De George, 1999).

Education thus has the dual role of transmitting moral practice as well as facilitating the ethical reflection of that practice. These two roles are included in many other tasks of education that one can find in the literature. A general description of education will sometimes include the fact that it is supposed to develop the person. Human beings are sometimes understood to have a natural thirst for knowledge (Galbraith, 1998); they want to develop the faculty of reason. Reason is the condition of judgement and prudence, which leads us back to virtue. The person, as the subject of ethics, needs a character that disposes him or her towards acting morally, and that character is developed in education (Gehlen, 1997).

There are several other aspects of education that have a moral quality. It has been a long-held view of many philosophers, starting with Socrates, that in order to achieve happiness, one must dedicate oneself to knowledge, truth, contemplation and thinking (Maritain, 1960). Education is also the basis of many of the central decisions in life, and in large part it determines individual opportunities. These individual opportunities then shape freedom and choices and thus the ability to act morally.

There is also a social viewpoint to these individual aspects of the ethical importance of education. Morality, as the set of rules that are valid in a given society, is a necessary condition of successful social interaction. A society will thus generally have an interest in instilling morality in its members. In order for morality to fulfil this stabilising and facilitating function, it must have a certain measure of validity and, thus, dependability. Most societies therefore develop measures and institutions for the moral socialisation of their members, and these tend to be integrated into the formal process of education.

Most of the above observations would be as true for a medieval or a tribal society as they are for the information society. However, it is important to note them in our context because they represent the background of a crucial component of education, namely its legitimacy. Education usually has a high degree of legitimacy, and educators are usually highly regarded by the public. The reasons for this are complex, but an important part of them is based on the moral quality of education. We rarely reflect expressly on the justification of education. However, one of the cornerstones of most educational systems, and especially those of western societies, is the fact that education is simply seen as good and legitimate in its own right. The growing importance of education in the information society is likely to enforce this aspect. The argument here is that the possible domination of the educational system, or parts of it, can threaten this legitimacy and thereby the entire structure of education as we know it.

E-teaching

In order to argue this point, the next step is to take a closer look at the aspect of education in question, namely e-teaching. The term 'e-teaching' stands for all uses of information technology in the process of education. The emphasis will be on the use of computers in post-secondary education. This includes computer labs, virtual learning environments, PDAs in classrooms, etc. As a starting point, one can note that e-teaching has become a reality in most universities. There are few universities today without extensive computer facilities, and these are increasingly used directly for teaching purposes, either for campus education using computers in class or for distance education (Tress, 2000).

The use of IT in teaching holds a huge amount of potential and promise (see Alexander, 2001). Most of these benefits are either directly or indirectly of a moral nature. In general, the argument for e-teaching is that it improves the learning process. 'At its best, technology can facilitate deep exploration and integration of information, high-level thinking, and profound engagement by allowing students to design, explore, experiment, access information, and model complex phenomena' (Goldman *et al.*, 1999). This means that traditional learning is supported, but also that the borders of traditional learning are transcended. Learning will become possible outside of traditional institutions and traditional frameworks. 'The world is their [the students'] classroom' (Goldman *et al.*, 1999). Borgmann (1999, p. 204) describes the desired advantages of e-teaching as follows:

> The student becomes the sovereign who can choose the material, the method of presentation, and the time and place of studying. But learners not only change from passive recipients to active choosers of information, they are also freed from the injuries that prejudices of gender, race, class, or physical appearance might otherwise have inflicted on them.

At the same time, empirical research has shown that the use of technology in the right circumstances can in fact improve learning success and overcome some of the barriers to learning found in traditional institutions (Piccoli *et al.*, 2001). While technology may not be a panacea, it 'can enable the effective application of constructive, cognitive, collaborative, and socio-cultural models of learning' (Leidner and Jarvenpaa, 1995, p. 288). One of the reasons for this success of e-teaching is that it is closely associated with one of the central features of all educational processes, namely communication. Communication is the basis of any successful education, no matter what learning model or underlying theory one chooses. Since IT is a tool for the improvement of communication, it stands to reason that its use will result in an improvement of education. Communication can be improved between learners and teachers (Tress, 2000), as well as between learners. The latter is highly important for all constructivist teaching theories and has been proved to significantly influence learning success (Alavi *et al.*, 1995).

Another expected advantage of e-teaching is that it can change the roles in the educational process. Traditionally, teaching in universities is teacher centred, and teachers used to be elevated far above learners. Both these aspects can be detrimental to learning. Through the use of computers, students' attitudes improve and learning becomes more student centred (Piccoli *et al.*, 2001). Traditional instructional modes are often not suited to the use of technologies and will therefore have to be changed (Alavi, 1994). The change of roles implies that the paradigm will change from push to pull, meaning that, while the students will be allowed and required to take greater control of their own education, the instructor's role will change to that of a facilitator or coach (Ives and Jarvenpaa, 1996). Yet while all these developments seem to increase the students' freedom and choice and should lead to empowerment, there is also a downside to e-teaching, which has some related moral problems.

The most general critique of e-teaching is that it does not live up to the promises listed in the preceding paragraphs. Concerning the efficiency argument, for example, research has shown that while most participants agree that e-teaching reduces cost, there is very little evidence to support those claims. Another fear is that even those improvements in student interest and attitude that can be measured are not in fact caused by the use of IT but only by the novelty of the situation (Alavi *et al.*, 1995; Leidner and Jarvenpaa, 1995). Generally, there seems to be a feeling that excessive enthusiasm about e-teaching is not appropriate. Davenport and Prusak's argument, which was originally aimed at knowledge management, is clearly applicable to e-teaching: 'The assumption that technology can replace human knowledge or create its equivalent has proven false time and again' (1998, p. xx).

Among the more specific points of criticism of e-teaching, there is the dilemma of technology versus content: the problem is that the attempt to use a new medium can lead to a disproportionate emphasis on the medium itself, which causes neglect of the educational content. The medium becomes the message. It is what Goldman *et al.* (1999) call the 'flash over substance' phenomenon. Even though most educators would probably agree that educational content is more important than technologies for delivering it, the real-life requirements often work in a different direction. A related problem is that transferring education from traditional methods to computer-mediated environments is not as simple as it may seem. The effort required can be extremely high, and this can turn the efficiency argument around. It could be argued the cost and effort expended on e-teaching are not justified by any resulting gain in educational improvement (Lytras and Pouloudi, 2001).

A final problem worth mentioning here is that in order for e-teaching to be successful, teachers and learners must fulfil several non-trivial conditions. They must have a certain level of proficiency in using computers. It has been shown that familiarity with computers is necessary for successful e-teaching (Piccoli *et al.*, 2001; Leidner and Jarvenpaa, 1995), but there are also other, less tangible conditions, such as computer self-efficacy. This refers to a judgement of one's capability to use a computer and it leads into the areas of psychological requirements, the ability to work unsupervised, a general attitude towards technology, etc. These requirements, if not met, can jeopardise even the best-prepared attempt at e-teaching (Compeau and Higgins, 1995).

Despite all these (potential) problems of e-teaching, one hears relatively little of them in public discourses. Strengths of e-teaching are emphasised, often without any sort of evidence, whereas weaknesses are systematically blended out, again disregarding any evidence. Discourse analysis of discourses relating to e-teaching has shown that published statements are one-sided and in favour of e-teaching (Cukier *et al.*, 2003).

E-teaching and business

There are several connections linking business and e-teaching. The domination of education by economic interests can produce ethical problems. I will first show that such an argument is tenable by showing that e-teaching is a huge market, that vocational training is increasingly replacing traditional education, that education is turning into a commodity, and, finally, by showing that economic interests are starting to dominate other aspects of the information society as well.

E-teaching as a market

If economic interests are seen as a threat to the moral integrity of e-teaching, then it has to be demonstrated that businesses have an interest in it in the first place. This can be done by showing that teaching in general, and e-teaching in particular, are businesses in their own right. Americans alone spend $740 billion annually on education and training (Tress, 2000). An increasing share of this ever-growing amount is going to be spent in those areas where information technology is used. It is predicted that education on demand, provided to homes, schools and workplaces, will be a relevantly bigger business than entertainment on demand (Ives and Jarvenpaa, 1996). This means that the size of the market alone will probably be enough to produce increasing competition between different players. Among them, one can find those service providers and businesses which are in the game to make profits. On the other hand, there are the educational institutions, especially tertiary education institutions such as colleges and universities. In fact, competition between universities for those students who are able and willing to pay for their services started long ago. Increasingly, universities have identified the use of new technologies in teaching and learning as a critical success factor. Many of them hope to be able to gain a competitive advantage by introducing technology. We are already at the point where the lack of technical facilities is a clear disadvantage. It seems to be beyond doubt that most universities are more or less willing participants in this competition (see Hesketh *et al.*, 1996; Tress, 2000; Ives and Jarvenpaa, 1996).

E-teaching and vocational training

Another aspect of the relationship of business interests and e-teaching is that of vocational training. Starting with the industrial revolution, the focus of education started changing from lofty humanist aims, such as enlightenment, personal happiness and knowledge for its own sake, to more mundane objectives. The industrialised economy needed workers with a higher level of skills, which led to pressure on educational institutions to provide those workers with the necessary skills. This development is still accelerating because of the pressures in the knowledge societies towards more skills and knowledge. Nowadays, few universities can resist the call to provide their students with skills that are deemed to be in demand in the labour market. This increased influence of business interests on education is being magnified by the use of information technology. IT is one of the reasons why additional skills are being sought. It is also part of the solution to the problem of how these skills can be transmitted.

Thus, it can be argued that the potential gains to be made from the market for e-teaching will encourage business interests to further align themselves with tertiary education institutions. If left unchecked, this could lead to the commodification of education. Such commodification could be problematic, given the ethical aspect of education. As soon as education becomes something to be bought and sold, it loses some of its ethical qualities, its normatively binding force and thus its legitimacy.

The commodification of information

In the past, information was something that could be either freely shared or closely guarded (as it could possibly provide its holder with power and riches). For most of human history, however, information has not been seen as property in a sense comparable to property in physical objects. This has changed in the wake of the international spread of capitalist economic frameworks and the increased importance of information as part of intellectual property.

This commodification of information has extended to everything related to information as well. 'What largely drives computer sprawl at the moment is the marketplace. Opportunities to make significant amounts of money are plentiful, and many, many people are aware of these opportunities' (Moor, 2000, p. 35). Moor is referring to the computing infrastructure, often called the Global Information Infrastructure (GII), as well as the entire socio-economic-technical system that we call the internet (see Chapman and Rotenberg, 1995). The economic exploitation of the internet requires information to be treated as a commodity and it also requires several other changes to our commonly shared definitions.

Ethical problems of the business domination of e-teaching

So far it has been argued that teaching is a moral activity and that business interests threaten to dominate it, especially through new developments such as e-teaching. In the final part of the argument I will attempt to demonstrate that these two aspects are contradictory – that is, that domination of education and e-teaching by business would run counter to the moral premise of education and thus might endanger the legitimacy of e-teaching.

The moral relevance of business interests

Why would business interest in education pose a moral problem? At the heart of the answer to this question is the idea of impartiality. All the great ethical theories from Aristotelian virtue ethics through utilitarianism to Kantian deontology emphasise the equality of all their subjects and the importance of the impartiality for the acceptability of moral judgements. Impartiality seems to be an axiom of our modern understanding of ethics, and without it no theory can lay claim to ethical acceptability. A similar claim can be made for education. Whether teaching is based on an objectivist or a constructivist world-view, its aim is always to convey knowledge and meaning in an independent, unbiased and unprejudiced way. That means that no single position should be preferred in teaching and that all the relevant viewpoints must be considered. This impartiality axiom of teaching and ethics is reflected in many of the approaches to applied ethics that are prevalent nowadays. The stakeholder approach to business ethics, for example, or the discursive approach to technological ethics, can easily be described as being based on the assumption that all the involved parties are equal and that the process that leads to moral outcomes must be impartial.

The dominance of any given voice in a discourse threatens this impartiality, and that is exactly what the strong position of business interests does in e-teaching. While businesses are a legitimate stakeholder in e-teaching, they are only one group among many, and arguably they are not the most important one. De George (2003b, p. 13) summarises the complex relationship between business and university as follows:

> The autonomy of the university is a paradox for some in that it is financially supported by the state or by donors and/or by the tuition and fees paid by students. Yet those who pay the piper do not get to call the tune. The university is accountable to its supporters; but it is primarily accountable for fulfilling its mission, which they presumably endorse.

At the same time as we see that business interests cannot have a decisive say in educational matters, there is evidence that strong business interests tend to take over the different areas they are interested in. In fact, in other fields the commercialisation and commodification that resulted from the strengthening of business interests have been described as negative and immoral. The most pertinent example in this case is the internet, whose originally libertarian framework is being completely remodelled as a result of, and in accordance with, business interests (see Yoon, 1996).

Consequences of business domination of e-teaching

As regards the problems arising from the mix of e-teaching and business interests, there are several areas one can look at. First, there is the question of the quality of education. While this is a difficult and highly contentious topic in the first place, it becomes even more difficult to handle in e-teaching. To give an example: most universities today offer some kind of introduction to computers, and that usually includes an introduction to the standard software used in business, namely Microsoft Office. This sort of education is especially suited for automation and e-teaching. The e-teaching applications for standard software tend to include automatic assessments which allow the students to check their progress but which can also be used for grading. In this scenario, where students learn something about software by using computers, getting graded automatically raises the questions regarding who determines what is taught, what the standards are, what the aim is, etc. The strong influence of business views can affect quality issues, and quality relates back to the moral legitimacy.

Another big area of moral problems that is related to business interests in e-teaching is the question of access. Access to education, especially higher education, is determined by many different factors. One of them is the financial aspect. The more expensive education is, the less likely the poorer members of a society are to be able to avail themselves of it. While different societies have different views on how access to education should be distributed, few would argue that being poor should be an insurmountable obstacle. Dominance of e-teaching by business interests would mean that the price of education would rise and that only those students who had the means to pay for it would be considered interesting. Of course, there could be grants, scholarships, etc. in order to alleviate the problem. As a general tendency, however, those students from a financially less well endowed background would probably be forced out of the system.

Another problem with access is that e-teaching uses the IT resources that are available and increasingly the internet. The internet is still very much US centred and requires skills and possessions which are distributed unequally. That means that the access problem appears not only at the level of an individual society but even more so on an international level. Again, business interests are not the only root of the problem, but it is clear that businesses have little incentive to do anything about it, since providing access to the Third World will not lead to profits. It is part of the constitution of market economies that business activity is aimed at those markets where profits can be made. The market for education in the Third World is generally not very promising. While one can agree with Fagin (2000) when he states that absolute equality of access to information is not achievable, the question remains how much equality of access is deemed desirable and should be provided by universities or states.

This leads to the last and most fundamental ethical problem of e-teaching: it changes our basic assumptions about education and moves it further down the line towards being a business. There are many tacit assumptions and consequences of e-teaching that we may or may not agree with, but that simply appear when it is introduced. On a very basic level, there is the question that needs to be asked whenever someone teaches someone else: what is the purpose of teaching? E-teaching often suggests a vocational purpose to education because it is mostly used to transfer specific skills. 'What we need to consider about the computer has nothing to do with its efficiency as a teaching tool. We need to know in what ways it is altering our conception of learning' (Postman, 1992, p. 19). E-teaching also presupposes a certain sort of metaphysics, usually an objectivist world-view, which is a particular view that cannot claim impartiality. The relationship between pedagogy, ethics and technology in education is complex and cannot be reduced to simple causalities (Jefferies *et al.*, 2007). However, the combination of e-teaching and business interests leads to a strengthening of the idea of competition in education. Although this can be a good thing, and competition between students is often seen as a way to improve results, we should realise that competition, by definition, produces losers, and there needs to be a discussion about how many losers in the educational game society is willing to accept and how it wants to deal with them. Finally, the move of e-teaching into universities seems unstoppable and it looks as though the moral questions regarding access, competition and impartiality have been taken out of the hands of decision makers. That would mean that our freedom is being reduced by e-teaching, which in itself is a moral problem.

None of these problems is unique to e-teaching. Questions of access, competition, content, examination, and especially the role and meaning of education are constants in every educational system. The argument here is that the use of e-teaching processes or tools has the potential to strengthen one interest group, namely business interests, to the detriment of others. E-teaching can lead to the exclusion of the less well-off, it can promote business interests in a clandestine way and it can change our perception of education without our becoming aware of it. This is where the danger lies and where this argument aims to promote discussion. The impartiality of education, which used to be guaranteed through formalisms and processes such as academic freedom, may come under threat without the main stakeholders noticing it. This is where e-teaching can pose a threat to education, and threat is what this chapter hopes to draw attention to.

In the second half of the chapter I will now develop a very similar argument concentrating on the problems arising from the application of economic ideas to the field of democratic government.

Framing e-government as e-commerce

Like e-teaching, e-government is a growth industry whose potential has been recognised by most of the big players in the hardware and software market, from IBM to Microsoft. Most industrialised societies have started to use ICT in government, and some have made considerable progress. In many respects the development of e-government seems to follow the example of e-commerce. High-level administrators or political leaders recognise the potential of a certain technology and decide to deploy it in their area of responsibility. Given that the systems as well as the vendors and their personnel are usually experienced in e-commerce or e-business, similar systems are used in e-government, and similar processes are installed. Furthermore, the rhetoric of e-government uses arguments and logic which stem from the business world. In many cases this happens deliberately and with the best of intentions. The perceived weaknesses of democratic governments and administrations include a high level of bureaucracy, a duplication of efforts in departments that do not communicate and a general sluggishness and lack of response. Given that businesses increasingly try to overcome these problems in order to become agile competitors, the hope is that the use of the paradigm of business in government, which is transported through the medium of e-government, will alleviate these problems.

I want to question this type of narrative by asking what the implications of the use of the commercial paradigm on e-government will be by concentrating on the moral basis of democracy. I will do this by discussing the moral foundation of democracy. I will then analyse the concept of e-government and introduce the important distinction between e-government as the technological delivery of administrative services and e-democracy as the technological enhancement of primary democratic processes. From there the chapter will proceed to take a look at e-commerce and why it seems to be a suitable paradigm for e-government. The use of this paradigm will then be analysed, and in particular the limits of its use will be discussed. The discussion will show that e-commerce is a legitimate paradigm in some respects because it stands for values such as efficiency gains or better distribution that are common to democracies. At the same time, business ideas can represent democratic processes only within relatively narrow limits. The central problem is that the conceptualisation of humans differs fundamentally between the business world and politics. In business, people are most importantly consumers, whereas in democracy, people are predominantly citizens. The danger of the commercial paradigm is that it implies that citizens can be reduced to consumers. This change in the conceptualisation of human beings creates a change from e-democracy to e-government, it excludes certain members from participating and it generally affects the character of democracy. This, it will be argued, threatens the moral legitimacy of democracy, which is the central basis of its acceptability and therefore of its success. The conclusion will therefore be that politicians as well as information systems professionals must make sure that they keep the sometimes fine line between business processes and political processes in mind in order to avoid a failure of the (political as well as technical) system and retain its legitimacy.

The ethics of democracy

I will argue that the commercial 'paradigm' can threaten the moral legitimacy of democracy. The choice of the term 'paradigm' here stands for a general world-view that emphasises the economic aspects of social reality. It is thus related to, but not as extensive as, the concept of paradigm discussed in Chapter 8 under the heading of philosophical aspects of CRIS. I will first clarify what democracy is and how it relates to ethics. This section will therefore start with a review of some of the defining aspects of democracy in order to then establish its relationship with ethics and morality. It will end by briefly looking at some of the weaknesses of democracy.

The concept of democracy

A look at the etymology of 'democracy' shows that it literally means 'rule of the people'. It is the conceptual opposite of forms of government where single persons or minorities rule. The concept of democratic government contains a number of implications and suppositions that need to be spelled out in order for us to understand the importance of ethics for democracy and also the conditions under which democracies can function and be stable.

One implication of democratic rule is that the will of the community is created bottom-up, that the individual members of society collaborate to determine what society does. Democracy is a formal process that leaves the outcome of the decision process mostly open. It only determines the external format necessary to make decisions. These decisions refer not only to actions but, more importantly, to intentions. Thus, democracy is the process of the collective forming of a political will as well as the way of realising this will (see Richardson, 1999).

This implies that every member of society is recognised as a person, that the rights of all persons are equal, that the individual is protected from the arbitrariness of society. At the same time, democracy stands for an attitude by individuals that implies responsibility for the commonwealth, tolerance, and courage (see Söderbaum, 2000). The very heart of democracy is the deliberative process that allows the forming of the political will. This is based on the idea that the members of the democratic society are willing and able to exchange ideas and arguments in such a way as to come to acceptable and legitimate majority decisions (Habermas, 1998a). Communication can thus be said to be the essence of democracy (Ricoeur, 1991).

Another possible approach to democracy is to look at its purpose. The formal and functional description of democracy I have given implies purposes but does not spell them out. One can, however, see democracy as a means to an end. The ends that democracy is supposed to realise could then be the safeguarding of internal peace and individual freedom (Hayek, 1994).

These few short remarks on democracy should point us in the direction of the ethical basis of democracy, to show us why accepted moral rules and their ethical justifications are of central importance to the functioning of democracy.

The ethical basis of democracy

There are different reasons why democracy is linked to ethics and morality. Maybe the most obvious one is that it is a system that distributes power. Power affects our moral rights and obligations and the way we can and should behave, and it is also of theoretical and reflective importance. It also establishes one link between democracy and critical theory. The most important aspect of ethics and power in democracies is that democratic processes give power legitimacy. Power as the ability to make others do one's bidding is a necessary part of any community, and it can only be held if the affected parties believe it to be justified and legitimate. In a modern society the source of legitimacy of power can only come from the assumption that democratic processes, albeit fallible, create the most reasonable results that can be expected (Habermas, 1998a). Power can always be misused, but democracies seem to be better at avoiding or ending misuse than authoritarian forms of government (Küng, 1997). Democracies are decentralised, and this decentralisation allows reasonable local solutions (Beck, 1986). The participation of individuals, which is constitutive for democracies, allows regulations which are acceptable to all (Kant, 1992; Tocqueville, 1998). In addition to the provision of a legitimate distribution and execution of power, democracies facilitate the change of power relationships in a peaceful and way.

A further link between ethics and democracy can be developed from the underlying anthropological assumptions. Democracy is based on a view of humans that is itself ethically charged. The citizens of democracy are modelled after the Enlightenment idea of humans as free, autonomous and moral agents. Democracy can only exist on the basis of this (sometimes counter-factual) view of its members. This anthropological view assumes moral values such as the fundamental equality of all citizens and it esteems the classical liberal individual as the basis of the community.

Finally, democracy promises to deliver moral values to society as a whole by forming the autonomous individual through socialisation and education. Democracy requires and disseminates knowledge and it provides the court of public exchange for the creation of knowledge (see Rauch, 1993). The institutions and members of democracy promise the achievement of progress in material, social, intellectual and many other respects. One important basis of this argument is the close link between democracy as a political framework and capitalism as the corresponding economic framework (Becker, 1976; Friedman, 1994b). Many of the moral arguments supporting democracy can be found in a similar form for capitalism. Democracy, with its emphasis on the individual, is supposed to give people the skills and the desire to perform well economically, and the aggregation of individual performance should lead to an improvement in general welfare. Only on the basis of a functioning economic system can wealth be redistributed to the needy which again strengthens the moral case for democracy (Rorty, 1996b). The combination of capitalism and democracy should not only increase welfare in individual states but also lead to an equalising effect between countries and, at least for those countries that participate, bring a generally high standard of living (Cohen, 1996).

As another moral advantage, democracy is supposed to be peaceful. Since the sovereign is the people itself, and the people (as opposed to the elites or aristocrats) suffer the most from a war, democracy is often depicted as intrinsically peaceful. Furthermore, war tends to disrupt commerce. Thus, the businesspeople in democratic states, who have a strong political influence, are supposed to be peaceful (Tocqueville, 1999).

Moral weaknesses of democracy

The last subsection may have struck the reader as overly optimistic, and, in fact, democracy may not always display the moral advantages just described. From the very beginning of democracy there has always been the suspicion that it is nothing but mob rule (Aristotle, 1998). It has often been suspected that democracies are intrinsically unstable, for different reasons. Rorty (1996b) suspects that democracies require a high level of material well-being to function; that they cannot survive real hardship. Maybe even worse is the material emptiness of democracies. Plato believed that they have to disintegrate because they know no boundaries, and the question is still open as to whether liberal democracies can provide humans with an idea of the 'good life' which has always been central to ethical thought (Postman, 1992).

There is the problem of theory and practice, the question whether democratic states can really live up to the expectations levelled at them. Experience tells us that the noble idea of free forming of the political will bottom-up may not work in practice. The view of humans that informs democracy will often not be displayed and reflected by democratic institutions. The welfare argument may be weak because experience shows that not everybody participates in the generation and sharing of wealth. Finally, it can even be argued that democracies are not peaceful but create perverse incentives which make them intrinsically more belligerent than autocratic regimes (Tocqueville, 1999).

While we should thus take the moral advantages of democracy with a grain of salt, we should be aware that they have one central function: they legitimise the democratic form of government. Whether fact or fiction, the moral side of democracy allows us to distribute power and resources, to find collective solutions, to create a shared vision of the good life. None of this is ever perfect. It can only work because the vast majority of the affected accept it as morally justified. Arguably, every form of government needs this sort of justification, and democracy seems best suited to provide it in the modern world. Admittedly, these are strong assumptions and might lead to a lengthy debate on political theory and practice. I will not be able to dwell on them here, and hope that the reader finds them sufficiently plausible to follow the rest of the argument, which is based on the assumption that ethics and morality play an essential role in legitimising democracy.

E-government and e-democracy

The term 'e-government' stands for the use of ICT in the realm of government. Clearly, the area covered by the term 'government' is immense and depends on the definition of government. In the widest sense it can stand for all the activities of municipal, regional or national governments and administrations. It can also include activities of the legislative and judicial power. The term 'e-government' is often used in such a wide sense, which can be problematic. I will distinguish between e-government as the administrative use of ICT and e-democracy as the use of ICT for genuine democratic purposes. This distinction is important because the use of the paradigm of business can hide or imply a shift from e-democracy to e-government and thereby threaten the legitimacy of the democratic form of government.

E-government and service delivery

E-government understood as the use of ICT for the purposes of the executive branch of government is advancing quickly and covering more and more areas in a geographic as well as a thematic sense. For what purposes is ICT used by governments? The answer to this question depends on the type and particularities of government. Generally, there seems to be a trend to include as much as possible within e-government. One can fundamentally distinguish between internal processes of governments and external relationships, where the latter can be divided into relationships with citizens or constituents and relationships with others, such as other governments or organisations. ICT can thus be used for purposes as different as internal data exchange for the streamlining of workflows or international development (Thompson, 2003).

While e-government could thus theoretically span a wide range of activities, it appears that governments and their bureaucracies have a strong tendency to favour activities that could broadly be described as service delivery. This is arguably the case because bureaucracies have the task of delivering services and because there is an intrinsic affinity between governments and ICT, which can also be called a technology of 'command and control' (Postman, 1992, p. 115). It is not possible to prove this point here, but, disregarding the reasons for the development, one can easily find that a large number of publications about the topic of e-government are concerned with service delivery. (For a plethora of examples, see the edited collection by Bannister and Remenyi, 2003.)

Most of us have come across examples of this trend. Municipalities post local information on the internet, tax returns can be done electronically, driving licences can be applied for online, etc. While this development is beneficial in many respects, it also seems to take away awareness of other applications of ICT, namely those that are directly linked to democratic processes, which I will call 'e-democracy' (Wastell, 2003).

E-democracy and the radicalisation of democratic processes

'E-democracy' stands for the use of ICT for the purposes of democratic deliberation and policy formulation. One can often find the idea that ICT, and specifically the internet, are inherently democratic technologies. The reasoning is that '(1) Democracy means power in the hands of individuals (the many); (2) information is power; (3) the Internet makes vast quantities of information available to individuals; (4) therefore, the Internet is democratic' (Johnson, 2001, p. 211; and see also Johnson, 2000). This democratic promise was one of the main motivators for the investment in internet technologies by government, most notably the internet backbones in the United States (Gore, 1995). One should note that this inherent democratic character of internet technology is often used as a moral argument to support its development and implementation (see Stichler and Hauptman, 1998). On this basis, some authors go so far as to develop grand visions of technological utopias where constant interaction leads to an ideal democracy which displays high ethical values (Lévy, 1997; Meeks, 2000).

Why is this form of democracy so desirable? Collectively, it allows for new forms of free and equal deliberation. Everybody can make his or her voice heard on all matters of interest. In fact, systems have been built that allow for public discourse on socially relevant topics which are based explicitly on the (ethical) principles of Habermasian discourse theory (Heng and de Moor, 2003). This means that ICT can be used to approximate the ideal speech situation where only the power of the better argument counts. This collective advantage can be translated into the maximisation of knowledge and therefore into an optimal viability of the outcomes of deliberations. At the same time, the participation of stakeholders guarantees the moral viability of discussions. Also, the chance to participate in discourses and thereby influence the outcome of democratic decisions is supposed to bring about the emancipation and empowerment of individuals (Hirschheim and Klein, 1994).

In the context of this discussion one should note that the introduction of this sort of online deliberation and policy formulation could have radical consequences. It leads away from the established representational model of democracy towards a more direct type of democracy. This can be seen as positive for the reasons I have given, but it can also be problematic. Either way, this vision of a more radical technology-mediated democracy is highly ethically charged. It affects the individual's rights and obligations, it is based on our view of human beings and it changes the distribution of power. This radical democracy could thus strengthen the moral legitimacy of democracy but it might also lead to problems.

Problems of e-government and e-democracy

Both e-government and e-democracy run into problems. The problems with e-government tend to be of a technical nature, whereas e-democracy faces more fundamental obstacles. E-government faces problems of technical implementation, of user involvement, of co-operation between different administrative departments, and the like. These are typical problems of systems design, implementation and use that we know about from the information systems literature. While they are not trivial, there are established ways of addressing them.

The problems with e-democracy are more serious. While the promises that it holds are immense, the criticism is just as impressive. Some authors state that e-democracy simply does not live up to its promises, that instead of promoting democracy, ICT has undemocratic effects (Breen, 1999), that instead of decentralising access, it centralises it (Yoon, 1996), that it stabilises power structures instead of changing them (Stallman, 1995; Weizenbaum, 1976). Another fundamental problem is that of the democratic ideal that seems to be promoted by ICT, namely direct democracy. This may appear attractive for several reasons, but it also threatens to turn into the plebiscite that, since Plato, has been feared as the ugly face of democracy (Ess, 1996; Paletz, 2000).

Apart from these problems, which cast doubt on whether e-democracy is really desirable at all, there are also numerous practical problems. Among these we find the nature of the internet, which is designed to avoid central control, which might make it difficult to regulate it to the extent that it might be suitable for e-democratic purposes (Lessig, 2001). Then there is the complex of problems caused by globalisation and the change of the nature of the state. E-democracy offers the vision of a world-wide democracy but at the same time we do not know how global problems can be addressed. Our political system and our democracies are based on the nation-state, whose future may be uncertain (see Castells, 1997).

The commercial paradigm in e-government and e-democracy

Thus far I have argued that the ethical qualities of e-democracy are of central importance for the legitimacy of democracy. I then discussed how ICT can be used in two fundamentally different ways within democracies: as a tool for administration and service delivery or as a means of changing the way democracy is conducted. The former, here called e-government, is less problematic as it only aims to change the modes of delivery of established processes. The latter, e-democracy, holds radical promises as well as potential pitfalls, both of which are closely linked to its moral foundation. What I am interested in is how the use of business as a paradigm influences the discussion, perception and use of ICT in a democracy.

Reasons for the use of the commercial paradigm

The reason why e-commerce may seem like a useful paradigm for the use of ICT in governments is its success. If e-commerce could be successful, so the argument goes, then e-government or e-democracy should copy the approaches and processes and thereby copy the success. Furthermore, business in general is perceived to be able to overcome problems inherent in democratic decision making and administration, and the adoption of the commercial paradigm is implied to improve this situation.

Spelled out in more detail, there are several explicit or implicit arguments for the adoption of the commercial paradigm. First, there is the technical one. Many of the commercially available systems have now reached a level of maturity that allows businesses to depend on them and to generate steady profits. Using such established systems (possible systems would include enterprise resource planning or customer relationship management) would allow administrations to avoid the tedious systems development process.

Apart from the technical side, there are organisational issues. Democratic institutions are often perceived to be bureaucratic and slow, to be inflexible and to disregard the needs of the citizens. Business in general and e-commerce in particular are viewed differently. Modern businesses need to be agile, to understand their environment, including competitors, suppliers and customers, and they can focus their efforts when necessary. Translated to governments, this would mean that decisions could be made more quickly while incorporating the important stakeholders. Commercial processes should overcome bureaucracies and allow a focus on the citizen. Last but not least, it should go some way towards addressing the problem of motivation. Civil servants and democratic politicians are often viewed as unsuitable for their jobs and not sufficiently motivated. The business world supposedly knows how to deal with this sort of problem through sophisticated management of incentives and human resources.

Then there are the commercial benefits based on market principles that could be translated into political benefits. Among them we find a greater liberty and more choice for the consumer. In terms of democracy, this might translate into competition between jurisdictions, or between organisations within jurisdictions. This should lead to more freedom and better services for the citizen.

While these are probably not the only advantages of the commercial paradigm, they encompass the most important ones. For the current argument, it is important to see that these contentions are of a moral nature. Whether it is the mere improvement of business processes, the saving of costs or the general overhaul of administrations, they all translate into moral goods such as freedom, welfare and distribution for the citizen.

Problems with the commercial paradigm

While there are good reasons to apply the commercial paradigm to ICT use in government and politics, some of which have a clear moral content, there are also plausible arguments to be raised against it. I will briefly look at the limits of the analogy of customer and citizen, at the problem of the analogy of business and politics, and finally at genuine political problems.

The first problem of the commercial paradigm is the equation of customers and citizens. This is useful in so far as citizens have the same role as customers, namely as recipients of services and goods. However, it is important to see that there are fundamental differences between customers and citizens. A company caters to the needs of customers but only when, or if, doing so is in its own interest. A customer who is overly troublesome, cannot pay, threatens the organisation's integrity, etc. has no right to be catered to. Conversely, citizens remain citizens no matter what. While a customer usually has a choice between suppliers, the same is rarely true for citizens. We cannot choose which country or state we want to live in. Furthermore, the state has a huge amount of power over the citizen, which is not comparable with the firm's power over the customer. Most importantly, customer and company are fundamentally separate entities, whereas citizen and state depend on one another. Ideally, in a democracy the government should represent the state, which is a manifestation of the people who are citizens of the state. A government thus has to accept citizens because it is (indirectly) acting on their behalf. Describing citizens as customers thus takes away their input and ownership in state and government, and thereby robs the state of its own power basis.

The next group of problems of the commercial paradigm consist of the analogy of political and economic system. Can the state be run like a company or a market and is political leadership like commercial management? There are some reasons to answer in the negative. First, there is the problem of competition. We have seen that the strength of the commercial paradigm is partly based on competition, which is supposed to create more motivation and better welfare. In politics there is the question of whether competition between governments is fundamentally possible or desirable. What should competition in government look like? Should we have to compare financial authorities and the one with the better tax rate wins? This seems unlikely. Competition is only possible between states, and even then it is questionable because citizens are not free to choose. Another problem of competition, when applied to citizens, is that, by definition, it produces losers. If citizens were to compete for state services, then some would not get them. This is sometimes possible and legitimate (e.g. for research grants), but in many cases the nature of state services makes it inevitable that some would have to lose (e.g. social welfare).

Second, there is the problem of efficiency. Efficiency is supposed to be one of the great strengths of businesses and something that politics and public administration lack. However, a closer look reveals that it is difficult to define efficiency. In economics it is usually held to be Pareto optimality (Sen, 1987), which means that a state is efficient where no more mutually beneficial exchanges are possible. The problem with this definition is that it neglects the question of justice, as a state where one person owned everything and nobody else owned anything would be 'efficient'. This definition of efficiency therefore does not seem useful, but others are not readily available.

Possibly even more serious than the problems of the comparability between economic and political sphere are the genuine political problems the commercial paradigm creates. Among them there is the question of public goods. While markets may be good at allocating scarce goods under competition, they are notoriously bad at dealing with public goods (such as the environment, public infrastructure, etc.) One of the legitimating aspects of democratic governments is that they are able to use an impartial perspective in the allocation and management of public goods such as network infrastructure (Chapman and Rotenberg, 1995). Similarly, it can be argued that the commercial realm is not good at providing other aspects which are vital for the ethical legitimacy of democracies. Among them one finds access, which is often discussed in terms of ICT and the digital divide (Breen, 1999; Trauth *et al.*, 2006) but which extends more generally to access to the political life. Even more important is the question of the distribution of power. Democracies require the fiction that everybody has equal access to power. While this is arguably not always the case, there still is a high degree of theoretical equality between citizens. The capitalist system has no intrinsic interest in equality of access and power (Introna, 2001), and its application to politics could thus jeopardise democratic legitimacy.

The most serious issue with regard to the political problems of the commercial paradigm is that it transports a more or less hidden political ideology, namely capitalist liberalism. The very idea that the state can be seen as an economic system implies that it should be left alone and is self-regulating, the way markets are usually described. This is an ideology, because it hides vested interests and describes as natural and unchangeable what is in fact human-made and contingent (Hirschheim and Klein, 1994). At the same time, this economic description of politics finds many proponents because it plays to the libertarian culture of the early internet (Fagin, 2000; Winner, 2000). The political culture of e-democracy as based on e-commerce is therefore not a neutral construct but carries with it a number of implications that are not necessarily accepted by everyone. Among these implications there is the suggestion that commercial exchange is the key social interaction, which in turn implies a commodification not only of knowledge and information (Yoon, 1996) but, at the extreme, of human relationships and political exchange.

E-teaching, e-government, e-democracy and critique

This chapter has taken up the ongoing stream of critique of capitalism that concentrates on the problematic influence that capitalist considerations can have on areas that are not necessarily, or not always, subject to market forces. In both cases, e-teaching and e-government/e-democracy, I have put forward the argument that there are important ethical underpinnings of the original activity, teaching and democratic government, and that the introduction of ICT can lead to an increased influx of market-oriented thinking, which can come into conflict with the original ethical justification of the area.

The argument seems fairly straightforward and it is probably hard to deny that there may be some merit to it. At the same time, it can also be somewhat problematic. Unless one wants to follow a technological determinist position, one needs to admit that these developments are not logically necessary and that the opposite may also be true. Teaching may become more fulfilling and emancipatory as a result of the use of technology, and democracy may be made more inclusive and fulfilling by the introduction of technology. Whether technology thus follows the problematic path outlined here therefore seems to be an empirical question. However, this is not something that a critical scholar will easily believe. Without denying the importance of more research into both e-teaching and e-government, one also needs to realise that it is more than likely that evidence of both alienating and emancipatory consequences of technology and its capitalist support is likely to be found. This brings us back to the question of the purpose of empirical research and how critical scholars can engage with it without losing sight of their critical aims. The only way such problems can be addressed, if not overcome, seems to be the reflexivity of critical research, which I have already alluded to in several places in this book. Reflexivity means that the researcher needs to continuously reflect on her or his role in the research and must remain open to questions about all aspects thereof. Critical researchers needs to be able to contextualise the ontological as well as the epistemological aspects of their work and to be able to refer the research findings or methods of analysis to the greater moral framework of critical research and its aim to improve the world.

In terms of e-teaching and e-government this means that the researcher should keep in mind that both of these have strong moral underpinnings and that those underpinnings form part of the ideology that legitimises them. Researchers need to be aware of such ideologies, even if they are ideologies they share or support, in order to prevent them from sedimenting into reifications which can hurt the critical enterprise. Furthermore, there must be awareness of differing and possibly contradictory ideologies, which can be imported into an area via technology. This chapter has argued that such an ideology import is not only possible but easily observable in such ubiquitous technology applications as e-teaching and e-government. There is nothing inherently capitalist about ICT and there is nothing inherently alienating about ICT use in teaching or democratic governance. However, the way current systems are designed needs to be understood in its capitalist frame of reference. A customer relationship management system, for example, is geared towards particular purposes, and these do not usually include the inclusion of marginalised groups. A simple transfer of such a technical system to a social system with different aims from the ones it was originally envisaged for can thus lead to ideological problems. The Critical Researchers should understand such problems and be able to reflect on their own influence on them. And clearly this influence is considerable. The academic profession has a high standing and can confer legitimacy on its research objects, and can therefore be used to mask the particular leanings associated with certain technologies or certain uses of technologies.

Reflexivity thus seems to be the key for critical research to be able to sustain its emancipatory claims and to retain the legitimating narratives on which it is built. This implies that any piece of critical research or scholarship needs to be open to reflection on its assumptions, background and contradictions. This is clearly true for a long and foundational text such as this one, which leads me to the final main part of the book, in which I will undertake a critical reflection of the narrative I have developed here.

Part IV
Reflection(s)

The criterion of reflexivity requires critical researchers to be open about their own background and prejudices. This background includes their motivations for doing critical research as well as an awareness of their shortcomings and limitations. Complete honesty is not possible because it would require complete knowledge of the self, which is not likely to be attainable. But that does not rule out the attempt to be frank and honest about the limitation of the critical narrative. In this final section, I will discuss some of the problems of critical research in general and critical research in information systems (CRIS) in particular. This discussion will prepare the ground for some suggestions as to what critical scholars should consider and how critical research in IS can be developed further.

15 Limitations of the critical approach

A first, and fundamental, observation with regard to this book is that its story, like any other story, is limited and excludes other stories. Throughout the book I have very much concentrated on matters of ethics and morality and linked these with critical theories on a number of levels. Critical theory is based on and motivated by moral views, often explicit ones, of the researcher. The main aim of critical research, emancipation, has a moral nature and requires ethical scrutiny and justification. Because of the ethical nature of critical research, any attempt to realise it runs into problems where its ethical base conflicts with other views of ethics. This is also one reason why empirical critical research is so problematic. Critical research claims never to be exclusively descriptive, while, at the same time, the normative component is difficult to accommodate in research design, and even more difficult to express in research publications. Despite the importance of ethics and morality for CRIS, I have also detailed where and how they can become a problem. Accepted morality is a main vehicle of ideology, and criticalists need to be careful in accepting moral claims and need to understand their provenance and be able to deconstruct them. The morality of critical research will often conflict with the morality of the research subjects, and there is no easy way to reconcile the two.

The emphasis on ethics and morality in critical research is one of the main contributions of this book. At the same time, this emphasis has crowded out a number of alternative narratives. My concentration on a small subset of critical theories has kept me from exploring other theories such as postcolonialism or different streams of postmodernism. I have tried to construct the current narrative in a linear fashion. The reader will, hopefully, agree that this book is reasonably coherent and contains few contradictions. This means, however, that I have followed the traditional academic style of writing and thereby constructed a reality that may not be shared or accepted by other critical scholars. I may be accused of promoting the Enlightenment style of straightforward rationality that may be the root cause of the ills of modernity, as Horkheimer and Adorno (2004) argued so powerfully over 60 years ago. My response, which I model on Habermas's ideas and which I discussed in more depth in Chapter 4 on the problems of cross-cultural emancipation, would be that there seems to be no way of escaping a communication-oriented rationality and that all we can do is remain open to alternative accounts.

This modernist approach is the one I am most familiar with and the one that I feel most comfortable with. This leads to the difficult problem of the role of the researcher and its influence on the possibility of reaching one's goals. There is a disconnection between some aspects of the arguments I have developed and my personal life. I have emphasised the role of capitalism in the alienation of individuals and have thereby drawn heavily on traditional Marxist figures of thought. This leads to associations of class struggle between capitalists and proletarians, which history arguably does not support, at least not in the way envisaged by Marx. And it leads to the problem of the role of critical intellectuals, which Marxists have grappled with for so long. I am probably not a capitalist in a strong sense of the word, but neither am I a proletarian. My life is that of a comfortable member of the middle class with a sufficient income and all the material niceties and lack of existential worries that one can associate with the middle class. I am thus a product and a beneficiary of the social system that I criticise, and this position creates cognitive tensions. Moreover, as a member of the academic community I have a range of privileges that others, including capitalists, can only dream of. As a member of this community I communicate with fellow members, and this book can best be understood as an attempt to do just that. While it is of course acceptable to share thoughts with the group one considers one's peers, there is at the same time the danger that this will lead to an elitist discourse, defining insiders and outsiders. The use of a certain vocabulary renders the arguments difficult to access by some. I also move in terrain familiar to myself (what else could I do?), which renders my work a possible contribution to elitist and Eurocentric thinking, thus opening it up to the charge of promoting its own ideology (Kincheloe and McLaren, 2005).

The role of the critical scholar or intellectual in the framework of critical thinking seems to be intrinsically problematic. There seems to be no way of exposing ideologies and overcoming reifications without replacing these with new ones. Our best hope is that criticalists are more honest about this and more open to being questioned in this regard than non-critical scholars.

There are further problems arising from the Marxist history of critical research. I have mentioned that the Marxist tradition of critical work is more widespread in continental Europe than in the Anglo-American world. By drawing on this tradition I have located this book in the wider area of Marxism, which raises the question of the continuing relevance of Marxist analyses. There is no doubt that Marxism, if taken as a collection of theoretical approaches to social reality, still has much to teach us, and there are good current examples of this in IS (Greenhill and Wilson, 2006). This leaves open the question of how much Marxist thought one should accept and to what degree one can disregard it because it is no longer relevant or has lost its plausibility.

A central question here is the evaluation of and consequent attitude towards capitalism. Marxism is highly critical of capitalism and sees the root cause of social problems in the capitalist constitution of the economy. The economy as the base of society influences the superstructure of all other fields of social activity such as education, culture, etc. This view is problematic for several reasons. First, it seems less believable now than it may have seemed 150 or even 50 years ago that the influence of the economy on society is a one-way street. Economic structures clearly have an influence on most areas of life, and several of my application examples above have alluded to this. However, there is also great influence from other sectors on the economy, and many such sectors are now main drivers of the economy. Education or creative activities have now become major industries and cannot be divorced from the economy.

One way of viewing this would be to interpret it as the victory of capitalism, which now pervades most walks of life. Capitalist thinking has entered not only healthcare and education but even formerly private relationships such as the economics of partner choice or economic considerations related to family policy. Yet while this is a possible and to some degree convincing view, it does not capture the whole phenomenon. Capitalism with its increasingly fine-tuned reward systems is perceived as a rich sphere of experience. There are still many instances of alienation, oppression and exploitation, but many members of modern societies seem to enjoy modern ways of living. Capitalism and globalisation are deeply problematic for the many, be they the forgotten in areas far from international exchange or the unemployed in industrial societies whose jobs have gone to areas with cheaper labour. However, there are also numerous winners who have the abilities to use the opportunities of an increasingly global market but also those of global ways of communicating and exchanging ideas. Many academics, including myself, are among those who are able to exploit these new opportunities. We are therefore well advised to be careful with blanket condemnations of capitalism.

A further aspect of the debate on capitalism is that capitalism is not an immovable and ancient block. One of the reasons for the success of capitalism seems to be its ability to change and adapt. This explicitly includes the ability to react to criticism and even incorporate critical views. An example of this is the environmental debate. For a long time it seemed that capitalism was the root cause of environmental problems. While this is certainly still true in many respects, one can also observe a change in capitalist rhetoric that allows an alternative expression of capitalism. Where natural resources are explicitly considered, capitalist ways of exchange seem capable of preserving nature. This is of course a much larger debate than I can capture. But it indicates one of the problems that critical scholars have with capitalism. Simple slogans just do not capture it.

A related observation is that capitalism is not always perceived by its subjects as problematic or alienating. Some of us may still slave away, but many enjoy the thrills of capitalism. Not only does it provide a substantial basis for sustenance and has at least contributed to the eradication of many diseases in the capitalist West and an enormous increase in life expectancy, but it can be positively fun (Thrift, 2005). This refers to the consumption of goods, which, albeit often unnecessary and frivolous, still evokes positive emotions in many of us.

More importantly, capitalism opens new ways of proving our abilities and exercising our strengths, ways that many individuals have learned to enjoy. The problem of the criticalist is here again how to judge such views. Traditional critical theory used to speak of false consciousness, and there still is the suspicion that people are being led to enjoy activities or goods which are detrimental to their true desires. There is some truth to this, but at the same time this type of view raises the problem that I have discussed under the heading or emancipation across cultures. Clearly, most of us do not really need another car and even more food. We see through the misleading promises of advertising but are still influenced by it. But on what grounds can the critical scholar put some values ahead of others and demand of others to follow this preference order?

Furthermore, capitalism is strongly linked to academia, in particular to business schools but also to other disciplines. Via these venues and via discourses such as the critical management studies one, critical thoughts are disseminated to business students, who can use them to create alternative conceptions of economic reality. This means that the privileged and external viewpoint that academics have on the economic sphere may simply no longer exist and that businesses may be much more advanced in theory and self-perceptions than critical scholars tend to give them credit for (Thrift, 2005).

All this leads to the problem of radicalism. Traditional critical theory, in particular the Marxist schools of thought were often radical. In effect they sought to overcome or even overthrow current social institutions and replace them with better, more just and emancipated ones. There are no doubt still many criticalists around who would sign up to such notions, but they are no longer the majority. This seems to be the case in critical management studies, and it is most certainly true for CRIS. Even those authors who explicitly reference Marx tend to use his work as a means to criticise a particular instance of injustice without demanding an overthrow of our current social institutions.

One of the main aims of critical research is liberalism, often equated with capitalism. Critical scholars of different disciplines tend to agree that liberalism is problematic. Also, liberal discourses are described as means of camouflaging underlying social problems that appear more soluble and less drastic if the liberal idea of ascribing responsibility to individuals is followed (Adam and Kreps, 2006). Clearly, this is problematic, and the liberal tradition linked with methodological individualism and unidimensional rationality go counter to much critical research. At the same time, some of the ideas of classical liberalism are arguably the condition of the possibility of critique of modern society. The critical intention to emancipate is deeply liberal. Indeed, the term 'liberal', with its etymological connection to 'freedom', epitomises the critical intention. In effect, this means that current critical research, even where it is critical of liberalism, is less critical of the ideals of liberalism than of the implementation and misuse of liberalism. One legitimate aim of critical scholarship is to point out the contradictions in liberalism (Adam, 2005), but that is a long way away from overthrowing society.

It seems to be true of CRIS, then, that it is not radical, that it does not aim to overthrow society but is content with pointing out the contradictions in society.

This leaves CRIS in the uncomfortable position of being distinctly close to interpretive research. And it may well be that the distinction between CRIS and interpretive IS research is less clear-cut than one might think. In the end, there is not even a strong reason to assume that critical research must be fundamentally different from a positivist stance, as even positivists may research discrepancies between claims and reality. I have already discussed this issue with regard to academic paradigms, and one could argue that it does not raise any problems. There remains the problem for critical scholars, however, of whether what they do is distinctive in any respect. If, as I have argued above, the intention to emancipate is the main criterion for critical research, then the only thing that may distinguish a critical research project from a non-critical one is the researcher's mindset. This leads to problems, given that we cannot know other people's thoughts and are often hard-pressed to know our own. It means that there may be no practical difference between critical and non-critical work, which leads us back to the issue of identity of critical research.

One possible solution to this is to move the focus of attention away from the researcher and towards the outcomes of the research. If critical research is to effect emancipation and overcome oppression, then one could argue that its most important characteristic should be the fulfilment of these goals. One problem with this position is the one discussed previously, namely that it is difficult to agree on what exactly emancipation means and that there may be a disagreement on emancipation between researcher and subject. This links in with the issue of capitalism. There is a strong assumption among intellectual circles that, for example, the passive consumption of trivial television programmes is alienating and should be overcome. There is a long tradition of critique of media use and consumption in critical research, and it extends to the use of new media, which are close to the interests of many critical IS scholars. However, how are we to argue that individuals should stop and overcome practices if they themselves do not feel alienated and even enjoy them?

A further problem of concentrating on the emancipatory outcomes of critical research is that it would put an additional onus on critical scholars which would put them at a disadvantage when compared to others. Assuming that it is possible to judge the emancipatory qualities of critical research (a shaky assumption at the best of times), the reliance on this measure for the evaluation of the success of critical research means that there would have to be an additional research cycle attached to each project. In practice this would make critical research more burdensome and it would be detrimental to the entire critical enterprise, at least in so far as it moves within the given boundaries of western academic institutions.

Despite these problems, one should not simply discard the notion of practical consequences. For logical reasons, a research approach that aims to change social realities should be questioned on how this can be done or is to be expected. There may not be any hard and fast answers to such a question, but that is no good reason for simply ignoring them. To put it differently, critical researchers are under a stronger expectation to consider the practical outcomes and the possibility of realising their work than their non-critical counterparts.

This leads to the issue of relevance. Within the IS discipline there has been much discussion on rigour versus relevance. This debates takes on a slightly different meaning when applied to critical research. Critical research does not have clear standards of rigour comparable to the ones accepted in positivist quantitative research. At the same time, its claims to relevance are arguably even stronger than in other approaches, owing to the fundamental claim to emancipation, liberation, and change of status quo. How such relevance is to be achieved is a different question.

16 The future of critical research in information systems

I have argued that CRIS is distinguished from other approaches by its intention to improve the world. This is arguably the main appeal of the approach but also its Achilles' heel. Critical scholars want to make a difference, but there is no agreement on what this difference is, how they could know about it or how it is to be achieved. In addition, such practical goals sit uncomfortably with the rules of academia, in which much critical scholarship is produced.

That does not mean, however, that there is no way of engaging with critical research in IS. An important aspect of being able to fulfil the self-imposed criterion of emancipation will be its conceptualisation and the reach of the claim raised by critical scholars. The solution may lie in a bit of modesty as regards critical claims. Rather than aiming at true emancipation of research subjects, critical scholars could view themselves as contributors to discourses whose eventual aim would be emancipation. Such a view would open more avenues for critical research and it would give critical work legitimacy in those cases where no straight line can be drawn between critical activity and practical emancipatory outcome.

Much of the conceptual work presented in this book, but also in other critical publications, will then find its justification in the quality of the argument rather than in practical impacts. Exposing ideologies, uncovering reifications or revealing commodifications are then aims in their own right which find their legitimacy in the underlying discursive structure of society. This view of critical research is based upon some sort of Enlightenment hope for rationality and the Habermasian optimism that the better argument can win. A Foucauldian understanding of discourse as a power game is more problematic here. However, at least for academic criticalists, this should not pose too much of a problem, given that the entire academic system is based on the hope that better arguments can be recognised and preferred over less good ones.

One might doubt the viability of this limited understanding of CRIS and raise the question of realisability again. If CRIS is just a voice in a complex chorus, can it truly claim to be critical, given that the potential result may be non-existent? The answer to this could be that this is all that can be expected. And while it may not look like a lot, one should also not underestimate the power of discursive interventions. A look at the history of critical research shows that critical contributions to a variety of discourses can have manifest results even when a direct causal link between a particular argument a specific outcome may be impossible to establish. One prominent example of this would be the 1968 student unrests which disrupted university life in much of Europe and North America. Based in large parts on the critical writings of the Frankfurt School, they were clearly not successful in all of their multi-faceted goals. But they did result in manifest changes in university education in many countries. They furthermore led to the legitimising of arguments and figures of thought much beyond this. A look at current western societies reveals that several of the aims of the students, including the recognition of alternative ways of expressing sexuality or of redefining power relationships in universities, have been achieved, at least in part. There are different influence factors as well, but one could argue that critical discourses contributed to the shaping of society.

The understanding of CRIS as a contribution to the discourse of information systems that emphasises emancipation, empowerment and freedom allows this body of work to fit within the existing disciplinary structure. While much critical work aims to show the weaknesses of current approaches, such an understanding would nevertheless see critical research as an integral part of the overall landscape. It would thus overcome the potential problem of being excluded, or of self-exclusion, from traditional discourses. One of the main problems of such an exclusion is that it precludes the criticalist from engaging in ongoing discussion and thus from changing current practices (Fournier and Grey, 2000). Critical research as a contribution to discourses would also overcome some of the internal issues of critical debate. There are ongoing and sometimes severe differences between different strands of critical scholarship, which have led the critical project to spend much time on internal debates where arguably the more important issue would have been to engage with external positions. Such internal debates are of course important, and I have engaged in them in this book. A larger picture of critical work as one contribution to societal discourse may reduce the overemphasis of such divisions.

My following suggestions on how critical research in IS could be developed and furthered should be seen in this light. I do not claim that these are the only possible ones or that they exclude other approaches. I realise that I am partial and that I follow a stream of critical scholarship, namely the Frankfurt School tradition with an emphasis on Habermas, which is contentious in many respects. However, I believe that the narratives developed throughout this book can make a useful contribution to the development of CRIS.

Since the one pervading thought of this book was that the importance of ethics and morality for CRIS needs to be recognised and discussed, I will use some of the ideas relating to this to suggest further development in the field. The earlier distinction between the French and the German ways of using the terms 'ethics' and 'morality' may serve as an indicator of some of the issues CRIS needs to address.

Let us start with the German tradition, in which morality stands for the accepted norms and ethics for the theory and justification of morality. I think that this distinction is helpful in identifying some of the problems of CRIS as well as possible solutions. One such problem is the status of emancipation. If we see emancipation as a moral notion in this context, which means as a material norm telling critical scholars what to do, then we run into all sorts of problems, as discussed earlier. We would have to figure out what exactly constitutes emancipation and how it can be implemented. A resulting likely problem would be a lack of agreement of the research subjects, leading to the danger of the dictatorship of the intellectual, which critical scholars cannot really aim for. The situation changes once we realise that critical work cannot aim directly to influence morality but has to take it into account as a possible alienating force. Some of the applications described earlier in the book, for example the ideological use of privacy and security, support this point. Critical scholars need to understand the importance of particular meanings of moral terms in given contexts, which can turn them into means of oppression. Marcuse (1964), for example, uses the example of the concept of liberty, which can be turned into a powerful instrument of domination under the rule of a repressive whole. Criticalists should be weary of moral concepts and terms, but the German tradition offers a way out short of discarding all ethical thoughts.

Rather than defining a particular morality and promoting it in the name of emancipation, critical scholars would be in a better position to ethically assess morality and intervene in such ethical discourses. This requires some degree of literacy in ethical theory but it also points towards a way to realise ethical ideas. If moral norms are the results of collective interaction, then the process of this interaction – what I, following Foucault and Habermas, have called discourse – is the place to be active. Much critical work can then be interpreted as a contribution to the shaping of our moral stances, which allows ethical engagement without moral dictatorship. This reintroduction of the concept of discourse this time as a means to address ethical issues in critical work raises some of the problems discussed earlier. What concept of discourse do we use, how do we engage in it, how do we analyse outcomes? My suggestion clearly points towards a Habermasian type of discourse, which by construction includes ethical components. But even a Foucauldian analysis of discourse is not a problem if fed back into the discourse by theoretically aware critical scholars. The rigour versus relevance debate in IS may be an example. One can clearly see it as a means to establish a regime of truth that favours particular aspects of IS research. However, a Foucauldian analysis of just this fact fed back into the discourse, as done by Introna (2003a), leads to a modification of understanding of the original contributions.

A further piece of guidance that the German distinction of ethics and morality can provide critical scholars with is that the only way to intervene in ethical matters that does not run afoul of existing moral notions is procedural. Modern ethical theories, a category that includes Kantian deontology just as much as utilitarianism, share the characteristic of being of a procedural nature. They do not tell people what to do but they tell them how they can come to an acceptable answer to the question. The same is true for critical research and its ethical intention. Interpreting emancipation as an ethical concept rather than a moral one, one could argue that emancipation requires the introduction of structures that will allow the identification of particular instances of emancipation rather than define it up front. This raises the question of what the structures are that allow for the implementation of emancipation as an ethical notion. It seems to me that some of them are relatively clear. Emancipation requires the input of those who are to be emancipated. They need to be able to voice their opinion and influence ongoing discussions regarding the design and use of technology. It thus seems reasonable to assume that this points towards participative approaches to system development and democratic views of managing organisations. Wilson's (1997) objection that this exchanges one type of ideology for another does not hold if the critical process ensures that relevant voices can be raised, even if they run counter to expectations. Critical scholarship then takes the form of promoting democratic structures, including the spreading of the conditions of democracy, throughout the field of its application. This is not a new thought (Cecez-Kecmanovic, 2005; Alvarez, 2005) but is now underpinned by ethical considerations which are at the core of critical work.

The French tradition of ethics and morality is also in a position to point out some areas where current CRIS work could benefit from further development. In the French tradition, ethics stands for the Aristotelian practice of debating the good life. This refers to one's individual life-plans but also to the collective view of how our society should be structured. This, I think, is an area where critical work needs to develop and where critical discourses should intensify. I have noted early in my definition of CRIS that currently there seems to be agreement that the existing social arrangements we find ourselves in are not always satisfactory and could be improved. The common denominator with regard to the good life thus seems to be a negative one, namely that we have not yet achieved it. This may not be enough to attract others to the critical view. The history of critical theory gives ample examples of a conception of the good life, most prominently in the form of the classless society envisaged by Marx and some of his followers. There seem to be few who still believe such a society is either possible or desirable. But if this is no longer the critical vision, then what is?

It seems obvious that such a deep question will not find a simple answer here. Critical theory gives some indication of the shape of the good life, however. It has to do with power and a more equal distribution thereof than we see today. Another aspect is that of economic distribution of goods but, more importantly, of life chances and possibilities to interact and develop oneself. An important aspect is that of education which will help individuals shape their own view of emancipation. Critical theory thus gives some pointers towards what the good life might look like. It is not likely that critical scholars will agree on the exact shape of a good society but it may be possible that some agreement can be reached on desirable institutions or processes. What seems to be important to me is that this type of debate should be held more prominently and that different views shall be made explicit. Otherwise there is the danger that the critical community assumes that there is a shared view of the central concept of the good life, whereas this may not be the case.

A final suggestion for further development of critical research in IS has to do with the French notion of morality. This was introduced as based on the recognition that the shared view of the good life requires rules and constraints in order to avoid individual domination and violence. To me this is an aspect that CRIS and critical research in general seems to engage in very little. One related thought is the one going back to Montaigne that moral norms are important and desirable and that their form is in the first instance of secondary importance. Morality is required to sustain order and allow the pursuit of the good life. Much critical theory has taken a different view and attempted to do away with established moral norms in the name of emancipation. And in many cases there will have been good reasons for this because the norms were oppressive. What critical theory has often lost sight of is the fact that moral norms will still be required. The question will be what form such norms should have. The reflection on such norms strikes me as an important contribution to the critical debate, which will be required if we want to engage with questions such as how critical thoughts are to be realised.

Overall, then, there seems much left to do for critical research in information systems. The field is still characterised by the dominance of positivism and purposive rationality. Critical scholars have an important contribution to make to overcome this dominant discourse and provide alternative narratives. This book has, hopefully, contributed to the foundation of this debate and provided some pointers to where further work could be headed.

Appendix A

Discourse analysis of the Egyptian information society

A1 Guiding questions to identify Habermasian validity claims (adapted from Cukier *et al*., 2003, 2004)

Truth: argumentation and evidence

T1 **What is said** about the technology?
T2 Are the issues and options **clearly defined**?
T3 What **costs and benefits** have been identified and assessed?
T4 What **evidence** has been provided to support these arguments?
T5 Has the relevant information been communicated without **distortion or omission**?
T6 Are there **ideological claims** which are unexamined?

Legitimacy: whose interests?

L1 **Who is speaking**, who is silent, what are their interests?
L2 **What is privileged**? What is not said about the technology?
L3 What is **assumed or implied**?
L4 What is **missing or suppressed** in the discourse?
L5 How are the decisions **legitimised**?
L6 **Who** is **involved**? Who is **not involved**?
L7 What are the **stakes and interests** involved or excluded?

Sincerity: metaphors and descriptors

S1 Do metaphors and connotative words promote or suppress understanding?
S2 Do **metaphors** and connotative words create **false assurances**?

Clarity

C1 Is there use of **jargon**?
C2 Are there **terms** that are **not explained**?
C3 Is there evidence of **obfuscation**?

A2 List of validity claims used for coding the text during critical discourse analysis

Validity claim	Sub-claim	Specific instance of claim	Number of claims (total number: 1,248)
Truth			557
	Definition		1
	Costs		14
		Economic costs	14
	Benefits		252
		Economic (growth, cost, efficiency)	110
		Development	2
		Literacy/education	37
		Healthcare	26
		Political benefits	25
		Other benefits	50
	Evidence		25
		Statistical evidence	4
		Research; science	1
		Other evidence	1
	Distortion		22
	Omission		9
	Ideology		112
		Market metaphysics	52
		Role of the government	56
		Other ideological statements	1
	Problems		123
		Access	27
		Language	8
		Digital Divide	4
		Failure	3
		Other problems	76
Legitimacy			487
	Speaker		3
	Non-speaker (who is silent)		1
	Assumptions (about technology)		28
		Technological determinism	18
	Legitimation (of argument, not benefits of technology)		166
		Local/regional interests	55
		Success	75
		Academic/scientific research	10
		Other means of legitimation	22
	Stakeholders		265
		Citizens	20

Validity claim	Sub-claim	Specific instance of claim	Number of claims (total number: 1,248)
		Companies	71
		Government	156
		NGOs	3
		Other stakeholders	12
	Missing stakeholders		17
Sincerity: Metaphors/ descriptors			70
	Metaphor		27
		Citizen as consumer	5
		Promotes understanding	2
		Suppresses understanding	11
	False assurances		42
		Technical solutions	35
Clarity			133
	Jargon		47
		Technical jargon	44
		Economic jargon	3
	Unexplained terms		11
	Obfuscation		47
		E-government as service delivery	29
	Irrelevant information		28
		Consultant-speak	21
		Developed world (does not apply to Egypt)	7

A3 List of texts used for discourse analysis

[1] 'ICT Trust Fund Projects', available www.mcit.gov.eg/brochures/ ICT.pdf [accessed 29 September 2004]

[2] 'Egypt's Message to the Global Information Society', available www.mcit.gov.eg/Egy_vis_mess.asp [accessed 28 September 2004]

[3] 'E-Bridges: Introduction', available www.mcit.gov.eg/Egy_vis_introd.asp [accessed 8 October 2004]

[4] 'The Information Society and National Development: The Information Society', available www.mcit.gov.eg/Egy_vis_soc1.asp [accessed 13 October 2004]

[5] 'The Information Society and National Development, the Digital Divide', available www.mcit.gov.eg/Egy_vis_soc2.asp [accessed 18 October 2004]

[6] 'The Information Society and National Development, Strategic Challenges and Opportunities for Egypt', available www.mcit.gov.eg/Egy_vis_soc3. asp [accessed 18 October 2004]

[7]   'The Egyptian Information Society Initiative – Summary', available www.mcit.gov.eg/Egy_vis_infosoc.asp [accessed 26 October 2004]

[8]   'E-Readiness – Equal Access for All: The E-Readiness Initiative Will:', available   www.mcit.gov.eg/Egy_vis_infosoc_1_1.asp   [accessed   26 October 2004]

[9]   'E-Readiness – Equal Access for All, Our Policy Guidelines Are', available www.mcit.gov.eg/Egy_vis_infosoc_1_2.asp [accessed 26 October 2004]

[10] 'E-Readiness – Equal Access for All, Challenges and Proposed Solutions', available   www.mcit.gov.eg/Egy_vis_infosoc_1_3.asp   [accessed   26 October 2004]

[11] 'E-Readiness – Equal Access for All, Where Are We Today', available www.mcit.gov.eg/Egy_vis_infosoc_1_4.asp [accessed 26 October 2004]

[12] 'E-Readiness – Equal Access for All, The Way Forward', available www.mcit.gov.eg/Egy_vis_infosoc_1_5.asp [accessed 26 October 2004]

[13] 'E-Learning – Nurturing Human Capital, The E-Learning Initiative Will:', available www.mcit.gov.eg/Egy_vis_infosoc_2_1.asp [accessed 2 November 2004]

[15] 'E-Learning – Nurturing Human Capital, The E-Learning Initiative Follows a Number of Guiding Principles', available www.mcit.gov.eg/ Egy_vis_infosoc_2_2.asp [accessed 2 November 2004]

[16] 'E-Learning – Nurturing Human Capital, Implementation of the E-Learning Initiative is Faced with a Number of Challenges', available www.mcit. gov.eg/Egy_vis_infosoc_2_3.asp [accessed 2 November 2004]

[17] 'E-Learning – Nurturing Human Capital, Where Are We Today', available www.mcit.gov.eg/Egy_vis_infosoc_2_4.asp [accessed 2 November 2004]

[18] 'E-Learning – Nurturing Human Capital, The Way Forward', available www.mcit.gov.eg/Egy_vis_infosoc_2_5.asp [accessed 2 November 2004]

[19] '19 E-Government – Government Now Delivers, The E-Government Initiative Will:', available www.mcit.gov.eg/Egy_vis_infosoc_3_1.asp [accessed 11 November 2004]

[20] '20 E-Government – Government Now Delivers, Our Objectives Are to Ensure the Following', available www.mcit.gov.eg/ Egy_vis_infosoc_3_2. asp [accessed 11 November 2004]

[21] '21 E-Government – Government Now Delivers, Challenges and Proposed Solutions',   available   www.mcit.gov.eg/Egy_vis_infosoc_3_3.asp [accessed 11 November 2004]

[22] '22 E-Government – Government Now Delivers, Where Are We Today', available   www.mcit.gov.eg/Egy_vis_infosoc_3_4.asp   [accessed   11 November 2004]

[23] '23 E-Government – Government Now Delivers, the Way Forward', available www.mcit.gov.eg/Egy_vis_infosoc_3_5.asp [accessed 11 November 2004]

[24] 'E-Business – A New Way of Doing Business, the E-Business Initiative Will:', available www.mcit.gov.eg/Egy_vis_infosoc_4_1.asp [accessed 17 November 2004]

[25] 'E-Business – A New Way of Doing Business, the Initiative's Objectives Are to:', available www.mcit.gov.eg/Egy_vis_infosoc_4_2.asp [accessed 17 November 2004]

[26] 'E-Business – A New Way of Doing Business, Challenges and Proposed Solutions', available www.mcit.gov.eg/Egy_vis_infosoc_4_3.asp [accessed 17 November 2004]

[27] 'E-Business – A New Way of Doing Business, Where Are We Today', available www.mcit.gov.eg/Egy_vis_infosoc_4_4.asp [accessed 17 November 2004]

[28] 'E-Business – A New Way of Doing Business, The Way Forward', available www.mcit.gov.eg/Egy_vis_infosoc_4_5.asp [accessed 17 November 2004]

[39] 'E-Health – Increasing Health Services Availability, The E-Health Initiative Will:', available www.mcit.gov.eg/Egy_vis_infosoc_5_1.asp [accessed 30 November 2004]

[40] 'E-Health – Increasing Health Services Availability, To Achieve Our Objectives, We Have Formulated the Following Policies', available www.mcit.gov.eg/Egy_vis_infosoc_5_2.asp [accessed 30 November 2004]

[41] 'E-Health – Increasing Health Services Availability, Challenges and Proposed Solutions', available www.mcit.gov.eg/Egy_vis_infosoc_5_3.asp [accessed 30 November 2004]

[42] 'E-Health – Increasing Health Services, Where Are We Today', available www.mcit.gov.eg/Egy_vis_infosoc_5_4.asp [accessed 30 November 2004]

[43] 'E-Health – Increasing Health Services, The Way Forward', available www.mcit.gov.eg/Egy_vis_infosoc_5_5.asp [accessed 30 November 2004]

[44] 'E-Culture – Promoting Egyptian Culture, The E-Culture Initiative Will:', available www.mcit.gov.eg/Egy_vis_infosoc_6_1.asp [accessed 8 December 2004]

[45] 'E-Culture – Promoting Egyptian Culture, to Achieve Those Objectives', available www.mcit.gov.eg/Egy_vis_infosoc_6_2.asp [accessed 8 December 2004]

[46] 'E-Culture – Promoting Egyptian Culture, Challenges and Proposed Solutions', available www.mcit.gov.eg/Egy_vis_infosoc_6_3.asp [accessed 8 December 2004]

[47] 'E-Culture – Promoting Egyptian Culture, Where Are We Today', available www.mcit.gov.eg/Egy_vis_infosoc_6_4.asp [accessed 8 December 2004]

[48] 'E-Culture – Promoting Egyptian Culture, the Way Forward', available www.mcit.gov.eg/Egy_vis_infosoc_6_5.asp [accessed 8 December 2004]

[49] 'ICT Export Initiative – Industry Development, the ICT Export Initiative will:', available www.mcit.gov.eg/Egy_vis_infosoc_7_1.asp [accessed 8 December 2004]

[50] 'ICT Export Initiative – Industry Development, in Order to Achieve These Objectives', available www.mcit.gov.eg/Egy_vis_infosoc_7_2.asp [accessed 8 December 2004]

[51] 'ICT Export Initiative – Industry Development, Challenges and Proposed Solutions', available www.mcit.gov.eg/Egy_vis_infosoc_7_3.asp [accessed 8 December 2004]

[52] 'ICT Export Initiative – Industry Development, Where Are We Today', available www.mcit.gov.eg/Egy_vis_infosoc_7_4.asp [accessed 8 December 2004]

[53] 'ICT Export Initiative – Industry Development, The Way Forward', available www.mcit.gov.eg/Egy_vis_infosoc_7_5.asp [accessed 8 December 2004]

[54] 'Building Bridges with the Global Information Society', available www.mcit.gov.eg/Egy_vis_brid.asp [accessed 8 December 2004]

Appendix B

List of validity claims used for coding the text during critical discourse analysis of e-commerce trust research

Validity claim	Sub-claim	Specific instance of claim	Number of claims (total number: 682)
Truth			440
	Benefits of e-commerce		3
	Benefits of trust		
		Facilitation of exchange	78
		Financial advantage of trust	30
	Definition		
		Benevolence	7
		Calculus, calculative trust	18
		Complexity reduction	7
		Conditions of trust	31
		Expectation/belief/psychological state	56
		Function of trust	1
		Moral/ethical nature of trust	21
		Relationship	9
		Risk management	62
		Vulnerability acceptance	6
	Evidence		
		Empirical evidence	14
	Ideology		
		Economic/purposive rationality	25
		Market metaphysics	1
	Omission		
		Ethical/moral side of trust	3
		Meaning of trust, understanding of subjects	5
		Other factors relevant to explain the phenomenon	15
	Problems of e-commerce		
		Anonymity online	2
		Fraud, illegal behaviour	1
		Information asymmetry	2

Validity claim	Sub-claim	Specific instance of claim	Number of claims (total number: 682)
		Lack of traditional forms of trust	13
		Security	3
		Technology as the problem of e-commerce	1
	Problems of trust		
		Conceptual problems	21
		Familiarity, lack thereof	3
		Misuse/abuse of trust	2
Legitimacy			226
	Assumption		
		Production of trust is possible/ desirable	71
		Quantifiable nature of trust	22
		Technology can create/support creation of trust	6
	Legitimation		
		Academic research/theory as legitimation	13
		Mathematical/statistical validity	1
	Research assumptions		
		Laboratory experiments are desirable	4
		Limitations of research	29
		Purpose of research	51
		Treatment of research subjects	10
	Stakeholders		
		Business	8
		Consumers	0
		Management	3
		Researchers	7
		State/government	0
		Users	1
Sincerity: Metaphors/ descriptors			0
	Metaphor		
	False assurances		
Clarity			16
	Irrelevant information	Triviality	1
	Jargon	Mathematical/statistical jargon	15
Meta claims			not quantified
	Audience		
	Objectivity		
	Quantifiability		

Notes

1 Critical research in information systems

1 The concept of 'paradigm' was originally popularised in academia by Kuhn (1996). Where it is used in IS research, however, it tends to rely on Burrell and Morgan's (1979) understanding of the term. These two are arguably very different types of paradigms, which leads to some confusion. In this chapter I will follow Orlikowski and Baroudi (1991, p. 2), for whom the paradigm debate refers to a 'consistent philosophical world view'.

9 Information systems as means of (dis)empowerment: the information society and decision support systems in local authorities in Egypt

1 The titles and references of these texts are summarised in Appendix A3. When they are referenced, they will be referenced using the numbers indicated in Appendix A3 (e.g. [17]).
2 The interviews were conducted, translated and transcribed were required by Dr Ibrahim Elbeltagi. Data analysis was supported by Dr Neil McBride. I would like to thank both for allowing me to use their research findings. I need to stress that the interpretations and inferences are mine.

10 Responsible and heroic management of workplace privacy: a critical view of ICT management

1 For a discussion of the complex relationship of responsibility with different ethical theories and traditions, see Stahl (2004a).

11 Trust as fetish: a critical theory perspective on research on trust in e-commerce

1 The concept of ideology will be discussed in more depth in the following chapter.

References

Abdat, S. and Pervan, G. P. (2000) 'Reducing the Negative Effects of Power Distance during Asynchronous Pre-meeting with Using Anonymity in Indonesian Culture.' In: F. Sudweeks and C. Ess (eds) *Proceedings of the Second International Conference on Cultural Attitudes towards Technology and Communication*, Murdoch University Press, Murdoch, Western Australia: 209–215

Achterberg, J. S., van Es, G. A. and Heng, M. S. H. (1991) 'Information Systems Research in the Postmodern Period.' In: Nissen, H.-E., Klein, H. K. and Hirschheim, R. (eds) *Information Systems Research: Contemporary Approaches & Emergent Traditions*, Amsterdam, North-Holland: 281–294

Ackoff, R. L. (1967) 'Management Misinformation Systems.' *Management Science* (14:4), 147–156

Adam, A. (2001a) 'Computer Ethics in a Different Voice'. *Information and Organization* (11:4), 235–261

Adam, A. (2001b) 'Gender and Computer Ethics.' In: Spinello, R. A. and Tavani, H. T. (eds) *Readings in Cyberethics*, Jones and Bartlett, Sudbury, MA: 63–76

Adam, A. (2001c) 'Heroes or Sibyls? Gender and Engineering Ethics.' *IEEE Technology and Society Magazine* (20:3), 39–46

Adam, A. (2002) 'Cyberstalking and Internet Pornography: Gender and the Gaze.' *Ethics and Information Technology* (4:2), 133–142

Adam, A. (2005) *Gender, Ethics and Information Technology*. Palgrave Macmillan, Basingstoke, UK

Adam, A. and Kreps, D. (2006) 'Web Accessibility: A Digital Divide for Disabled People?' In: Trauth, E. M., Howcroft, D., Butler, T., Fitzgerald, B. and DeGross, J. I. (eds) *Social Inclusion: Societal and Organizational Implications for Information Systems*. IFIP vol. 208. Springer, New York: 217–228

Alavi, M. (1994) 'Computer-Mediated Collaborative Learning: An Empirical Evaluation.' *MIS Quarterly* (18:2), 159–174

Alavi, M., Wheeler, B. C. and Valacich, J. S. (1995) 'Using IT to Reengineer Business Education: An Exploratory Investigation of Collaborative Telelearning.' *MIS Quarterly* (19:3), 293–312

Alexander, S. (2001) 'E-Learning Developments and experiences.' *Education + Training* (43:4, 5), 240–238

Alpern, K. D. (1997) 'What Do We Want Trust to Be?' *Business and Professional Ethics Journal* (16:1–3), Special Issue on Trust and Business: Barriers and Bridges, ed. by D. Koehn: 29–46

Alvarez, R. (2005) 'Taking a Critical Linguistic Turn: Using Critical Discourse Analysis for the Study of Information Systems.' In: Howcroft, D. and Trauth, E. M. (eds) *Handbook of Critical Information Systems Research: Theory and Application*. Edward Elgar, Cheltenham, UK: 104–122

Alvesson, M. and Deetz, S. (2000) *Doing Critical Management Research*. Sage, London

Alvesson, M. and Willmott, H. (1992) 'On the Idea of Emancipation in Management and Organization Studies'. *Academy of Management Review* (17:3), 432–464

Anderson, R. (2004) 'Cryptography and Competition Policy: Issues with "Trusted Computing".' In: Camp, L. J. and Lewis, S. (eds) *Economics of Information Security*. Kluwer, Dordrecht: 35–52

Anonymous (2004A) 'Two for TE? It's Been an Exciting Year for the Telecommunications Industry.' *Annual Business Economic and Political Review: Egypt*, available www.oxfordbusinessgroup.com [accessed 1 November 2004]: 125–128

Anonymous (2004b) 'Wind of Change: Egypt Says It Wants to Reform, but How Much?' *Annual Business Economic and Political Review: Egypt*, available: www.oxfordbusinessgroup.com [accessed 1 November 2004]: 23–24

Apel, K.-O. (1980) 'The A Priori of the Communication Community and the Foundations of Ethics: The Problem of a Rational Foundation of Ethics in the Scientific Age.' In: Apel, K.-O., *Towards a Transformation of Philosophy*. Routledge & Kegan Paul, London: 225–300

Apel, K.-O. (1988) *Diskurs und Verantwortung: Das Problem des Übergangs zur postkonventionellen Moral* (3rd edn 1997). Suhrkamp, Frankfurt am Main

Argyris, C. (1971) 'Management Information Systems: The Challenge to Rationality and Emotionality.' *Management Science* (17:6), 275–292

Aristotle (1998) *The Nicomachean Ethics*, trans. with an introduction by David Ross; rev. J. L. Ackrill and J. O. Urmson. Oxford University Press, Oxford

Ashendon, S. and Owen, D. (1999) 'Introduction: Foucault, Habermas and the Politics of Critique.' In: Ashenden, S. and Owen, D. (eds) *Foucault contra Habermas: Recasting the Dialogue between Genealogy and Critical Theory*. Sage, London: 1–20

Attias, B. A. (2004) 'Technology and the Great Refusal: The Information Age and Critical Social Theory.' In: Tabachnick, D. and Koivukoski, T. (eds) *Globalization, Technology, and Philosophy*. State University of New York Press, Albany: 43–56

Avgerou, C. (2005) 'Doing Critical Research in Information Systems: Some Further Thoughts.' *Information Systems Journal* (15): 103–109

Avgerou, C. and McGrath, K. (2005) 'Rationalities and Emotions in IS Innovation.' In: Howcroft, D. and Trauth, E. M. (eds) *Handbook of Critical Information Systems Research: Theory and Application*. Edward Elgar, Cheltenham, UK: 299–324

Avgerou, C. and McGrath, K. (2007) 'Power, Rationality, and the Art of Living through Socio-technical Change.' *MIS Quarterly* (31:2), 295–315

Ba, S. and Pavlou, P. A. (2001) 'Evidence of the Effects of Trust Building Technology in Electronic Markets: Price Premiums and Buyer Behavior.' *MIS Quarterly* (26:3), 243–268

Ba, S., Whinston, A. B. and Zhang, H. (1998) 'Building Trust in the Electronic Market through an Economic Incentive Mechanism.' *Proceedings of the International Conference on Information Systems*, Charlotte, NC, 12–15 December: 208–213

Backhouse, J. and Dhillon, G. (1996) 'Structures of Responsibility and Security in Information Systems.' *European Journal of Information Systems* (5), 2–9

Ball, K. (2003) 'The Labours of Surveillance.' *Surveillance & Society* (1:2), 125–137

Bannister, F. and Remenyi, D. (eds) *Proceedings of the 3rd European Conference on e-Government*, Trinity College, Dublin, 3–4 June 2003

Barber, B. R. (1995) *Jihad versus McWorld*. Times Books, New York

Baskerville, R. (2001) 'Conducting Action Research: High Risk and High Reward in Theory and Practice.' In: Trauth, E. M. (ed.) *Qualitative Research in IS: Issues and Trends*. Idea Group Publishing, Hershey, PA: 192–217

Bayertz, K. (1993) *Evolution und Ethik*. Reclam, Stuttgart

Beavers, A. F. (2002) 'Phenomenology and Artificial Intelligence.' *Metaphilosophy* (33:1/2), Special Issue: *Cyberphilosophy: The Intersection of Philosophy and Computing*, ed. J. H. Moor and T. W. Bynum: 70–82

Bechtel, W. (1985) 'Attributing Responsibility to Computer Systems.' *Metaphilosophy* (16:4), 296–305

Beck, U. (1986) *Risikogesellschaft: Auf dem Weg in eine andere Moderne*, Suhrkamp, Frankfurt am Main

Beck, U. (1998) *Was ist Globalisierung? Irrtümer des Globalismus – Antworten auf Globalisierung*, 5th edn. Suhrkamp, am Main

Becker, G. S. (1976) *The Economic Approach to Human Behavior*, University of Chicago Press, Chicago

Bedau, M. A. (1998) 'Philosophical Content and Method of Artificial Life.' In: Bynum, T. W. and Moor, J. H. (eds) *The Digital Phoenix: How Computers Are Changing Philosophy*. Blackwell, Oxford: 135–152

Bell, F. and Adam, A. (2004) 'Whatever Happened to Information Systems Ethics? Caught between the Devil and the Deep Blue Sea.' In: Kaplan, B., Truex, D. P., Wastell, D., Wood-Harper, A. T. and DeGross, J. (eds) *Information Systems Research: Relevant Theory and Informed Practice*. IFIP 8.2 Proceedings. Kluwer, Dordrecht: 159–174

Benbasat, I. and Weber, R. (1996) 'Research Commentary: Rethinking "Diversity" in Information Systems Research.' *Information Systems Research* (7:4), 389–399

Benbasat, I. and Zmud, R. W. (1999) 'Empirical Research in Information Systems: The Practice of Relevance.' *MIS Quarterly* (23:1), 3–16

Benbasat, I. and Zmud, R. W. (2003) 'The Identity Crisis within the IS Discipline: Defending and Communicating the Discipline's Core Properties.' *MIS Quarterly* (27:2): 183–194

Berendt, B., Günther, O. and Spiekermann, S. (2005) 'Privacy in E-Commerce: Stated Preferences vs. Actual Behavior.' *Communications of the ACM* (48:4), 101–106

Berg, T. C. and Kalish, G. I. (1997) 'Trust and Ethics in Employee-Owned Companies.' *Business and Professional Ethics Journal* (16:1–3), Special Issue on Trust and Business: Barriers and Bridges, ed. D. Koehn: 211–224

Berleur, J. and Poullet, Y. (2006) 'What Governance and Regulations for the Internet? Ethical Issues.' In: Zielinski, C., Duquenoy, P. and Kimppa, K. (eds) *Information Society: Emerging Landscapes*. IFIP WG 9.2 Proceedings. Springer, New York: 169–191

Berne, R. W. (2003) 'Recognizing Religious Mythology in Visions of New Technology.' *IEEE Technology and Society Magazine* (22:1), 34–39

Beu, D. and Buckley, M. R. (2001) 'The Hypothesized Relationship between Accountability and Ethical Behavior.' *Journal of Business Ethics* (34), 57–73

Bews, N. and Rossouw, G. J.(2002) 'A Role for Business Ethics in Facilitating Trustworthiness.' *Journal of Business Ethics* (39), 377–390

Bhattacherjee, A. (2002) 'Individual Trust in Online Firms: Scale Development and Initial Test.' *Journal of Management Information Systems* (19:1), 211–241

Bissett, A. (2002) 'Surgical Strikes: Ideological Weaponry.' In: Alvarez, I., Bynum, T. W., Álvaro de Assis Lobes, J. and Rogerson, S. (eds) *The Transformation of Organisations in the Information Age: Social and Ethical Implications*. Proceedings of the sixth ETHICOMP Conference, 13–15 November, Lisbon. Universidade Lusiada, Lisbon: 747 756

Block, W. (2001) 'Cyberslacking, Business Ethics and Managerial Economics.' *Journal of Business Ethics* (33), 225–231

Bloomfeld, B. P. and Coombs, R. (1992) 'Information Technology, Control, and Power: The Centralization and Decentralization Debate Revisited.' *Journal of Management Studies* (29:4), 459–484

Boehm, B. W. and Ross, R. (1989) 'Software Project Management: Principles and Examples.' *IEEE Transactions on Software Engineering* (15:7), 902–916

Boland, R. J. Jr (1985) 'Phenomenology: A Preferred Approach to Research on Information Systems.' In: Mumford, E., Hirschheim, R., Fitzgerald, G. and Wood-Harper, T. (eds) *Research Methods in Information Systems*. IFIP 8.2 Proceedings. Amsterdam, North-Holland: 193–201

Boncella, R. J. (2001) 'Internet Privacy – at Home and at Work.' *Communications of the Association for Information Systems* (7)

Borgmann, A. (1999) *Holding On to Reality: The Nature of Information at the Turn of the Millennium*. University of Chicago Press, London

Bourlakis, C. A. and Bourlakis, M. A. (2003) 'Logistics, Information Technology and Retail Internationalisation: The Formation of International Strategic Retail Networks.' In: Joia, L. A. (ed.) *IT-Based Management: Challenges and Solutions*. Idea Group Publishing, Hershey, MA: 257–276

Bowie, N. E. (1999) *Business Ethics: A Kantian Perspective*. Blackwell, Oxford

Brandt, R. B. (1959) *Ethical Theory: The Problems of Normative and Critical Ethics*. Prentice Hall, Englewood Cliffs, NJ

Breen, M. (1999) 'Counterrevolution in the Infrastructure: A Cultural Study of Technoscientific Impoverishment.' In: Pourciau, L. J. (ed.) *Ethics and Electronic Information in the 21st Century*. Purdue University Press, West Lafayette, IN: 29–45

Brenkert, G. (1997) 'Marketing Trust: Barriers and Bridges.' *Business and Professional Ethics Journal* (16:1–3), Special Issue on Trust and Business: Barriers and Bridges, ed. D. Koehn: 77–98

Brenkert, G. (1998) 'Trust, Business and Business Ethics: An Introduction.' *Business Ethics Quarterly* (8:2), 195–203

Bringsjord, S. (2001) 'Are We Evolved Computers? A Critical Review of Steven Pinker's *How the Mind Works*.' *Philosophical Psychology* (14:2), 227–243

Britz, J. J. (1999) 'Ethical Guidelines for Meeting the Challenges of the Information Age.' In: Pourciau, L. J. (ed.) *Ethics and Electronic Information in the 21st Century*, Purdue University Press, West Lafayette, IN: 9–28

Brock, F. J. and Dhillon, G. S. (2001) 'Managerial Information, the Basics.' *Journal of International Information Management* (10:2), 45–59

Brooke, C. (2002a) 'What Does it Mean to be 'Critical' in IS Research?' *Journal of Information Technology* (17), 49–57

Brooke, C. (2002b) 'Critical Perspectives on Information Systems: An Impression of the Research Landscape.' *Journal of Information Technology* (17), 271–283

Brown, H. G., Scott Poole, M. and Rodgers, T. L. (2004) 'Interpersonal Traits, Complementarity, and Trust in Virtual Collaboration.' *Journal of Management Information Systems* (20:4), 115–137

Brown, W. S. (2000) 'Ontological Security, Existential Anxiety and Workplace Privacy.' *Journal of Business Ethics* (23) 61–65

Browne, M. N. and Blank, L. (1997) 'The Contrast between Friendship and Business-Consumer Relationships: Trust Is an Earned Attribute.' *Business and Professional Ethics Journal* (16:1–3), special issue on Trust and Business: Barriers and Bridges, ed. D. Koehn: 155–170

Burrell, G. (1994) 'Modernism, Postmodernism and Organizational Analysis 4: The Contribution of Jürgen Habermas.' *Organization Studies* (15:1): 1–19

Burrell, G. and Dale, K. (2003) 'Building Better Worlds? Architecture and Critical Management Studies.' In: Alvesson, M. and Willmott, H. (eds) *Studying Management Critically*. Sage, London: 177–196

Burrell, G. and Morgan, G. (1979) *Sociological Paradigms and Organizational Analysis*. Heinemann: London

Bynum, T. W. (2006) 'Flourishing Ethics.' *Ethics and Information Technology* (8:4): 157–173

Calás, M. B. and Smircich, L. (1999) 'Past Postmodernism? Reflections and Tentative Directions.' *Academy of Management Review* (24:4): 649–671

Camp, L. J. (2001) 'Web Security and Privacy: An American Perspective.' In: Spinello, R. A. and Tavani, H. T. (eds) *Readings in Cyberethics*. Jones and Bartlett, Sudbury, MA: 474–486

Camp, L. J. and Lewis, S. (eds) (2004) *Economics of Information Security*. Kluwer, Dordrecht

Camp, L. J. and Wolfram, C. (2004) 'Pricing Security: A Market in Vulnerabilities.' In: Camp, L. J. and Lewis, S. (eds) *Economics of Information Security*. Kluwer, Dordrecht: 17–34

Cantrell, S. (2000) 'E-Market Trust Mechanisms.' *Accenture Research Note: E-Commerce Networks* (11), 1–3

Capurro, R. and Pingel, C. (2002) 'Ethical Issues of Online Communication Research.' *Ethics and Information Technology* (4:3), Special Issue on *Internet Research Ethics*, ed. C. Ess: 189–194

Carnap, R. (1980) 'Empiricism, Semantics, and Ontology.' In: Morick, H. (ed.) *Challenges to Empiricism*. Methuen, London: 28–46

Casacuberta, D. (2005) 'Loaded Metaphors: Legal Explanations on Monitoring the Workplace in Spain.' In: Weckert, J. (ed.) *Electronic Monitoring in the Workplace: Controversies and Solutions*. Idea Group Publishing, Hershey, PA: 158–170

Castells, M. (1997) *The Information Age: Economy, Society, and Culture*. Vol. 2: *The Power of Identity*. Blackwell, Oxford

Castells, M. (2000a) *The Information Age: Economy, Society, and Culture*. Vol. 1: *The Rise of the Network Society*, 2nd edn, Oxford, Blackwell

Castells, M. (2000b) *The Information Age: Economy, Society, and Culture*. Vol. 3: *End of Millennium*, 2nd edn, Oxford, Blackwell

Catudal, J. N. (2001) 'Censorship, the Internet, and the Child Pornography Law of 1996: A Critique.' In: Spinello, R. A. and Tavani, H. T. (eds) *Readings in CyberEthics*. , Jones and Bartlett, Sudbury, MA: 170–187

Cavaye, A. L. M. (1996) 'Case Study Research: A Multi-faceted Research Approach for IS.' *Information Systems Journal* (6), 227–242

Cavusoglu, H. (2004) 'Economics of IT Security Management.' In: Camp, L. J. and Lewis, S. (eds) *Economics of Information Security*. Kluwer, Dordrecht: 71–83

Cecez-Kecmanovic, D. (2001a) 'Doing Critical IS Research: The Question of Methodology.' In: Trauth, E. M. (ed.) *Qualitative Research in IS: Issues and Trends.* Idea Group Publishing, Hershey, MA: 141–162

Cecez-Kecmanovic, D. (2001b) 'Critical Information Systems Research: A Habermasian Approach.' *Proceedings of the 9th European Conference on Information Systems,* Bled, Slovenia, 27–29 June 2001: 253–263

Cecez-Kecmanovic, D. (2005) 'Basic Assumptions of the Critical Research Perspectives in Information Systems.' In: Howcroft, D. and Trauth, E. M. (eds) *Handbook of Critical Information Systems Research: Theory and Application.* Edward Elgar, Cheltenham, UK: 19–46

Cecez-Kecmanovic, D., Janson, M. and Brown, A. (2002) 'The Rationality Framework for a Critical Study of Information Systems.' *Journal of Information Technology* (17), 215–227

Chan, A. (2000) 'Redirecting Critique in Postmodern Organization Studies: The Perspective of Foucault.' *Organization Studies* (21:6), 1059–1075

Chapman, G. and Rotenberg, M. (1995) 'The National Information Infrastructure: A Public Interest Opportunity.' In: Johnson, D. G. and Nissenbaum, H. (eds) *Computers, Ethics & Social Values.* Prentice Hall, Upper Saddle River, NJ: 628–644

Cheskin Research and Studio Archetype/Sapient (1999) *eCommerce Trust Study.* Available: www.studioarchetype.com/cheskin/ [accessed 1 August 2001]

Chomsky, N. (1998/1999) *Language and Responsibility.* Reprinted in: Chomsky, N. *On Language.* The New York Press, New York

Chouliaraki, L. and Fairclough, N. (1999) *Discourse in Late Modernity: Rethinking Critical Discourse Analysis.* Edinburgh University Press, Edinburgh

Chua, W. F. (1986) 'Radical Developments in Accounting Thought.' *Accounting Review* (61:4), 601–632

Ciborra, C. (2000) 'A Critical Review of the Literature on the Management of Corporate Information Infrastructure.' In: Ciborra, C. and Associates, *From Control to Drift: The Dynamics of Corporate Information Infrastructures.* Oxford University Press, Oxford: 15–40

Ciborra, C. (2002) *The Labyrinths of Information: Challenging the Wisdom of Systems.* Oxford University Press, Oxford

Ciborra, C. (2004) *Digital Technologies and the Duality of Risk.* Discussion Paper 27. ESRC Centre for Analysis of Risk and Regulation, London

Cohen, M. G. (1996) 'Democracy and the Future of Nations. Challenges for Disadvantaged Women and Minorities' In: Boyer, R. and Drache, D. (eds) *States against Markets: The Limits of Globalization.* Routledge, London: 399–414

Compeau, D. and Higgins, C. A. (1995) 'Computer Self-Efficacy: Development of a Measure and Initial Test.' *MIS Quarterly* (19:2), 189–211

Conway, D. W. (1999) 'Pas de Deux: Habermas and Foucault in Genealogical Communication.' In: Ashenden, S. and Owen, D. (eds) *Foucault contra Habermas: Recasting the Dialogue between Genealogy and Critical Theory.* Sage, London: 60–90

Copeland, D. G. and McKenney, J. L. (1988) 'Airline Reservation Systems: Lessons from History.' *MIS Quarterly* (12:3), 353–370

Couillard, J. (1995) 'The Role of Project Risk in Determining Project Management Approach.' *Project Management Journal* (26:4), 3–15

Coyote (2006) 'Slow Leadership: Heroic Management.' Available: www.slowleadership. org/2006/04/heroic-management.html [accessed 30 April 2007]

Cukier, W., Bauer, R. and Middleton, C. (2004) 'Applying Habermas' Validity Claims as a Standard for Critical Discourse Analysis.' In: Kaplan, B., Truex, D., Wood-Harper, T. and DeGross, J. (eds) *Information Systems Research: Relevant Theory and Informed Practice*. Kluwer Academic Publishers, Dordrecht: 233–258

Cukier, W., Middleton, C. and Bauer, R. (2003) 'The Discourse of Learning Technology in Canada: Understanding Communication Distortions and the Implications for Decision Making.' In: Wynn, E., Whitley, E., Myers, M. D. and DeGross, J. (eds) *Global and Organizational Discourse about Information Technology*. Kluwer Academic Publishers, Dordrecht: 197–221

Culnan, M. J. (1993) ' "How Did They Get My Name?": An Exploratory Investigation of Consumer Attitudes toward Secondary Information Use.' *MIS Quarterly* (17:3), 341–363

Dahlbom, B. (2000) 'Postface: From Infrastructure to Networking.' In: Ciborra, C. and Associates, *From Control to Drift: The Dynamics of Corporate Information Infrastructures*. Oxford University Press, Oxford: 212–226

Darke, P., Shanks, G. and Broadbent, M. (1998) 'Successfully Completing Case Study Research: Combining Rigour, Relevance and Pragmatism.' *Information Systems Journal* (8), 273–289

Dasgupta, P. (2000) 'Trust as a Commodity.' In: Gambetta, D. (ed.) *Trust: Making and Breaking Cooperative Relations*. Department of Sociology, University of Oxford, 49–72, electronic edition Oxford, available www.sociology.ox.ac.uk/papers/ dasgupta49-72.pdf [accessed 17 August 2006]

Davenport, T. H. and Prusak, L. (1998) *Working Knowledge: How Organizations Manage What they Know*. Harvard Business School Press, Boston, MA

Davison, R. M., Clarke, R., Smith, H. J., Langford, D. and Kuo, F.-Y. (2003) 'Information Privacy in a Globally Networked Society: Implications for IS Research.' *Communications of the Association for Information Systems* (12), 341–365

Dawson, R. J. and Newman, I. A. (2002) 'Empowerment in IT Education.' *Journal of Information Technology Education* (1:2), 125–141

De George, R. T. (1999) *Business Ethics* 5th edn. Prentice Hall, Upper Saddle River, NJ

De George, R. T. (2003a) The *Ethics of Information Technology and Business*. Blackwell, Oxford

De George, R. T. (2003b) 'Ethics, Academic Freedom and Academic Tenure.' *Journal of Academic Ethics* (1), 11–25

Deetz, S. (1992) 'Disciplinary Power in the Modern Corporation.' In: Alvesson, M. and Willmott, H. (eds) *Critical Management Studies*. Sage, London: 21–45

Dewey, E. J. and Hurlbutt, R. H. III (1978) *An Introduction to Ethics*. Macmillan, New York

Dirks, K. T. and Ferrin, D. L. (2001) 'The Role of Trust in Organizational Settings.' *Organization Science* (12:4), 450–467

Doherty, N. F. and King, M. (2001) 'An Investigation of the Factors Affecting the Successful Treatment of Organisational Issues in Systems Development Projects.' *European Journal of Information Systems* (10), 147–160

Donaldson, T. and Dunfee, T. W. (1999) *Ties That Bind: A Social Contracts Approach to Business Ethics*. Harvard Business School Press, Boston, MA

Donaldson, T. and Preston, L. E. (1995) 'The Stakeholder Theory of the Corporation: Concepts, Evidence, and Implications.' *Academy of Management Review* (20:1), 65–91

Doolin, B. (2004) 'Power and Resistance in the Implementation of a Medical Management Information System.' *Information Systems Journal* (14), 343–362

Doolin, B. and McLeod, L. (2005) 'Towards Critical Interpretivism in IS Research.' In: Howcroft, D. and Trauth, E. M. (eds) *Handbook of Critical Information Systems Research: Theory and Application*. Edward Elgar, Cheltenham, UK: 244–271

Doorewaard, H. and van Bijsterveld, M. (2001) 'The Osmosis of Ideas: An Analysis of the Integrated Approach to IT Management from a Translation Theory Perspective.' *Organization* (81): 55–76

Dreyfus, H. L. (1993) *What Computers Still Can't Do*. MIT Press, Cambridge, MA

Dribben, M. R. (2004) 'Exploring the Processual Nature of Trust and Cooperation in Organisations: A Whiteheadian Analysis.' *Philosophy of Management* (4:1), Special Issue on Organisation and Decision Processes, ed. L. Leonard Minkes and T. Gear, 25–39

Dummett, M. (1963) *Realism*, reprinted in: *Truth and Other Enigmas*, Harvard University Press, Cambridge, NA (1978): 145–165

Edenius, M. (2003) 'Discourse on E-Mail in Use.' In: Wynn, E., Whitley, E., Myers, M. D. and DeGross, J. (eds) *Global and Organizational Discourse about Information Technology*, Kluwer Academic Publishers, Dordrecht: 73–90

Egger, F. N. (2001) 'Affective Design of E-Commerce User Interfaces: How to Maximise Perceived Trustworthiness.' In: Helander, M. G., Khalid, H. M. and Tham, M. P. (eds) *Proceedings of the International Conference on Affective Human Factors Design*, Singapore, 26–29 June. ASEAN Academic Press, London: 317–324

Egypt (2004) 'Political System', available www.presidency.gov.eg/html/political_system.html [accessed: 16 November 2004]

Eisenhardt, K. M. (1989) 'Building Theories from Case Study Research.' *Academy of Management Review* (14:4), 632–550

El Sayed, H. and Westrup, C. (2003) 'Egypt and ICTs: How ICTs Bring National Initiatives, Global Organizations and Local Companies Together.' *Information Technology & People* (16:1), 76–92

El Sherif, H. and El Sawy, O. A. (1988) 'Issue-Based Decision Support Systems for the Egyptian Cabinet.' *MIS Quarterly* (12:4), 551–569

Elbeltagi, I., McBride, N. and Hardaker, G. (2005) 'Evaluating the Factors Affecting DSS Usage by Senior Managers in Local Authorities in Egypt.' *Journal of Global Information Management* (13:2), 42–65

Elgesem, D. (1996) 'Privacy, Respect for Persons, and Risk.' In: Ess, C. (ed.) *Philosophical Perspectives on Computer-Mediated Communication*. State University of New York Press, Albany: 45–66

Elkjaer, B., Flensburg, P., Mouritsen, J. and Willmott, H. (1991) 'The Commodification of Expertise: The Case of Systems Development Consulting.' *Accounting, Management and Information Technologies* (1:2), 139–156

Encarta World English Dictionary (1999), Bloomsbury: London

Environ (2002) *Minister Cullen Announces Roll Out Of Electronic Voting for 2004 Local Government and European Parliament Elections*, Department of the Environment, Heritage and Local Government, available www.environ.ie/DOEI/DOEIPub.nsf/6fb57b90102ce64c80256d12003a7a0d/97488b6e000fe85380256d2d005e48b1?Open Document [accessed 11 August 1004]

Environ (2003) *Cullen Invites All Party Oireachtas Committee for Electronic Voting Demonstration: 6 Independent Studies Verify Security of Electronic Voting*, Department of the Environment, Heritage and Local Government, available www.environ.ie/DOEI/DOEIPub.nsf/wfInfo/15d88ab7fad648ce80256dd300540874?OpenDocument [accessed 11 August 2004]

Escobar, A. (1995) *Development*, Princeton University Press, Princeton, NJ

Ess, C. (1996) 'The Political Computer: Democracy, CMC, and Habermas.' In: Ess, C. (ed.) *Philosophical Perspectives on Computer-Mediated Communication*. State University of New York Press, Albany: 197–230

Ess, C. (2001) 'Introduction: What's Culture Got to Do with It? Cultural Collisions in the Electronic Global Village, Creative Inferences, and the Rise of Culturally-Mediated Computing.' In: Ess, C. (ed.) with F. Sudweeks, *Culture, Technology, Communication: Towards an Intercultural Global Village*. : State University of New York Press, Albany: 1–52

Fagin, B. (2000) 'Liberty and Community Online.' In: Baird, R. M., Ramsower, R. and Rosenbaum, S. E. (eds) *Cyberethics: Social and Moral Issues in the Computer Age*. Prometheus Books, New York: 332–352

Fairclough, N. (1993) 'Critical Discourse Analysis and the Marketization of Public Discourse: The Universities.' *Discourse & Society* (4:2), 133–168

Fairclough, N. (2003) *Analysing Discourse: Textual Analysis for Social Research*. Routledge, London

Faldetta, G. (2002) 'The Content of Freedom in Resources: The Open Source Model.' *Journal of Business Ethics* (39), 179–188

Feenberg, A. (1991) *Critical Theory of Technology*. Oxford University Press, New York

Feenberg, A. (1999) *Questioning Technology*. Routledge, London

Feyerabend, P. K. (1980) 'How to Be a Good Empiricist. A Plea for Tolerance in Matters Epistemological.' In: Morick, H. (ed.) *Challenges to Empiricism*. Methuen, London: 164–193

Fineman, S. (2001) 'Fashioning the Environment.' *Organization* (8:1), 17–31

Fischer, J. M. and Martin, J. (1999) 'Recent Work on Moral Responsibility.' *Ethics* (110:1), 93–139

Flores, F. L. and Solomon, R. C. (1997) 'Rethinking Trust.' *Business znd Professional Ethics Journal* (16:1–3), special interest on Trust and Business: Barriers and Bridges, ed. D. Koehn: 47–76

Flores, F. and Solomon, R. C. (1998) 'Creating Trust.' *Business Ethics Quarterly* (8:2), 205–232

Floridi, L. (1999) *Philosophy and Computing: An Introduction*. Routledge, London

Forester, J. (1992) 'Critical Ethnography: On Fieldwork in a Habermasian Way.' In: Alvesson, M. and Willmott, H. (eds) *Critical Management Studies*. Sage, London: 46–65

Forester, T. and Morrison, P. (1994) *Computer Ethics: Cautionary Tales and Ethical Dilemmas in Computing*, 2nd edn. MIT Press, Cambridge, MA

Foucault, M. (1971) *L'Ordre du discours*, Gallimard, Paris

Foucault, M. (1975) *Surveiller et punir: Naissance de la prison*, Gallimard, Paris

Foucault, M. (1976) *Histoire de la sexualité I: La Volonté de savoir*, Gallimard, Paris

Foucault, M. (1994a) 'Two Lectures.' In: Kelly, M. (ed.) *Critique and Power: Recasting the Foucault/Habermas Debate*. MIT Press, Cambridge, MA: 17–46

Foucault, M. (1994b) 'The Art of Telling the Truth.' In: Kelly, M. (ed.) *Critique and Power: Recasting the Foucault/Habermas Debate*. MIT Press, Cambridge, MA: 139–148

Fournier, V. and Grey, C. (2000) 'At the Critical Moment: Conditions and Prospects for Critical Management Studies.' *Human Relations* (53:1): 7–32

Freeden, M. (2003) *Ideology: A Very Short Introduction*. Oxford: Oxford University Press

French, J. A. (1990) *The Business Knowledge Investment: Building Architected Information.* Yourdon Press, Englewood Cliffs, NJ

French, P. A. (1992) *Responsibility Matters.* University Press of Kansas, Lawrence

Friedman, M. (1994a) 'The Methodology of Positive Economics.' In: Hausman, D. M. (ed.) *The Philosophy of Economics: An Anthology,* 2nd edn. Cambridge University Press, Cambridge: 180–213

Friedman, M. (1994b) 'Introduction to the Fiftieth Anniversary Edition.' In: Hayek, F. A., *The Road to Serfdom,* 50th anniversary edition. University of Chicago Press, Chicago

Fukuyama, F. (1998) *The Virtual Handshake: E-Commerce and the Challenge of Trust.* The Merrill Lynch Forum, New York

Gadamer, H.-G. (1990) *Wahrheit und Methode: Grundzüge einer philosophischen Hermeneutik,* 6th edn. J. C. B. Mohr (Paul Siebeck), Tübingen

Galbraith, J. K. (1998/1958) *The Affluent Society,* 40th anniversary edition. New York: Mariner Books, Boston, MA

Gallivan, M. J. (2001) 'Striking a Balance between Trust and Control in a Virtual Organization: A Content Analysis of Open Source Software Case Studies.' *Information Systems Journal* (11:4), 277–304

Gallivan, M. J. and Depledge, G. (2003) 'Trust, Control and the Role of Interorganizational Systems in Electronic Partnerships.' *Information Systems Journal* (13), 159–190

Garson, J. (2003) 'Modal Logic.' In: *The Stanford Encyclopedia of Philosophy,* Winter 2003 edn, ed. E. N. Zalta, available http://plato.stanford.edu/archives/win2003/entries/-logic-modal/ [accessed 9 September 2004]

Gauthier, D. (1986) *Morals by Agreement.* Clarendon Press, Oxford

Gavison, R. (1995) 'Privacy and Limits of Law.' In: Johnson, D. G. and Nissenbaum, H. (eds) *Computers, Ethics & Social Values.* Prentice Hall, NJ, Upper Saddle River: 332–351

Gefen, D. (2000) 'E-Commerce: The Role of Familiarity and Trust.' *Omega* (28:6), 725–737

Gefen, D. (2004) 'What Makes an ERP Implementation Relationship Worthwhile: Linking Trust Mechanisms and ERP Usefulness.' *Journal of Management Information Systems* (21:1), 263–288

Gefen, D., Karahanna, E. and Straub, D. W. (2003) 'Trust and TAM in Online Shopping: An Integrated Model.' *MIS Quarterly* (27:1), 51–90

Gehlen, A. (1997) *Der Mensch: Seine Natur und seine Stellung in der Welt,* 13th edn. UTB, Wiesbaden

Gergen, K. J. (1999) *An Invitation to Social Construction.* Sage, London

Gibson, K. (2000) 'The Moral Basis of Stakeholder Theory.' *Journal of Business Ethics* (26), 245–257

Giddens, A. (1984) *The Constitution of Society: Outline of the Theory of Structuration.* Polity Press, Cambridge

Glasersfeld, E. von (2000) 'Konstruktion der Wirklichkeit und des Begriffs der Objektivität.' In: C. F. von Siemens Stiftung (ed.) *Einführung in den Konstruktivismus,* 5th edn. Piper, Munich: 9–40

Goldman, A. I. (1999) 'Why Citizens Should Vote: A Causal Responsibility Approach.' In: Paul, E. F., Miller, F. D. and Paul, J. (eds) *Responsibility.* Cambridge University Press, Cambridge: 201–217

Goldman, S., Cole, K. and Syer, C. (1999) 'The Technology/Content Dilemma.' The Secretary's Conference on Educational Technology – 1999, available www.ed.gov/Technology/TechConf/1999/ [accessed 23 October 2001]

Goles, T. and Hirschheim, R. (2000) 'The Paradigm Is Dead, the Paradigm Is Dead ... Long Live the Paradigm: The Legacy of Burrell and Morgan.' *Omega* (28:3), 249–268

Gomart, E. and Hennion, A. (1999) 'A Sociology of Attachment: Music, Amateurs, Drug Users.' In: Law, J. and Hassard, J. (eds) *Actor Network Theory and After*. Blackwell, Oxford: 220–247

Goold, B. J. (2003) 'Public Area Surveillance and Police Work: The Impact of CCTV on Police Behaviour and Autonomy.' *Surveillance & Society* (1:2), 191–203

Gore, A. (1995) 'Global Information Infrastructure.' In: Johnson, D. G. and Nissenbaum, H. (eds) *Computers, Ethics & Social Values*. Prentice Hall, Upper Saddle River, 620–628

Gosling, J. and Mintzberg, H. (2003) 'The Five Minds of a Manager.' *Harvard Business Review* (81:11), 54–63

Gouldner, A. W. (1976) *The Dialectic of Ideology and Technology: The Origins, Grammar and Future of Ideology*. Macmillan, London

Grabner-Kräuter, S. (2002) 'The Role of Consumers' Trust in Online-Shopping.' *Journal of Business Ethics* (39), 43–50

Greenaway, K. E. and Chan, Y. E. (2005 'Theoretical Explanations for Firms' Information Privacy Behaviors.' *Journal of the Association for Information Systems* (6:6), 171–198

Greenhill, A. and Wilson, M. (2006) 'Haven or Hell? Telework, Flexibility and Family in the E-Society: A Marxist Analysis.' *European Journal of Information Systems* (15:3), 379–388

Gregor, S. (2006) 'The Nature of Theory in IS.' *MIS Quarterly* (30:3): 611–642

Grey, C. (2005) 'Critical Management Studies: Towards a More Mature Politics.' In: Howcroft, D. and Trauth, E. M. (eds) *Handbook of Critical Information Systems Research: Theory and Application*.: Edward Elgar, Cheltenham, UK: 174–194

Grim, P., St Denis, P. and Kokalis, T. (2004) 'Information and Meaning: Use-Based Models in Arrays of Neural Nets.' *Minds and Machines* (14:1), 43–66

Grint, K. and Woolgar, S. (1997) *The Machine at Work: Technology, Work, and Organization*. Blackwell, Oxford

Habermas, J. (1969) *Technik und Wissenschaft als 'Ideologie'*. Suhrkamp, Frankfurt am Main

Habermas, J. (1981) *Theorie des kommunikativen Handelns* – Band I/II, Suhrkamp, Frankfurt am Main

Habermas, J. (1983) *Moralbewußtsein und kommunikatives Handeln*. Suhrkamp, Frankfurt am Main

Habermas, J. (1985) *Die neue Unübersichtlichkeit*. Suhrkamp, Frankfurt am Main

Habermas, J. (1984) *Vorstudien und Ergänzungen zur Theorie des kommunikativen Handelns*. Suhrkamp, Frankfurt am Main

Habermas, J. (1991) *Erläuterungen zur Diskursethik*. Suhrkamp, Frankfurt am Main

Habermas, J. (1994a) 'The Critique of Reason as an Unmasking of the Human Sciences: Michel Foucault.' In: Kelly, M. (ed.) *Critique and Power: Recasting the Foucault/Habermas Debate*. MIT Press, Cambridge, MA: 47–78

Habermas, J. (1994b) 'Some Questions Concerning the Theory of Power: Foucault Again.' In: Kelly, M. (ed.) *Critique and Power: Recasting the Foucault/Habermas Debate*. MIT Press, Cambridge, MA: 79–108

Habermas, J. (1996) *Die Einbeziehung des Anderen: Studien zur politischen Theorie*. Suhrkamp, Frankfurt am Main

Habermas, J. (1998a) *Faktizität und Geltung: Beiträge zur Diskurstheorie des Rechts und des demokratischen Rechtsstaats*. Suhrkamp, Frankfurt am Main

Habermas, J. (1998b) 'Recht und Moral (Tanner Lectures 1986).' In: Habermas, J. (1998) *Faktizität und Geltung: Beiträge zur Diskurstheorie des Rechts und des demokratischen Rechtsstaats*. Suhrkamp, Frankfurt am Main: 541–599

Hajek, P. (2002) 'Fuzzy Logic.' In: *The Stanford Encyclopedia of Philosophy* (Fall 2002 edition), ed. E. N. Zalta, http://plato.stanford.edu/archives/fall2002/entries/logic-fuzzy/ [accessed 9 September 2004]

Hanseth, O. (2000) 'The Economics of Standards.' In: Ciborra, Claudio and Associates (eds) *From Control to Drift: The Dynamics of Corporate Information Infrastructures*. Oxford University Press, Oxford: 56–70

Harris, H., Carapiet, S. and Provis, C. (2004) ' "Adaptive and Agile Organisations": Do They Actually Exist? *Philosophy of Management* (4:1), Special Issue on Organisation and Decision Processes, ed. L. Minkes and T. Gear, 3–11

Hart, H. L. A. (1948) 'The Ascription of Responsibility and Rights.' *Proceedings of the Aristotelian Society* (49), 171–194

Hartman, L. (2001) 'Technology and Ethics: Privacy in the Workplace.' *Business and Society Review* (106:1), 1–27

Harvey, L. (1990) *Critical Social Research*. London: Unwin Hyman

Hastedt, H. (1994) *Aufklärung und Technik. Grundprobleme einer Ethik der Technik*. Suhrkamp, Frankfurt am Main

Hausman, D. M. (ed.) (1994) *The Philosophy of Economics: An Anthology*, 2nd edn. Cambridge University Press, Cambridge

Hausman, D. M. and McPherson, M. S. (1996) *Economic Analysis and Moral Philosophy*. Cambridge University Press: Cambridge

Hawkes, D. (2003) *Ideology*, 2nd edn. Routledge, London

Hayek, F. A. von (1994) *The Road to Serfdom*, fiftieth anniversary edition. University of Chicago Press, Chicago

Heaton, L. (2001) 'Preserving Communication Context: Virtual Workspace and Interpersonal Space in Japanese CSCW.' In: Ess, C. (ed.) with Fay Sudweeks *Culture, Technology, Communication: Towards an Intercultural Global Village*. State University of New York Press, Albany: 213–240

Heidegger, M. (1993) *Sein und Zeit*, 17th edn. Max Niemeyer Verlag, Tübingen

Heng, M. S. H. and de Moor, A. (2003) 'From Habermas's Communicative Theory to Practice on the Internet.' *Information Systems Journal* (13): 331–352

Hennessy, M. and Brennock, M. (2004) 'E-Voting Abandoned for Elections in June.' *Irish Times*, 1 May

Hesketh, B., Gosper, M., Andrews, J. and Sabaz, M. (1996) *Computer-Mediated Communication in University Teaching*. Australian Government Publishing Service, Canberra

Hinman, M. L. (1998) *Ethics: A Pluralistic Approach to Moral Theory*, Harcourt, Fort Worth, TX

Hirschheim, R. A. (1985) 'Information Systems Epistemology: An Historical Perspective.' In: Mumford, E., Hirschheim, R., Fitzgerald, G. and Wood-Harper, T. (eds) *Research Methods in Information Systems*. IFIP 8.2 Proceedings. Amsterdam, North-Holland: 13–36

Hirschheim, R. and Klein, H. K (1989) 'Four Paradigms of Information Systems Development.' *Communications of the ACM* (32:10), 1199–1216

Hirschheim, R. and Klein, H. K. (1994) 'Realizing Emancipatory Principles in Information Systems Development: The Case for ETHICS.' *MIS Quarterly* (18:1), 83–109

Hirschheim, R. and Klein, H. K. (2003) 'Crisis in the IS Field? A Critical Reflection on the State of the Discipline.' *Journal of the Association for Information Systems* (4:5), 237–293

Hirschheim, R. and Newman, M. (1991) 'Symbolism and Information Systems Development: Myth, Metaphor and Magic.' *Information Systems Research* (2:1), 29–62

Hirschheim, R., Klein, H. K. and Lyytinen, K. (1995) *Information Systems Developing and Data Modeling: Conceptual and Philosophical Foundations.* Cambridge University Press, Cambridge

Hjørland, B. (2004) 'Arguments for Philosophical Realism in Library and Information Science.' *Library Trends* (52:3), 488–506

Höffe, O. (1995) *Moral als Preis der Moderne: Ein Versuch über Wissenschaft, Technik und Umwelt*, 3rd edn. Suhrkamp, Frankfurt am Main

Hoffman, D. L., Novak, T. P. and Peralta, M. (1999) 'Building Consumer Trust Online.' *Communications of the ACM* (42:4), 80–87

Hollis, M. (1994) *The Philosophy of Social Science: An Introduction.* Cambridge University Press, Cambridge

Homann, K. and Blome-Drees, F. (1992) *Wirtschafts- und Unternehmensethik*, Vandenhoek & Ruprecht, Göttingen

Horkheimer, M. and Adorno, T. W. (2004) *Dialektik der Aufklärung: Philosophische Fragmente*, 15th edn. Fischer, Frankfurt am Main

Hosmeh, L. T. (1995) 'Trust: The Connecting Link between Organizational Theory and Philosophical Ethics.' *Academy of Management Review* (20:2), 379–403

Howcroft, D. and Trauth, E. M. (eds) (2005) *Handbook of Critical Information Systems Research: Theory and Application.* Edward Elgar, Cheltenham, UK

Howcroft, D. and Wilson, M. (2003) 'Paradoxes of Participatory Practices: The Janus Role of the Systems Developer.' *Information and Organization* (13:1), 1–24

Howcroft, D., Mitev, N. and Wilson, M. (2004) 'What We May Learn from the Social Shaping of Technology Approach.' In: Mingers, J. and Willcocks, L. (eds) *Social Theory and Philosophy for Information Systems.* Wiley, Chichester, UK: 329–371

Hughes, J. A., Rouncefield, M. and Tolmie, P. (2002) 'The Day-to-Day Work of Standardization: A Sceptical Note on the Reliance on IT in a Retail Bank.' In: Woolgar, S. (ed.) *Virtual Society? Technology, Cyberbole, Reality.* Oxford University Press, Oxford: 247–263

Hume, D. (1948) *Hume's Moral and Political Philosophy (1711–1776)*, ed. with an introduction by H. D. Aiken. Hafner, New York

Huntington, S. (1993) 'The Clash of Civilisations?' *Foreign Affairs* (72:3): 22–49

Husted, B. W. (1998) 'The Ethical Limits of Trust in Business Relations.' *Business Ethics Quarterly* (8:2), 233–248

Iivari, J., Hirschheim, R. and Klein, H. K. (1998) 'A Paradigmatic Analysis Contrasting Information Systems Development Approaches and Methodologies.' *Information Systems Research* (9:2), 164–193

Introna, L. (1997) *Management, Information and Power: A Narrative of the Involved Manager.* Macmillan, London

Introna, L. (2000) 'Privacy and the Computer: Why We Need Privacy in the Information Society.' In: Baird, R. M., Ramsower, R. and Rosenbaum, S. E. (eds) *Cyberethics: Social and Moral Issues in the Computer Age.* Prometheus Books, New York: 188–199

Introna, L. (2001) 'Workplace Surveillance, Privacy, and Distributive Justice' In: Spinello, R. A. and Tavani, H. T. (eds) *Readings in CyberEthics.* Jones and Bartlett, Sudbury, MA: 418–429

Introna, L. (2003a) 'Disciplining Information Systems: Truth and its Regimes.' *European Journal of Information Systems* (12), 235–240

Introna, L. (2003b) 'Workplace Surveillance 'IS' Unethical and Unfair.' *Surveillance & Society* (1:2), 210–216

Introna, L. D. and Whittaker, L. (2003) 'The Phenomenology of Information Systems Evaluation: Overcoming the Subject/Object Dualism.' In: Wynn, E., Whitley, E., Myers, M. D. and DeGross, J. (eds) *Global and Organizational Discourse about Information Technology*. Kluwer Academic Publishers, Dordrecht: 156–175

Introna, L. and Whittaker, L. (2004) 'Truth, Journals, and Politics: The Case of the MIS Quarterly.' In: Kaplan, B., Truex, D. P., Wastell, D., Wood-Harper, T. and DeGross, J. (eds) *Information Systems Research: Relevant Theory and Informed Practice*. Kluwer, Dordrecht: 103–120

ISDO (2005) Information Society Development Office 'Mission Statement.' available www.isdo.gov.eg/mission.asp [accessed 16 March 2005]

Ives, B. and Jarvenpaa, S. L. (1996) 'Will the Internet Revolutionize Business Education and Research?' *Sloan Management Review* (37:3), 33–41

Ives, B., Parks, M. S., Porra, J. and Silva, L. (2004) 'Phylogeny and Power in the IS Domain: A Response to Benbasat and Zmud's Call for Returning to the IT Artifact.' *Journal of the Association for Information Systems* (5:3): 108–124

Janson, M. and Cecez-Kecmanovic, D. (2005) 'Making Sense of E-Commerce as Social Action.' *Information Technology and People* (18:4), 311–342

Jarvenpaa, S. L., Shaw, T. R. and Staples, S. D. (2004) 'Toward Contextualized Theories of Trust: The Role of Trust in Global Virtual Teams.' *Information Systems Research* (15:3), 250–267

Jefferies, P., Stahl, B. C. and McRobb, S. (2007) 'Exploring the Relationships between Pedagogy, Ethics & Technology: Building a Framework for Strategy Development.' *Technology, Pedagogy and Education* (16:1), 111–126

Jenkins, M. A. (1985) 'Research Methodologies and MIS Research.' In: Mumford, E., Hirschheim, R., Fitzgerald, G. and Wood-Harper, T. (eds) *Research Methods in Information Systems*. IFIP 8.2 Proceedings. Amsterdam, North-Holland: 103–117

Johnson, D. G. (2000) 'Democratic Values and the Internet.' In: Langford, D. (ed.) *Internet Ethics*. Macmillan, London: 181–196

Johnson, D. G. (2001) *Computer Ethics*, 3rd edn. Prentice Hall, Upper Saddle River, NJ

Johnstone, J. (2007) 'Technology as Empowerment: A Capability Approach to Computer Ethics.' *Ethics and Information Technology* (9:1): 73–87

Jones, S. (2001) 'Understanding Micropolis and Compunity.' In: Ess, C. (ed.) with F. Sudweeks, *Culture, Technology, Communication: Towards an Intercultural Global Village*. State University of New York Press, Albany: 53–66

Jones, S., Wilikens, M., Morris, P. and Masera, M. (2000) 'Trust Requirements in E-Business: A Conceptual Framework for Understanding the Needs and Concerns of Different Stakeholders.' *Communications of the ACM* (43:12), 80–87

Jones, T. M and Bowie, N. E. (1998) 'Moral Hazards on the Road to the "Virtual" Corporation.' *Business Ethics Quarterly* (8:2), 273–292

Jönsson, S. (1991) 'Action Research.' In: Nissen, H.-E., Klein, H. K. and Hirschheim, R. (eds) *Information Systems Research: Contemporary Approaches & Emergent Traditions*. Amsterdam, North-Holland: 371–396

Kahin, B. (1997) 'The U.S. National Information Infrastructure Initiative: The Market, the Web, and the Virtual Project.' In: Kahin, B. and Wilson, E. J. (eds) *National Information Infrastructure Initiatives Vision and Policy Design*. MIT Press, Cambridge, MA: 150–189

Kambartel, F. (1998) 'Bemerkungen zur Politischen Ökonomie.' In: Kambartel, F.,

Philosophie und politische Ökonomei: Essener kulturwissenschaftliche Vorträge 2. Wallstein, Göttingen

Kant, I. (1985) *Was ist Aufklärung? Aufsätze zur Geschichte und Philosophie,* ed. and introduced by Jürgen Zehbe, 3rd edn. Vandenhoeck und Ruprecht, Göttingen

Kant, I. (1992) *Über den Gemeinspruch: Das mag in der Theorie richtig sein, taugt aber nicht für die Praxis,* Meiner, Hamburg

Kant, I. (1995) *Kritik der praktischen Vernunft: Grundlegung zur Metaphysik der Sitten,* Suhrkamp, Frankfurt

Keen, P. G. W. (1991) 'Relevance and Rigor in Information Systems Research: Improving Quality, Confidence, Cohesion and Impact.' In: Nissen, H.-E., Klein, H. K. and Hirschheim, R. (eds) *Information Systems Research: Contemporary Approaches & Emergent Traditions.* Amsterdam, North-Holland: 27–49

Keil, M., Tiwana, A. and Bush, A. (2002) 'Reconciling User and Project Manager Perceptions of IT Project Risk: A Delphi Study.' *Information Systems Journal* (12), 103–119

Kelly, M. (ed.) (1994) *Critique and Power: Recasting the Foucault/Habermas Debate.* MIT Press, Cambridge, MA

Kemerling, G. (2000) *Kant: The Moral Order,* available www.philosophypages.com/hy/5i.htm [accessed 15 November 2000]

Khare, R. and Rifkin, A. (1998) 'Trust Management on the World Wide Web.' *First Monday* (3:6), available www.firstmonday.dk

Khlentzos, Drew (2004) *Naturalistic Realism and the Antirealist Challenge.* MIT Press, Cambridge, MA

Kincheloe, J. L. and McLaren, P. (2005) 'Rethinking Critical Theory and Qualitative Research.' In: Denzin, N. K and Lincoln, Y. S. (eds) *The Sage Handbook of Qualitative Research,* 3rd edn. Sage, Thousand Oaks, CA: 305–342

Kishore, R., Ramesh, R. and Sharman, R. (eds) (2007) *Ontologies: A Handbook of Principles, Concepts and Applications in Information Systems.* Springer, New York

Kishore, R., Sharman, R. and Ramesh, R. (2004a) 'Computational Ontologies and Information Systems: I. Foundations.' *Communications of the Association for Information Systems* (14), 158–183

Kishore, R., Sharman, R. and Ramesh, R. (2004b) 'Computational Ontologies and Information Systems: II. Formal Specifications.' *Communications of the Association for Information Systems* (14), 184–205

Klang, M. (2003) 'A Critical Look at the Regulation of Computer Viruses.' *International Journal of Law and Information Technology* (11), 162–183

Klecun, E. (2005) 'Competing Rationalities: A Critical Study of Telehealth in the UK.' In: Howcroft, D. and Trauth, E. M. (eds) *Handbook of Critical Information Systems Research: Theory and Application.* Edward Elgar, Cheltenham, UK: 388–416

Klecun, E. and Cornford, T. (2005) 'A Critical Approach to Evaluation.' *European Journal of Information Systems* (14), 229–243

Klein, H. K. and Lyytinen, K. (1985) 'The Poverty of Scientism in Information Systems.' In: Mumford, E., Hirschheim, R., Fitzgerald, G. and Wood-Harper, T. (eds) *Research Methods in Information Systems.* IFIP 8.2 Proceedings. Amsterdam, North-Holland: 131–161

Klein, H. K. and Myers, M. D. (1999) 'A Set of Principles for Conducting and Evaluating Interpretive Field Studies in Information Systems.' *MIS Quarterly* (23:1), 67–94

Klein, H. K. and Myers, M. D. (2001) 'A Classification Scheme for Interpretive Research in Information Systems'. In: Trauth, E. (ed.) *Qualitative Research in IS: Issues and Trends.* Idea Group Publishing, Hershey, MA: 218–239

Klein, H. K., Hirschheim, R. and Nissen, H.-E. (1991) 'A Pluralist Perspective of the Information Systems Research Arena.' In: Nissen, H.-E., Klein, H. K. and Hirschheim, R. (eds) *Information Systems Research: Contemporary Approaches & Emergent Traditions*, Amsterdam, North-Holland: 1–17

Klenow, P. J. and Rodríguez-Clare, A. (1997) 'Economic Growth: A Review Essay.' *Journal of Monetary Economics* (40), 597–617

Knights, D. and Morgan, G. (1991) 'Corporate Strategy, Organizations, and Subjectivity: A Critique.' *Organization Studies* (12:2): 251–273

Knights, D. and Willmott, H. (1999) *Management Lives: Power and Identity in Organizations*. Sage, London

Kock, N. (2005) 'Media Richness or Media Naturalness? The Evolution of our Biological Communication Apparatus and its Influence on our Behavior toward E-Communication Tools.' *IEEE Transactions on Professional Communication* (48:2), 117–130

Koehn, D. (1997) 'Trust and Business: Barriers and Bridges.' *Business and Professional Ethics Journal* (16:1–3), Special Issue on Trust and Business: Barriers and Bridges, ed. D. Koehn: 7–28

Koehn, D. (2003) 'The Nature of and Conditions for Online Trust.' *Journal of Business Ethics* (43), 3–19

Kohlberg, L. (1981) *The Philosophy of Moral Development: Moral Stages and the Idea of Justice*. Harper & Row, San Francisco

Kolb, D. (1996) 'Discourse across Links.' In: Ess, C. (ed.) *Philosophical Perspectives on Computer-Mediated Communication*. State University of New York Press, Albany: 15–26

Kuhn, T. S. (1996) *The Structure of Scientific Revolutions*, 3rd edn. University of Chicago Press, Chicago

Kumar, K., van Dissel, H. G. and Bielli, P. (1998) 'The Merchant of Prato – Revisited: Toward a Third Rationality of Information Systems.' *MIS Quarterly* (22:2): 199–226

Küng, H. (1997) *Weltethos für Weltpolitik und Weltwirtschaft*, 3rd edn. Pieper Verlag, Munich

Kursawe, K. and Wolf, C. (2006) 'Trusted Computing, or the Gatekeeper.' In: Zielinski, C., Duquenoy, P. and Kimppa, K. (eds) *The Information Society: Emerging Landscapes*. IFIP WG 9.2 Proceedings. Springer, New York: 339–354

Kvasny, L. and Trauth, E. (2003) 'The Digital Divide at Work and Home: The Discourse about Power and Underrepresented Groups in the Information Society.' In: Wynn, E., Whitley, E., Myers, M. D. and DeGross, J. (eds) *Global and Organizational Discourse About Information Technology*. Ifip Tc8/Wg8.2 Conference. Kluwer Academic Publishers, Dordrecht: 273–291

Ladd, J. (2000) 'Ethics and the Computer World: A New Challenge for Philosophers.' In: Baird, R. M., Ramsower, R. and Rosenbaum, S. E. (eds) *Cyberethics: Social and Moral Issues in the Computer Age*, Prometheus Books, New York: 44–55

Landry, M. and Banville, C. (1992) 'A Disciplined Methodological Pluralism for MIS Research.' *Accounting, Management & Information Technology* (2:2), 77–92

Landwehr, C. E. (1981) *A Survey of Formal Models for Computer Security*, NRL Report 8489. Naval Research Laboratory, Washington, DC

Landwehr, C. E., Heitmeyer, C. L. and McLean, J. D. (2001) *A Security Model for Military Message Systems: Retrospective*, available http://chacs.nrl.navy.mil/publications/CHACS/2001/2001landwehr-ACSAC.pdf [accessed 4 January 2006]

Lane, C. and Bachmann, R. (1996) 'The Social Construction of Trust: Supplier Relations in Britain and Germany.' *Organization Studies* (17:3), 365–395

Laudon, K. C. and Laudon, J. P. (1999) *Essentials of Management Information Systems*, 4th edn. Prentice Hall, London

Lawler, J. (2004) 'Meaning and Being: Existentialist Concepts in Leadership.' *International Journal of Management Concepts and Philosophy* (1:1), 61–72

Lee, A. S. (1991) 'Integrating Positivist and Interpretive Approaches to Organizational Research.' *Organization Science* (2:4), 342–365

Lee, A. S. (1994) 'Electronic Mail as a Medium for Rich Communication: An Empirical Investigation using Hermeneutic Interpretation.' *MIS Quarterly* (18:2): 143–157

Lee, A. S. (2001) 'Challenges to Qualitative Researchers in IS.' In: Trauth, E. (ed.) *Qualitative Research in IS: Issues and Trends*. Idea Group Publishing, Hershey, MA: 240–270

Lee, A. S. (2004) 'Thinking about Social Theory and Philosophy for Information Systems.' In: Mingers, J. and Willcocks, L. (eds) *Social Theory and Philosophy for Information Systems*. Wiley, Chichester, UK: 1–26

Lee, A. S and Baskerville, R. L. (2003) 'Generalizing Generalizability in Information Systems Research.' *Information Systems Research* (14:3), 221–243

Leidner, D. E. and Jarvenpaa, S. L. (1995) 'The Use of Information Technology to Enhance Management School Education: A Theoretical View.' *MIS Quarterly* (19:3), 265–291

Lenk, H. (ed.) (1991) *Wissenschaft und Ethik*. Reclam, Stuttgart

Lenk, H. and Maring, M. (1995) 'Wer soll Verantwortung tragen? Probleme der Verantwortungsverteilung in komplexen (soziotechnischen-sozioökonomischen) Systemen.' In: Bayertz, K. (ed.) *Verantwortung: Prinzip oder Problem?* Wissenschaftliche Buchgesellschaft, Darmstadt: 241–286

Lenoir, F. (ed.) (1991) *Le Temps de la responsabilité: Entretiens sur l'éthique*, Fayard, Paris

Lessig, L. (2001) 'The Laws of Cyberspace.' In: Spinello, R. A. and Tavani, H. T. (eds) *Readings in Cyberethics*. Jones and Bartlett, Sudbury, MA: 124–134

Levary, R. R. and Niederman, F. (2003) 'Managing the Virtual Corporation using IT.' In: Joia, L. A. (ed.) *IT-Based Management: Challenges and Solutions*. Idea Group Publishing, Hershey, MA: 143–159

Levy, D. L., Alvesson, M. and Willmott, H. (2003) 'Critical Approaches to Strategic Management.' In: Alvesson, M. and Willmott, H. (eds) *Studying Management Critically*. Sage, London: 92–110

Lévy, P. (1997) *Cyberculture*, Éditions Odile Jacob, Paris

Lewicki, R. J. and Stevenson, M. A. (1997) 'Trust Development in Negotiation: Proposed Actions and Research Agenda.' *Business and Professional Ethics Journal* (16:1–3), Special Issue on Trust and Business: Barriers and Bridges, ed. D. Koehn, 99–132

Lewis, H. D. (1972) 'The Non-moral Notion of Collective Responsibility.' In: French, P. (ed.) *Individual and Collective Responsibility: Massacre at My Lai*. Schenkman, Cambridge, MA: 116–144

Lyon, D. (2002) 'Surveillance Studies: Understanding Visibility, Mobility and the Phenetic Fix.' *Surveillance & Society* (1:1), 1–7

Lyon, D. (2003) *Surveillance after September 11*. Polity Press, Cambridge

Lyotard, J.-F. (1993) *Die Phänomenologie*. Junius Verlag, Hamburg

Lytras, M. D. and Pouloudi, A. (2001) 'E-Learning: Just a Waste of Time.' *Proceedings of the Seventh Americas Conference on Information Systems 2001*: 216–222

Lyytinen, K. (1992) 'Information Systems and Critical Theory.' in Alvesson, M. and Willmott, H. (eds) *Critical Management Studies*. Sage, London: 159–180

Lyytinen, K. and Hirschheim, R. (1988) 'Information Systems as Rational Discourse: An Application of Habermas Theory of Communicative Action.' *Scandinavian Journal of Management* (4:1/2): 19 30

Lyytinen, K. J. and Klein, H. K. (1985) 'The Critical Theory of Jürgen Habermas as a Basis for a Theory of Information Systems.' In: Mumford, E., Hirschheim, R., Fitzgerald, G. and Wood-Harper, T. (eds) *Research Methods in Information Systems*. IFIP 8.2 Proceedings. Amsterdam, North-Holland: 219–236

McAulay, L., Doherty, N. and Keval, N. (2002) 'The Stakeholder Dimension in Information Systems Evaluation.' *Journal of Information Technology* (17), 241–255

McBride, N. K. (2005) 'Chaos Theory as a Model for Interpreting Information Systems in Organizations.' *Information Systems Journal* (15), 233–254

MacDoand, C., McDonald, M. and Norman, W. (2002) 'Charitable Conflicts of Interest.' *Journal of Business Ethics* (39), 67–74

MacDonald, C. (1997) 'Trust in the Marketplace: An Exploratory Computer Simulation.' *Business and Professional Ethics Journal* (16:1–3), special issue on Trust and Business; Barriers and Bridges, ed. D. Koehn: 225–238

McGaley, M. and Gibson, P. (2003) *Electronic Voting: A Safety Critical System*, available www.cs.may.ie/~pgibson/Research/Publications/E-Copies/NUIM-CS-TR2003–02. pdf [accessed 6 August 2004]

McGrath, K. (2003) 'In a Mood to Make Sense of Technology: A Longitudinal Study of Discursive Practices at the London Ambulance Service.' In: Wynn, E., Whitley, E., Myers, M. D. and DeGross, J. (eds) *Global and Organizational Discourse about Information Technology*. Kluwer Academic Publishers, Dordrecht: 485–506

McGrath, K. (2005) 'Doing Critical Research in Information Systems: A Case of Theory and Practice not Informing Each Other.' *Information Systems Journal* (15), 85–101

McGrath, K. (2006) 'Affection not Affliction: The Role of Emotions in Information Systems and Organizational Change.' *Information and Organization* (16:4), 277–303

McGregor, D. (1985) *The Human Side of Enterprise*, 25th anniversary printing. McGraw-Hill, London

MacIntyre, A. (1998) *A Short History of Ethics: A History of Moral Philosophy from the Homeric Age to the Twentieth Century*, 2nd edn. Routledge, London

McKnight, D. H. and Chervany, N. L. (2000) 'What Is Trust? A Conceptual Analysis and an Interdisciplinary Model.' *Proceedings of the Americas Conference on Information Systems 2000*, 827–833

McKnight, D. H., Choudhury, V. and Kacmar, C. (2002) 'Developing and Validating Trust Measures for E-Commerce: An Integrative Typology.' *Information Systems Research* (13:3), 334–359

McLellan, D. (1995) *Ideology*, 2nd edn. Open University Press, Buckingham

McRobb, S. and Rogerson, S. (2004) 'Are They Really Listening? An Investigation into Published Online Privacy Policies at the Beginning of the Third Millennium.' *Information Technology & People* (17:4), 442–461

Mahon, M. (1992) *Foucault's Nietzschean Genealogy: Truth, Power, and the Subject*. State University Press of New York, Albany

Maitland, C. F. and Bauer, J. M. (2001) 'National Level Culture and Global Diffusion: The Case of the Internet.' In: Ess, C. (ed.) with F. Sudweeks *Culture, Technology, Communication: Towards an Intercultural Global Village*. State University Press of New York, Albany: 87–129

Mansell, W., Meteyard, B. and Thomson, A. (1999) *A Critical Introduction to Law*, 2nd edn. Cavendish Publishing, London

Marcuse, H. (1964) *One-Dimensional Man*. Routledge Classics, London

Maritain, J. (1960) *La philosophie morale: Examen historique et critique des grands systèmes*. Librarie Gallimard, Paris

Marturano, A. (2002) 'The Role of Metaethics and the Future of Computer Ethics.' *Ethics and Information Technology* (4:1), 71–78

Marx, K. (1964) *Karl Marx/Friedrich Engels Studienausgabe*, ed. I. Fetscher. Fischer Philosophie, Frankfurt am Main

Marx, K. (1969) *Manifest der Kommunistischen Partei*. Reclam, Stuttgart

Marx, K. (1998) *Das Kapital: Kritik der politischen Ökonomie*, 3 Bd, Band 1, MEW Bd 23, 16th edn. Dietz, Berlin

Mason, R. O. (1986) 'Four Ethical Issues of the Information Age.' *MIS Quarterly* (10), 5–12

Mason, R. O., Mason, F. and Culnan, M. J. (1995) *Ethics of Information Management*. SAGE, Thousand Oaks, CA

Mayasandra, R., Pan, S. L. and Myers, M. D. (2006) 'Viewing Information Technology Outsourcing Organizations through a Postcolonial Lens.' In: Trauth, E. M., Howcroft, D., Butler, T., Fitzgerald, B. and DeGross, J. I. (eds) *Social Inclusion: Societal and Organizational Implications for Information Systems*. IFIP Vol. 208. Springer, New York: 381–396

Mayer, R. C., Davis, J. H. and Schoorman, F. D. (1995) 'An Integrative Model of Organizational Trust.' *Academy of Management Review* (20:3), 709–734

Meeks, B. N. (2000) 'Better Democracy through Technology.' In: Baird, R. M., Ramsower, R. and Rosenbaum, S. E. (eds) *Cyberethics: Social and Moral Issues in the Computer Age*, Prometheus Books, New York: 288–294

Mejias, R. J., Palmer, J. W. and Harvey, M. G. (1999) 'Emerging Technologies, IT Infrastructure, and Economic Development in Mexico.' *Journal of Global Information Technology Management* (2:1), 31–54

Mercuri, R. (2002a) 'A Better Ballot Box?' *IEEE Spectrum Online*, October, www. spectrum.ieee.org/WEBONLY/publicfeature/oct02/evot.html

Mercuri, R. (2002b) 'Florida 2002: Sluggish Systems, Vanishing Votes.' *Communication of the ACM* (45:11), p. 136

Metcalfe, M. and Lynch, M. (2003) 'Arguing for Information Systems Project Definition.' In: Wynn, E., Whitley, E., Myers, M. D. and DeGross, J. (eds) *Global and Organizational Discourse about Information Technology*. Kluwer Academic Publishers, Dordrecht: 295–321

Mingers, J. (1992) Technical, Practical and Critical OR – Past, Present and Future?' In: Alversson, M. and Willmott, H. (eds) *Critical Management Studies*. Sage, London: 90–113

Mingers, J. (2001a) 'Embodying Information Systems: The Contribution of Phenomenology.' *Information and Organization* (11:2), 103–128

Mingers, J. (2001b) 'Combining IS Research Methods: Towards a Pluralist Methodology.' *Information Systems Research* (12:3), 240–259

Mintzberg, H. (1973) *The Nature of Managerial Work*, Harper & Row, New York

Mintzberg, H. (2004) *Managers Not MBAs: A Hard Look at the Soft Practice of Managing and Management Development*, Prentice Hall, London

Miranda, S. M. and Saunders, C. S. (2003) 'The Social Construction of Meaning: An Alternative Perspective on Information Sharing.' *Information Systems Research* (14:1), 87–106

Mitev, N. N. (2005) 'Are Social Constructivist Approaches Critical? The Case of IS Failure.' In: Howcroft, D. and Trauth, E. M. (eds) *Handbook of Critical Information Systems Research: Theory and Application*. Edward Elgar, Cheltenham, UK: 70–103

Montaigne, M. de (1910) *Essays*, vols 1–3, trans. J. Florio. Everyman's Library, London, 1910

Montealegre, R. (1998) 'Waves of Change in Adopting the Internet: Lessons from Four Latin American Countries.' *Information Technology & People* (11:3), 235–260

Moor, J. H. (1985) 'What Is Computer Ethics?' *Metaphilosophy* (16:4), 266–275

Moor, J. H. (2000) 'If Aristotle were a Computing Professional.' In: Baird, R. M., Ramsower, R. and Rosenbaum, S. E. (eds) *Cyberethics: Social and Moral Issues in the Computer Age*, Prometheus Books, New York: 34–40

Moor, J. H. (2004) 'Reason, Relativity, and Responsibility in Computer Ethics.' In: Bynum, T. W. and Rogerson, S. (eds) *Computer Ethics and Professional Responsibility*, Blackwell, Oxford: 21–38

Moores, T. (2005) 'Do Consumers Understand the Role of Privacy Seals in E-Commerce?' *Communications of the ACM* (48:3), 86–91

Moran, D. (2000) *Introduction to Phenomenology*, Routledge, London

Morick, H. (1980) 'Introduction: The Critique of Contemporary Empiricism.' In: Morick, H. (ed.) *Challenges to Empiricism*. Methuen, London, 1–25

Mubarak, H. (1999) Address by President Muhammad Hosni Mubarak to the National Conference on the Promotion of Technology and Information. 13 September, available www.presidency.gov.eg/html/13_9.htm [accessed 16 November 2004]

Mubarak, H. (2000) President Mubarak's Speech at the Lunch Hosted in his Honor by Virginia's Governor, 27 March, available www.presidency.gov.eg/html/27-Mar2000_speech.htm [accessed 21 December 2004]

Mui, L. *et al.* (2002) 'A Computational Model of Trust and Reputation.' In: *Proceedings of the 35th Annual Hawaii International Conference on Systems Sciences*, Hawaii, 7–10 January

Mumford, E. (1996) *Systems Design: Ethical Tools for Ethical Change*. Macmillan, London

Mumford, E. (2001) 'Action Research: Helping Organizations to Change.' In: Trauth, E. M. (ed.) *Qualitative Research in IS: Issues and Trends*. Idea Group Publishing, Hershey, MA: 46–77

Mumford, E. (2003) *Redesigning Human Systems*. Information Science Publishing: Hershey, PA

Mumford, E. and Ward, T. B. (1968) *Computers: Planning for People*. Batsford, London

Mumford, E., Hirschheim, R., Fitzgerald, G. and Wood-Harper, T. (eds) (1985) *Research Methods in Information Systems*. IFIP 8.2 Proceedings. North-Holland, Amsterdam

Myers, M. D. and Avison, D. (2002) 'An Introduction to Qualitative Research in Information Systems.' In: Myers, M. and Avison, D. (eds) *Qualitative Research in Information Systems: A Reader*. Sage, London: 3–12

Newell, S., Swan, J. and Kautz, K. (2001) 'The Role of Funding Bodies in the Creation and Diffusion of Management Fads and Fashions.' *Organization* (8:1), 97–120

Ngwenyama, O. K (1991) 'The Critical Social Theory Approach to Information Systems: Problems and Challenges.' In: Nissen, H.-E., Klein, H. K. and Hirschheim, R. (eds) *Information Systems Research: Contemporary Approaches & Emergent Traditions* Amsterdam, North-Holland: 267–280

Nidumolu, S. R., Goodman, S. E., Vogel, D. R. and Danowitz, A. K. (1996) 'Information

Technology for Local Administration Support: The Governorates Project in Egypt.' *MIS Quarterly* (20:2), 197–224

Nissen, H.-E. (1985) 'Acquiring Knowledge of Information Systems: Research in a Methodological Quagmire.' In: Mumford, E., Hirschheim, R., Fitzgerald, G. and Wood-Harper, T. (eds) *Research Methods in Information Systems*. IFIP 8.2 Proceedings. Amsterdam, North-Holland: 39–51

Nissenbaum, H. (1999) 'Can Trust Be Secured Online? A Theoretical Perspective.' *Etica & Politica* (1:2), www.units.it/~etica/ [accessed: 26 May 2006]

Nissenbaum, H. (2001) 'Toward an Approach to Privacy in Public: Challenges of Information Technology.' In: Spinello, R. A. and Tavani, H. T. (eds) *Readings in CyberEthics*. Jones and Bartlett, Sudbury, MA: 392–403

Nissenbaum, H. (2005) 'Where Computer Security Meets National Security.' *Ethics and Information Technology* (7:2), 61–73

Nye, D. (2002) 'The "privacy in employment" critique: a consideration of some of the arguments for "ethical" HRM professional practice.' *Business Ethics: A European Review* (11:3), 224–232

Nygaard, K. (2002) 'An Emergency Toolkit: Foreword to "The Labyrinths of Information: Challenging the Wisdom of Systems".' Ciborra, C., *The Labyriths of Information: Challenging the Wisdom of Systems*. Oxford University Press, Oxford: v–x

O'Duffy, M. (2004) *The ICS Calls for Audit Trail in E-Voting System*, Irish Computer Society, available www.ics.ie/article-027.shtml [accessed 20 August 2004]

Olaison, J. (1991) 'Pluralism or Positivistic Trivialism: Important Trends in Contemporary Philosophy of Science.' In: Nissen, H.-E., Klein, H. K. and Hirschheim, R. (eds) *Information Systems Research: Contemporary Approaches & Emergent Traditions*. Amsterdam, North-Holland: 235–264

Olson, J. and Olson, G. M. (2000) 'i2i Trust in E-Commerce.' *Communications of the ACM* (43:12), 41–44

Orlikowski, W. J. and Baroudi, J. J. (1991) 'Studying Information Technology in Organizations: Research Approaches and Assumptions.' *Information Systems Research* (2:1), 1–28

Orlikowski, W. J. and Iacono, C. S. (2001) 'Research Commentary: Desperately Seeking the "IT" in IT Research – A Call to Theorizing the IT Artifact.' *Information Systems Research* (12:2): 121–134

Owen, D. (1999) 'Orientation and Enlightenment: An Essay on Critique and Genealogy.' In: Ashenden, S. and Owen, D. (eds) *Foucault contra Habermas: Recasting the Dialogue between Genealogy and Critical Theory*. Sage, London: 21–44

Paletz, D. L. (2000) 'Advanced Information Technology and Political Communication.' In: Baird, R. M., Ramsower, R. and Rosenbaum, S. E. (eds) *Cyberethics: Social and Moral Issues in the Computer Age*, Prometheus Books, New York: 285–287

Panko, R. R. and Beh, H. G. (2002) 'Monitoring for Pornography and Sexual Harassment.' *Communications of the ACM* (45:1), 84–87

Pauleen, D. J. (2003) 'An Inductively Derived Model of Leader-Initiated Relationship Building with Virtual Team Members.' *Journal of Management Information Systems* (20:3), 227–256

Pavlou, P. and Gefen, D. (2004) 'Building Effective Online Marketplaces with Institution-Based Trust.' *Information Systems Research* (15:1), 3–59

Pennington, R., Wilcox, H. D. and Grover, V. (2004) 'The Role of System Trust in Business-to-Consumer Transactions.' *Journal of Management Information Systems* (20:3), 197–226

Petter, S. C. and Gallivan, M. J. (2004) 'Toward a Framework for Classifying and Guiding Mixed Method Research in Information Systems.' In: *Proceedings of the 37th Annual Hawaii International Conference on Systems Sciences*, Hawaii, 5–8 January

Pettigrew, A. (1985) 'Contextualist Research and the Study of Organisational Change Processes.' In: Mumford, E., Hirschheim, R., Fitzgerald, G. and Wood-Harper, T. (eds) *Research Methods in Information Systems*. IFIP 8.2 Proceedings. Amsterdam, North-Holland: 53–78

Piccoli, G., Ahmad, R. and Ives, B. (2001) Web-Based Virtual Learning Environments: A Research Framework and a Preliminary Assessment of Effectiveness in Basic IT Skills Training.' *MIS Quarterly* (25:4), 401–426

Pieters, W. (2006) 'Internet Voting: A Conceptual Challenge to Democracy.' In: Trauth, E. M., Howcroft, D., Butler, T., Fitzgerald, B. and DeGross, J. I. (eds) *Social Inclusion: Societal and Organizational Implications for Information Systems*. IFIP Vol. 208. Springer, New York: 89–103

Popper, K. R. (1980) 'Science: Conjectures and Refutations.' In: Morick, H. (ed.) *Challenges to Empiricism*. Methuen, London: 128–160

Postman, N. (1992) *Technopoly – The Surrender of Culture to Technology*. Vintage Books, New York

Preece, J. (2002) 'Supporting Community and Building Social Capital.' *Communications of the ACM* (45:4), 37–39

Probert, S. K. (2002a) 'Ethics, Authenticity and Emancipation in Information Systems Development.' In: Salehnia, A. (ed.) *Ethical Issues of Information Systems* IRM Press, Hershey, MA: 249–254

Probert, S. K. (2002b) 'Critical Theory and Empirical Studies in IS Research: Theoretical and Practical Considerations.' *Proceedings of the Eighth Americas Conference on Information Systems*: 1651–1658

Probert, S. K. (2004a) 'Adorno: A Critical Theory for IS Research.' In: Mingers, J. and Willcocks, L. (eds) *Social Theory and Philosophy for Information Systems*. Wiley, Chichester, UK: 129–156

Probert, S. K. (2004b) 'What Is an Information System? A Critical Perspective.' *Proceedings of the Tenth Americas Conference on Information Systems*, New York, August : 4352–4360

Quine, W. V. O. (1980) 'Two Dogmas of Empiricism.' In: Morick, H. (ed.) *Challenges to Empiricism*. Methuen, London: 46–70

Rachels, J. (1995) 'Why Privacy Is important.' In: Johnson, D. G. and Nissenbaum, H. (eds) *Computers, Ethics & Social Values*. Prentice Hall, Upper Saddle River, NJ: 351–357

Rauch, J. (1993) *Kindly Inquisitors: The New Attacks on Free Thought*. University of Chicago Press, Chicago

Rawls, J. (2001) *Justice as Fairness: A Restatement*, ed. E. Kelly. Cambridge, Belknap, Harvard, Cambridge, MA

Reagle, J. M. Jr (1996) 'Trust in Electronic Markets.' *First Monday* (1:2), available www.firstmonday.dk

Rey, L. (2001) 'Cultural Attitudes toward Technology and Communication: A Study in the "Multi-cultural" Environment of Switzerland.' In: Ess, C. (ed.) with F. Sudweeks, *Culture, Technology, Communication: Towards an Intercultural Global Village*. State University of New York Press, Albany: 151–160

Richardson, H. S. (1999) 'Institutionally Divided Moral Responsibility.' In: Paul, E. F.,

Miller, F. D. and Paul, J. (eds) *Responsibility*, Cambridge University Press, Cambridge: 218–249

Richardson, H. (2005) 'Consuming Passion in the "'Global Knowledge Economy".' In: Howcroft, D. and Trauth, E. M. (eds) *Handbook of Critical Information Systems Research: Theory and Application*. Edward Elgar, Cheltenham, UK: 272–298

Ricoeur, P. (1983) *Tems et récit – 1. L'Intrigue et le récit historique*. Seuil, Paris

Ricoeur, P. (1990) *Soi-même comme un autre*. Seuil, Paris

Ricoeur, P. (1991) *Lectures 1: Autour du politique*. Seuil, Paris

Ricoeur, P. (1994) 'Entretien avec Paul Ricoeur.' In: Aeschlimann, J.-C. (ed.) *Éthique et responsabilité – Paul Ricoeur*, Éditions de la Baconnière, Boudry-Neuchâtel, Switzerland: 11–34

Ricoeur, P. (2001) 'De la morale à l'éthique et aux éthiques.' In: Ricoeur, P., *Le Juste 2*. Éditions Esprit, Paris: 55–68

Riis, A. M. (1997) 'The Information Welfare Society: An Assessment of Danish Governmental Initiatives Preparing for the Information Age.' In: Kahin, B. and Wilson, E. J. (eds) *National Information Infrastructure: Initiatives Vision and Policy Design*. MIT Press, Cambridge, MA: 424–456

Robey, D. and Azevedo, A. (1994) 'Cultural Analysis of the Organizational Consequences of Information Technology.' *Accounting, Management and Information Technologies* (4:1): 23–37

Robinson, S. and Watson, J. (2001) 'Female Entrepreneur Underperformance: A Puzzle for the Information Age.' *Journal of International Information Management* (10:1), 45–56

Rookby, E. (ed.) (2006) *Information Technology and Social Justice*. Idea Group, Hershey, PA

Ropohl, G. (1996) *Ethik und Technikbewertung*. Suhrkamp, Frankfurt am Main

Rorty, R. (1982) *Consequences of Pragmatism (Essays 1972–1980)*, fifth printing 1991. University of Minnesota Press, Minneapolis

Rorty, R. (1989) *Contingency, Irony, and Solidarity*. Cambridge University Press, Cambridge

Rorty, R. (1996a) 'On Moral Obligation, Truth, and Common Sense.' In: Niznik, J. and Sanders, J. T. (eds) *Debating the State of Philosophy: Habermas, Rorty and Kolakowski*. Praeger, Westport, CT: 48–52

Rorty, R. (1996b) 'The Notion of Rationality' In: Niznik, J. and Sanders, J. T. (eds) *Debating the State of Philosophy: Habermas, Rorty and Kolakowski*. Praeger, Westport, CT: 84–88

Rorty, R. (1998) *Das Kommunistische Manifest – 150 Jahre danach*. Suhrkamp, Frankfurt am Main

Rousseau, D. M., Sitkin, S. B., Burt, R. S. and Camerer, C. (1998) 'Not So Different after All: A Cross-Discipline View of Trust.' *Academy of Management Review* (23:3), 393–404

Russ, J. (1995) *La Pensée éthique contemporaine*, 10th corrected edn. Presses Universitaires de France, Paris

Rutter, J. (2001) 'From the Sociology of Trust towards a Sociology of "E-Trust".' *International Journal of New Product Development & Innovation Management* (2:4) 371–385

Sahay, S. (2004) 'Beyond Utopian and Nostalgic Views of Information Technology and Education: Implications for Research and Practice.' *Journal of the Association for Information Systems* (5:7), 282–313

Salam, A. F., Iyer, L., Palvia, P. and Singh, R. (2005) 'Trust in E-Commerce.' *Communications of the ACM* (48:2), 73–77

Saravanamuthu, K. (2002a) 'Information Technology and Ideology.' *Journal of Information Technology* (17), 79–87

Saravanamuthu, K. (2002b) 'The Political Lacuna in Participatory Systems Design.' *Journal of Information Technology* (17), 185–198

Schiller, D. (1999) *Digital Capitalism: Networking the Global Market System.* MIT Press, Cambridge, MA

Schulman, M. (2000) 'Little Brother Is Watching You.' In: Baird, R. M., Ramsower, R. and Rosenbaum, S. E. (eds) *Cyberethics: Social and Moral Issues in the Computer Age.* Prometheus Books, New York: 155–161

Schultze, U. (2001) 'Reflexive Ethnography in IS Research.' In: Trauth, E. (ed.) *Qualitative Research in IS: Issues and Trends.* Idea Group Publishing, Hershey, MA: 78–103

Schultze, U. and Leidner, D. (2002) 'Studying Knowledge Management in Information Systems Research: Discourses and Theoretical Assumptions.' *MIS Quarterly* (26:3), 213–242

Schumpeter, J. (1994) 'Science and Ideology.' In: Hausman, D. M. (ed.) *The Philosophy of Economics: An Anthology*, 2nd edn. Cambridge University Press, Cambridge: 224–238

Sen, A. (1987) *On Ethics and Economics*, Basil Blackwell, Oxford

Settle, A. and Berthiaume, A. (2002) 'Debating E-Commerce: Engaging Students in Current Events.' *Journal of Information Systems Education* (13:4): 279–285

Severson, R. J. (1997) *The Principles of Information Ethics.* M. E. Sharpe, Armonk, NY

Shin, N. (2003) 'Productivity Gains from IT's Reduction of Coordination Costs.' In: Shin, N. (ed.) *Creating Business Value with Information Technology: Challenges and Solutions.* London: Idea Group Publishing, Hershey, PA: 125–145

Shoib, G. M. and Jones, M. R. (2003) 'Focusing on the Invisible: The Representation of IS in Egypt.' *Information Technology & People* (16:4), 440–460

Shostack, A. and Syverson, P. (2004) 'What Price Privacy? (and Why Identity Theft Is about Neither Identity nor Theft).' In: Camp, L. J. and Lewis, S. (eds) *Economics of Information Security.* Kluwer, Dordrecht: 129–142

Siau, K., Nah, F. F.-H. and Tang, L. (2002) 'Acceptable Internet Use Policy.' *Communications of the ACM* (45:1), 75–79

Silva, L. O. (2005) 'Theoretical Approaches for Researching Power and Information Systems: The Benefit of a Machiavellian View.' In: Howcroft, D. and Trauth, E. M. (eds) *Handbook of Critical Information Systems Research*: *Theory and Application.* Edward Elgar, Cheltenham, UK: 47–69

Simons, R., Mintzberg, H. and Basu, K. (2002) 'Memo to: CEOs.' *Fast Company* 59, May, available www.fastcompany.com/magazine/59/ceo.html [accessed 2 May 2007]

Singh, M. P. (2001) 'An Evolutionary Look at E-Commerce.' *IEEE Internet Computing* (5:2), 6–7

Sloan, P. (2005) 'Evolution.' *The Stanford Encyclopedia of Philosophy*, Summer 2005 edn, ed. E. N. Zalta, http://plato.stanford.edu/archives/sum2005/entries/evolution/ [accessed 7 December 2007]

Smith, A. (1986/1776) *The Wealth of Nations*, books I–III. Penguin Classics, Classics

Söderbaum, P. (2000) 'Institutional Theory in Relation to Environment and Development: On Individuals as Actors Guided by an Ideological Orientation.' In: Grenholm,

C.-H. and Helgesson, G. (eds) *Efficiency, Justice, and Stability: Ethical Perspectives in Economic Analysis and Practice*. University of Uppsala: Uppsala, 37–50

Solomon, R. C. (1992) *Ethics and Excellence: Cooperation and Integrity in Business*. Oxford University Press, Oxford

Solomon, R. C. and Flores, F. (2001) *Building Trust in Business, Politics, Relationships, and Life*. Oxford University Press, Oxford

Soule, E. (1998) 'Trust and Managerial Responsibility.' *Business Ethics Quarterly* (8:2), 249–272

Spinello, R. (2000) *Cyberethics: Morality and Law in Cyberspace*. Jones and Bartlett, London

Staddon, J. (1999) 'On Responsibility in Science and Law.' In: Paul, E. F., Miller, F. D. and Paul, J. (eds) *Responsibility*. Cambridge University Press, Cambridge: 146–174

Stahl, B. C. (2002a) 'Ethical Issues in E-Teaching : A Theoretical Framework.' In: King, G., Ross, M., Staples, G. and Twomey, C. T. (eds) *Proceedings of INSPIRE VII: Quality in Learning and Delivery Techniques*, Limerick, Ireland, 25–27 March 2002, British Computer Society, 135–148

Stahl, B. C. (2002b) 'Ethics and E-Teaching: The Students' Perspective.' *Communications of the IIMA* (2:3), 51–62

Stahl, B. C. (2003) 'How we Invent what we Measure: A Constructionist Critique of the Empiricist Bias in IS Research. In: *Proceedings of the Ninth Americas Conference on Information Systems*, Tampa, 4–6 August: 2878–2884

Stahl, B. C. (2004) *Responsible Management of Information Systems*. Idea Group Publishing, Hershey, MA

Stahl, B. C. (2005) 'A Critical View of the Ethical Nature of Interpretive Research: Paul Ricœur and the Other.' Paper given at the 13th European Conference on Information Systems, 'Information Systems in a Rapidly Changing Economy.' Regensburg, Germany, 26–28 May 2005

Stahl, B. C. (2007) 'Ethics, Morality and Critique: An Essay on Enid Mumford's Socio-Technical Approach.' *Journal of the Association for Information Systems* (8:9): 479–490

Stahl, B. C. and Elbeltagi, I. (2004) 'Cultural Universality versus Particularity in CMC.' *Journal of Global Information Technology Management* (7:4): 47–65

Stahl, B. C., Prior, M., Wilford, S. and Collins, D. (2005) 'Electronic Monitoring in the Workplace: If People Don't Care, then What Is the Relevance?' In: Weckert, J. (ed.) *Electronic Monitoring in the Workplace: Controversies and Solutions*. Idea Group Publishing, Hershey, PA: 50–78

Stalder, F. (2002) 'Privacy Is Not the Antidote to Surveillance.' *Surveillance & Society* (1:1), 120–124

Stallman, R. (1995) 'Are Computer Property Rights Absolute?' In: Johnson, D. G. and Nissenbaum, H. (eds) *Computers, Ethics & Social Values*. Prentice Hall, Upper Saddle River, NJ: 115–119

Stanton, J. M. and Stam, K. R. (2003) 'Information Technology, Privacy, and Power within Organizations: A View from Boundary Theory and Social Exchange Perspectives.' *Surveillance & Society* (1:2), 152–190

Stegmaier, W. (1995) 'Ethik als Hemmung und Befreiung.' In: Endreß, M. (ed.) *Zur Grundlegung einer integrativen Ethik*. Suhrkamp, Frankfurt am Main

Steinmann, H. and Löhr, A. (1994) *Grundlagen der Unternehmensethik*, 2nd edn. Schäffer Poeschel, Stuttgart

Steup, M. (2001) 'The Analysis of Knowledge.' *The Stanford Encyclopedia of Philosophy*, Spring 2001 edn, ed. E. N. Zalta, http://plato.stanford.edu/archives/spr2001/entries/knowledge-analysis/ [accessed 1 June 2004]

Stewart, C. M., Shields, S. F. and Sen, N. (2001) 'Diversity in On-Line Discussions: A Study of Cultural and Gender Differences in Listservs.' In: Ess, C. (ed.) with Sudweeks, F., *Culture, Technology, Communication: Towards an Intercultural Global Village*, State University of New York Press, Albany: 161–186

Stichler, R. N. (1998) 'Ethics in the Information Market.' In: Stichler, R. N. and Hauptman, R. (eds) *Ethics, Information and Technology: Readings*. McFarland, Jefferson, NC: 169–183

Stichler, R. N. and Hauptman, R. (eds) (1998) *Ethics, Information and Technology: Readings*. McFarland, Jefferson, NC

Straub, D. W. and Collins, R. W. (1990) 'Key Information Liability Issues Facing Managers: Software Piracy, Proprietary Databases, and Individual Rights to Privacy.' *MIS Quarterly* (14), 143–156

Stuart, S. (2002) 'A Radical Notion of Embeddedness: A Logically Necessary Precondition for Agency and Self-Awareness.' *Metaphilosophy* (33:1/2), Special Issue: *Cyberphilosophy: The Intersection of Philosophy and Computing*, ed. J. H. Moor and T. W. Bynum: 98–109

Suchman, M. C. (1995) 'Managing Legitimacy: Strategic and Institutional Approaches.' *Academy of Management Review* (20:3), 571–610

Tapia, A. H. (2004) 'Resistance of Deviance? A High-Tech Workplace during the Bursting of the Dot-Com Bubble.' In Kaplan, B., Truex, D. P., Wastell, D., Wood-Harper, A. T. and DeGross, J. (eds) *Information Systems Research: Relevant Theory and Informed Practice*. IFIP 8.2 Proceedings. Kluwer, Dordrecht: 577–596

Tarantino, D. A. (1994) 'Trust + Ethics = Competitiveness.' In: The Conference Board (ed.) *Business Ethics: Generating Trust in the 1990s and Beyond*. The Conference Board, New York: 15–16

Tavani, H. (2000) 'Privacy and Security.' In: Langford, D (ed.) *Internet Ethics*. Macmillan, London: 65–89

Tavani, H. (2003) 'Ethical Reflections on the Digital Divide.' *Journal of Information, Communication & Ethics in Society* (1:2), 99–108

Tavani, H. T. and Moor, J. T. (2001) 'Privacy Protection, Control of Information, and Privacy-Enhancing Technologies.' In: Spinello, R. A. and Tavani, H. T. (eds) *Readings in CyberEthics*. Jones and Bartlett, Sudbury, MA: 378–391

Taylor, F. W. (1911) *The Principles of Scientific Management*. Harper, New York

Thomas, R. J. (1999) 'What Machines Can't Do: Politics and Technology in the Industrial Enterprise.' In: MacKenzie, D. and Wajcman, J. (eds) *The Social Shaping of Technology*, 2nd edn. Open University Press, Maidenhead, UK: 199–221

Thompson, M. (2003) 'ICT, Power, and Developmental Discourse: A Critical Analysis.' In: Wynn, E., Whitley, E., Myers, M. D. and DeGross, J. (eds) Kluwer Academic Publishers, Dordrecht: 347–373

Thrift, N. (2005) *Knowing Capitalism*. Sage, London

Tocqueville, A. (1998) *De la démocratie en Amérique* I. Gallimard, Paris

Tocqueville, A. (1999) *De la démocratie en Amérique* II. Gallimard, Paris

Trauth, E. M. (2001) 'Choosing Qualitative Methods in IS Research: Lessons Learned.' In: Trauth, E. M. (ed.) *Qualitative Research in IS: Issues and Trends*. Idea Group Publishing, Hershey, MA: 271–287

Trauth, E. M. and Jessup, L. M. (2000) 'Understanding Computer-Mediated Discussions:

Positivist and Interpretive Analyses of Group Support System Use.' *MIS Quarterly* (24:1), 43–79

Trauth, E. M. and O'Connor, B. (1991) 'A Study of the Interaction between Information Technology and Society: An Illustration of Combined Qualitative Research Methods.' In: Nissen, H.-E., Klein, H. K. and Hirschheim, R. (eds) *Information Systems Research: Contemporary Approaches & Emergent Traditions*. Amsterdam, North-Holland: 131–144

Trauth, E. M., Howcroft, D., Butler, T., Fitzgerald, B. and DeGross, J. I. (eds) (2006) *Social Inclusion: Societal & Organizational Implications for Information Systems*. Springer, Boston

Tress, M. (2000) *E-Learning Accelerates and Transforms Business School Pedagogy – A Special Report to the AACSB Annual Meeting*, San Diego, CA, 9 April, SmartForce

Truex, D., Holmström, J. and Keil, M. (2006) 'Theorizing in Information Systems Research: A Reflexive Analysis of the Adaptation of Theory in Information Systems Research.' *Journal of the Association for Information Systems* (7:12), 797–821

Ulrich, P. (1997) *Integrative Wirtschaftsethik: Grundlagen einer lebensdienlichen Ökonomie*, Haupt, Berne

Ulrich, W. (2001a) 'A Philosophical Staircase for Information Systems Definition, Design, and Development. *Journal of Information Technology Theory and Application* (3:3), 55–84

Ulrich, W. (2001b) 'Critical Systemic Discourse.' *Journal of Information Technology Theory and Application* (3:3), 85–106

Urbaczewski, A. and Jessup, L. M. (2002) 'Does Electronic Monitoring of Employee Internet Usage Work?' *Communications of the ACM* (45:1), 80–83

Urquhart, C. (2001) 'An Encounter with Grounded Theory: Tackling the Practical and Philosophical Problems.' In: Trauth, E. M. (ed.) *Qualitative Research in IS: Issues and Trends*. Idea Group Publishing, Hershey, MA: 104–140

Vallance, E. (1992) 'Never the Twain? Ethics and Economics in Eastern and Western Europe.' In: Mahoney, J. and Vallance, E. (eds) *Business Ethics in a New Europe*. Kluwer Academic Publishers, Dordrecht: 36–46

van den Hoeven, J. (2001) 'Privacy and the Varieties of Informational Wrongdoing.' In: Spinello, R. A. and Tavani, H. T. (eds) *Readings in CyberEthics*. Jones and Bartlett, Sudbury, MA: 430–442

van der Blonk, H. (2003) 'Writing Case Studies in Information Systems Research.' *Journal of Information Technology* (18), 45–52

Varey, R. J., Wood-Harper, T. and Wood, B. (2002) 'A Theoretical Review of Management and Information Systems using a Critical Communications Theory.' *Journal of Information Technology* (17), 229–239

Velasquez, M. (1998) *Business Ethics: Concepts and Cases*, 4th edn. Prentice Hall, Upper Saddle River, NeJ

Viega, J., Kohno, T. and Potter, B. (2001) 'Trust (and Mistrust) in Secure Applications.' *Communications of the ACM* (44:2), 31–36

Visala, S. (1991) 'Broadening the Empirical Framework of Information Systems Research.' In: Nissen, H.-E., Klein, H. K. and Hirschheim, R. (eds) *Information Systems Research: Contemporary Approaches & Emergent Traditions*, Amsterdam, North-Holland: 347–364

Vitalari, N. P. (1985) 'The Need for Longitudinal Designs in the Study of Computing Environments.' In: Mumford, E., Hirschheim, R., Fitzgerald, G. and Wood-Harper,

T. (eds) *Research Methods in Information Systems*. IFIP 8.2 Proceedings. Amsterdam, North-Holland: 243–265

Wall, C. and Paroff, J. (2005) 'Cracking the Computer Forensics Mystery.' *The Computer & Internet Lawyer* (22:4), 1–6

Walsham, G. (1993) *Interpreting Information Systems in Organizations*. Wiley, Chichester, UK

Walsham, G. (1995a) 'Interpretive Case Studies in IS Research: Nature and Method.' *European Journal of Information Systems* (4), 74–81

Walsham, G. (1995b) 'The Emergence of Interpretivism in IS Research.' *Information Systems Research* (6:4), 376–394

Walsham, G. (2001) *Making a World of Difference: IT in a Global Context*. Wiley, Chichester, UK

Walsham, G. (2002) 'Cross-cultural Software Production and Use: A Structurational Analysis.' *MIS Quarterly* (26:4): 359–380

Walsham, G. (2005a) 'Learning about Being Critical.' *Information Systems Journal* (15): 111–117

Walsham, G. (2005b) 'Critical Engagement: Why, What and How?' In: Howcroft, D. and Trauth, E. M. (eds) *Handbook of Critical Information Systems Research: Theory and Application*. Edward Elgar, Cheltenham, UK: 225–243

Ward, J. and Peppard, J. (1996) 'Reconciling the IT/business relationship: A Troubled Marriage in Need of Guidance.' *Journal of Strategic Information Systems* (5), 37–65

Waring, T. (2004) 'From Critical Theory into Information Systems Practice: A Case Study of a Payroll–Personnel System.' In: Kaplan, B., Truex, D. P., Wastell, D., Wood-Harper, A. T. and DeGross, J. (eds) *Information Systems Research: Relevant Theory and Informed Practice*. IFIP 8.2 Proceedings. Kluwer, Dordrecht: 556–575

Warren, S. D. and Brandeis, L. D. (1890) 'The Right to Privacy.' *Harvard Law Review* (5), 193–220

Warschauer, M. (2003) 'Dissecting the "Digital Divide": A Case Study in Egypt.' *The Information Society* (19), 297–304

Wastell, D. G. (1996) 'The Fetish of Technique: Methodology as a Social Defence.' *Information Systems Journal* (6), 25–40

Wastell, D. G. (2003) 'Organizational Discourse as a Social Defense: Taming the Tiger of Electronic Government.' In: Wynn, E., Whitley, E., Myers, M. D. and DeGross, J. (eds) *Global and Organizational Discourse about Information Technology*. Kluwer Academic Publishers: Dordrecht: 179–195

Watzlawik, P. (ed.) (2001) *Die erfundene Wirklichkeit*, 13th edn. Piper, Munich

Weber, M. (1994) 'Objectivity and Understanding in Economics.' In: Hausman, D. M. (ed.) *The Philosophy of Economics: An Anthology*, 2nd edn. Cambridge University Press, Cambridge: 69–82

Weber, R. (2003) 'Theoretically Speaking (Editor's Comment).' *MIS Quarterly* (27:3), iii–xii

Weber, R. (2004) 'The Rhetoric of Positivism versus Interpretivism: A Personal View (Editor's Comment).' *MIS Quarterly* (28:1), iii–xii

Weckert, J. and Adeney, D. (1997) *Computer and Information Ethics*. Greenwood Press, Westport, CT

Weick, K. E. (1989) 'Theory Construction as Disciplined Imagination.' *Academy of Management Review* (14:4), 516–531

Weil, É. (1998/1960) *Philosophie morale*, 5th edn. Librairie Philosophique J. Vrin, Paris

Weisinger, J. Y. and Trauth, E. (2002) 'Situating Culture in the Global Information Sector.' *Information Technology & People* (15:4): 306–320

Weizenbaum, J. (1976) *Computer Power and Human Reason.* W. H. Freeman, San Francisco

Welty, B. and Becerra-Fernandez, I. (2001) 'Managing Trust and Commitment in Collaborative Supply Chain Relationships.' *Communications of the ACM* (44:6), 67–73

Westland, J. C. (2004) 'The IS Core XII: Authority, Dogma and Positive Science in Information Systems Research.' *Communications of the Association for Information Systems* (13), 136–157

Westrup, C. (2003) 'Discourse, Management Fashions, and ERP Systems.' In: Wynn, E., Whitley, E., Myers, M. D. and DeGross, J. (eds) *Global and Organizational Discourse about Information Technology.* Kluwer Academic Publishers, Dordrecht: 401–418

Westrup, C. (2005) 'Management Fashions and Information Systems.' In: Howcroft, D. and Trauth, E. M. (eds) *Handbook of Critical Information Systems Research: Theory and Application.* Edward Elgar, Cheltenham, UK: 132–151

Wheeler, D. L. (2001) 'New Technologies, Old Culture: A Look at Women, Gender, and the Internet in Kuwait.' In: Ess, C. (ed.) with F. Sudweeks, *Culture, Technology, Communication: Towards an Intercultural Global Village* State University of New York, Albany: 187–212

Wheeler, D. L. (2006) 'Gender Sensitivity and the Drive for IT: Lessons from the Net-Corps Jordan Project.' *Ethics and Information Technology* (8:3), 131–142

White, K. B. (1985) 'Perceptions and Deceptions: Issues for Information Systems Research.' In: Mumford, E., Hirschheim, R., Fitzgerald, G. and Wood-Harper, T. (eds) *Research Methods in Information Systems.* IFIP 8.2 Proceedings. Amsterdam, North-Holland: 237–242

Wiener, N. (1954) *The Human Use of Human Beings: Cybernetics and Society.* Double-day Anchor Books, Garden City, NY

Wiggershaus, R. (2001) *Die Frankfurter Schule: Geschichte, theoretische Entwicklung, politische Bedeutung.* Munich dtv

Willcocks, L. (2004) 'Foucault, Power/Knowledge and Information Systems: Reconstructing the Present.' In: Mingers, J. and Willcocks, L. (eds) *Social Theory and Philosophy for Information Systems.* Wiley, Chichester, UK: 238–296

Wilson, F. A. (1997) 'The Truth Is Out There: The Search for Emancipatory Principles in Information Systems Design.' *Information Technology & People* (10:3), 187–204

Wilson, M. (2003) 'Rhetoric of Enrollment and Acts of Resistance: Information Technology as Text.' In: Wynn, E. H., Whitley, E. A., Myers, M. D. and DeGross, J. I. (eds) *Global and Organizational Discourse About Information Technology,* Kluwer Academic Publishers, Dordrecht: 225–248

Wilson, M. and Howcroft, D. (2002) 'Re-conceptualising Failure: Social Shaping Meets IS Research.' *European Journal of Information Systems* (11), 236–250

Winner, L. (2000) 'Cyberlibertarian Myts and the Prospects for Community' In: Baird, R. M., Ramsower, R. and Rosenbaum, S. E. (eds) *Cyberethics: Social and Moral Issues in the Computer Age,* Prometheus Books, New York: 319–331

Wolff, J. (2003) Karl Marx, *The Stanford Encyclopedia of Philosophy,* Fall 2003 edn, ed. E. N. Zalta, http://plato.stanford.edu/archives/fall2003/entries/marx/ [accessed 11 December 2005]

Wong, J. (2002) 'Sapere Aude: Foucault and Understanding Values.' Presentation given at the 20th Society for Applied Philosophy Conference, Mansfield College, Oxford, 28–30 June

Wunenburger, J.-J. (1993) *Questions d'éthique*. Presses Universitaires de France, Paris

Wyatt, S., Thomas, G. and Terranova, T. (2002) 'They Came, They Surfed, They Went Back to the Beach: Conceptualizing Use and Non-Use of the Internet.' In: Woolgar, S. (ed.) *Virtual Society? Technology, Cyberbole, Reality*. Oxford University Press, Oxford. 23–40

Wynn, E. (2001) 'Möbius Transitions in the Dilemma of Legitimacy.' In: Trauth, E. M. (ed.) *Qualitative Research in IS: Issues and Trends*. Idea Group Publishing, Hershey, MA: 20–44

Yee, G., El-Khatib, K., Korba, L., Patrick, A. S., Song, R. and Xu, Y. (2005) 'Privacy and Trust in E-Government.' In: Huang, W., Siau, K. and Wei, K. K. (eds) *Electronic Government Strategies and Implementation*. Idea Group Publishing, Hershey, MA: 145–189

Yin, R. K. (2003) *Case Study Research: Design and Methods*, 3rd edn. Sage, Thousand Oaks, CA

Yoon, S.-H. (1996) 'Power Online: A Post-structuralist Perspective on Computer-Mediated Communication.' In: Ess, C. (ed.) *Philosophical Perspectives on Computer-Mediated Communication*. State University of New York Press, Albany: 171–196

Yoon, S.-H. (2001) 'Internet Discourse and the Habitus of Korea's New Generation.' In: Ess, C. (ed.) with Sudweeks, F., *Culture, Technology, Communication: Towards an Intercultural Global Village*. State University of New York Press, Albany: 241–260

Zerdick, A., Picot, A. and Schrape, K. (2001) *European Communication Counciel Report: Die Internet-Ökonomie: Strategien für die digitale Wirtschaft*, 3rd edn. Springer, Berlin

Zuboff, S. (1988) *In the Age of the Smart Machine: The Future of Work and Power*. Basic Books, New York

Zucker, L. G. (1986) 'Production of Trust: Institutional Sources of Economic Structure, 1840–1920.' *Research in Organizational Behavior* (8), 53–111

Index